Communicative Activities for EAP

Cambridge Handbooks for Language Teachers

This series, now with over 40 titles, offers practical ideas, techniques and activities for the teaching of English and other languages providing inspiration for both teachers and trainers.

Recent titles in this series:

Communicative Activities for EAP

Jenni Guse

Consultant and editor: Scott Thornbury

 CAMBRIDGE
UNIVERSITY PRESS

CAMBRIDGE UNIVERSITY PRESS
Cambridge, New York, Melbourne, Madrid, Cape Town,
Singapore, São Paulo, Delhi, Mexico City

Cambridge University Press
The Edinburgh Building, Cambridge CB2 8RU, UK

www.cambridge.org
Information on this title: www.cambridge.org/9780521140577

First published 2011
Reprinted 2013

Printed and bound in the United Kingdom by the MPG Books Group

A catalogue record for this publication is available from the British Library

Library of Congress Cataloguing in Publication data

Guse, Jenni.
    Communicative activities for EAP / Jenni Guse; consultant and editor:
Scott Thornbury
        p. cm. – (Cambridge handbooks for language teachers)
    Includes index.
    ISBN 9780521140577WW
    1. English language–Study and teaching–Foreign speakers. 2. English language–Spoken English–Study and
teaching. I. Thornbury, Scott, 1950-II. Title. III. Series.

    PE1128.A2G87 2011
    428. 2'4–dc22   2010040748

ISBN 978-0-521-14057-7 Paperback and CD-ROM

Contents

Thanks and acknowledgements

I have heard it said that effective teachers are also good learners. I believe in lifelong learning, but this is not a solitary path. There are guides, supporters, advisers and cheerleaders along the way, and it is these people I would like to acknowledge here. For their friendship, professional support and timely advice, I am grateful to Sally Ashton-Hay, Sally Lewis, Marion Whittaker, Jennifer Alford and Suzanne Courtice. To Scott Thornbury, my series editor, I owe a great debt of gratitude for his patience, perseverance and expert guidance. I am also very thankful to the students who have allowed me to use their material: Lillian (Kai Lian), Zac Tooth, Kaitlin Rutledge and Leigh Staines, along with my own students who keep me on my toes and teach me so much. I would like to acknowledge Professor Alan Luke who has supported my use of the Four Resources Model as a framework for a large proportion of the activities. The folk at Cambridge University Press – Roslyn Henderson and Ruth Atkinson – have been generous in their professional advice, and I am very thankful for their support as well as that of my copy-editor Jacque French. And while I have never met Olwyn Alexander, Sue Argent or Jenifer Spencer, their book, *EAP Essentials* (Garner 2008), has been of great value in writing this book. Finally, to my partner, Allan – thank you for being the most enthusiastic cheerleader of all.

Text

p. 42: © Deb Illingworth, 2008; p. 45: VicTESOL; p. 66: Transcript taken from 'The Philosopher's Zone' courtesy of ABC Radio National, www.abc.net.au/rn.; p. 73 and 91: Reproduced by kind permission of Videojug Corporation Limited (www.videojug.com); p. 79: Transcript from 'The Judges' by Justice Michael Kirby, The Boyer Collection, 2003; p. 83: Transcript from 'The Placebo Effect' by Dr. Norman Swan; pp. 86 and 87–88: Courtesy of Lord Broers; p. 97 and 291: All in the Mind, ABC Radio National, Australian Broadcasting Corporation http://abc.net.au/rn/allinthemind; p. 100: Transcript of lecture 'The Web of Criminal Law' by Roma Mitchell, The Boyer Collection, 1975; pp. 105–106: Transcript from 'Stealing History' by Piotr Bienowski, 2005, The Liverpool Museum; p. 110: Robert N. Barger, *Computer Ethics. A Case-based Approach*, (2008), © Robert Newton Barger 2008, published by Cambridge University Press, reproduced with permission; pp. 119–120: Alan McKee, *The Public Sphere. An Introduction* (2005). © Alan McKee 2005, published by Cambridge University Press, reproduced with permission; p. 124: Poshek Fu, David Desser (eds), *The Cinema of Hong Kong, History, Arts, Identity*, (2000), © Cambridge University Press 2000, reproduced with permission; p. 127: Gene Bellinger; p. 137: University of Sydney website (http://www.health.usyd.edu.au) Used with permission.; p. 143: Vero Vanden-Abeele and Veerie Van Rompaey; p. 147: Taken from Dolnicar, S., and Schafer, A., (2006) 'Public perception of desalination versus recycled water in Australia' (Electronic Version), in CD Proceedings of the AWWA Desalination Symposium 2006, Faculty of Commerce, University of Wollongong; p. 158 and 174: R. McCall, S. O'Neill, F. Carroll, D. Benyson, M. Smyth, 'Responsive environments, place and presence', Journal, Vol. 3, No. 1, 2005: 35–73 Rod McCall; p. 161 and 204: Kai Lian (Lillian), Model intro. Unpublished paper, 2008. Used with permission; pp. 168–169: Michael Hutter, David Throsby (eds), *Beyond Price. Value in Culture. Economics and the Arts*, (2008) © Cambridge University Press 2008, reproduced with permission; pp. 183–184: L. Staines, 'Analysis of heat integration and process retrofit options for improved natural gas liquids recovery', Master's thesis. Monash University; pp. 190–191: © The Joint Commission, 2010. Reprinted with permission; p. 202: Suzanne Courtice (2009). Used with permission; p. 238: Image from the Visual Thesaurus, http://www.visualthesaurus.com, Copyright © 1998–2010 Thinkmap, Inc. All rights reserved; p. 241 and 270: Data cited herein have been extracted from the British National Corpus,

Introduction

Purpose, scope and use of this book

The aim of *Communicative Activities for EAP* is to provide communicative opportunities to notice, experiment with, analyse, produce and practise the language and skills that are essential to the study of English for Academic Purposes (EAP). The activities comprising this book also cater for students who are preparing for English tests such as the International English Language Testing System (IELTS) and Test of English as a Foreign Language (TOEFL). Students of EAP are to be admired for their courage, determination and commitment to extending their language skills and proficiency. They tend to be ambitious, motivated students who need to broaden their linguistic skills beyond social English in order to participate in academic study, and this book is designed to be a practical resource for their teachers.

I envisage that this series of communicative activities will reinforce the language and skills represented in most quality EAP textbooks and enable teachers to meet the learning needs of individual students within an established syllabus. Teachers of EAP in both English as a Second Language / English as an Additional Language (ESL/EAL) and English as a Foreign Language (EFL) settings will be able to draw on *Communicative Activities for EAP* to supplement their coursebook, challenge and extend their more able students and cater for any gaps they observe in the language and skills of less able students.

This book can be used in a number of ways. Teachers can choose an activity and work with the whole class to reinforce a language item or skill contained in their required syllabus or textbook. Alternatively, should some students need coaching in a particular skill, a point of grammar or vocabulary, teachers can conduct an activity aimed at the specific needs of a small group while the remainder of the class is engaged in an independent activity. Activities have been framed to be easily incorporated into the classroom teacher's overall planning. They can also be used to revitalise class interest and motivation, or when a teacher is called upon to take a class at short notice.

The audience for this book

This book is a handbook for EAP teachers of both ESL and EFL students. ESL learners find themselves in a context where English is the main language spoken outside the classroom, whereas EFL learners are most likely to encounter English only in their classroom. Some students receive EAP support as they prepare to enter a tertiary institution, while others receive support during their professional studies. The book provides communicative ideas for both experienced and new EAP teachers, as well as for those who speak English as an additional language.

Frameworks for communicative EAP activities

Framework for the four macro skills: speaking, listening, reading, writing

Chapters 1 to 4 contain activities which address the four macro skills: speaking, listening, reading and writing. As a framework for organizing these macro skills, I have drawn on the Four Resources Model developed by Freebody and Luke (1990). I chose this model because it provides a broad repertoire of textual practices for both oral and written language. The model offers teachers a wide range of activity types that assist students to produce and receive meaningful language. The Four Resources Model suggests that readers have access to four resources or roles: coding competence as 'Code breaker', semantic competence as 'Text participant' or 'Meaning maker', pragmatic competence as 'Text user' and critical competence as 'Text analyst' or 'Text critic'. I have adopted this model in Chapter 3 (*Reading*) and Chapter 2 (*Listening*). For the purposes of organizing the productive skills (speaking and writing), I have adapted the Four Resources Model so that the roles of speaker and writer mirror the roles of the reader and listener. The productive roles have been described as 'Code user', 'Text maker', 'Text user' and 'Text agent'. For a more detailed description of this framework, see Appendix 1 at the back of the book.

Framework for vocabulary and grammar

Vocabulary and grammar activities have been organized within three phases of learning which could be broadly described as (1) Noticing, (2) Experimenting and (3) Producing. The phases trace the development of vocabulary and grammar from input, through to acquisition and finally to access and output. See Appendix 2 for a summary of the knowledge and skills within these three phases of learning.

The philosophy underpinning the activities

When deciding on what activities to include in this book, I have been guided by four key principles: *communication, authenticity, learner autonomy* and *critical thinking and analysis*. Each activity engenders genuine communication in the class while still addressing the learner's need to produce and explore academic English. The activities also provide opportunities for students to interact with authentic texts and to develop independence and critical thinking and analysis as they learn. These guiding principles are described in more detail below.

Communication

In all of the activities, the focus is on communication. This methodology is realized either through ways of working, e.g. pair work, group work, individual work, whole-class work, or through tasks such as discussion, interactive games, information gap activities, problem-solving tasks, project work or role plays. The activities therefore provide the tools to promote meaningful, authentic language use in the classroom.

Authenticity

While interacting with authentic texts, students are encouraged to think about the context of written and oral texts, the purpose for speaking or writing, and the audience who will read or listen to these texts. The activities also lead students to an understanding of different academic genres and how speakers and writers can achieve their purposes through their choice of language features such as grammar or vocabulary. Through the activities, they also learn how texts are structured and what holds a text together as a cohesive whole.

Whether students are studying academic English as a preparation for future study, or as a support subject while participating in tertiary study, their language learning is more meaningful if the content of their class is linked to their academic field. For this reason, the activities in this book have been designed so that the teacher can choose the content area and the related authentic texts which best meet the needs of each class.

The dilemma for EAP teachers is to find suitable texts that reflect the rhetorical structures, linguistic features and content to meet the academic language needs and interests of the class. While the choice of text is always the decision of the teacher, *Communicative Activities for EAP* provides model texts from a range of content areas including law, the social sciences, medical science, the built environment, economics, engineering, science, business and finance, information technology and the arts. I have addressed the challenge of authenticity in a number of ways. Firstly, most activities include a range of short, authentic model texts which have been carefully selected to reflect academic register. In some instances, however, I have modified authentic texts to cater for the language needs of learners, while very occasionally I use my own original texts specifically written to illustrate a particular language objective within an academic register.

Learner autonomy

Empowering EAP students as they reflect on their learning and the academic context is also an objective of EAP classes. Learner autonomy is one way to promote such empowerment. Throughout the activities in the book, students are encouraged to supply texts of interest rather than relying solely on the teacher's choice. Students also monitor their own work, work cooperatively with peers and engage in peer tutoring. In addition, students have the opportunity to suggest the future directions of the class. In Activity 1.8: *Group seminars*, for example, students engage in peer feedback following a seminar and, based on their analysis of their performance, make suggestions for the focus of future speaking classes.

Critical thinking

The Four Resources Model, which acts as a framework for speaking, listening, reading and writing, also inspires activities that engage students in thinking critically about texts. These activities add to their sense of autonomy and empowerment and equip them with the critical thinking and analytical skills essential to academic study. Activity 3.17: *Multiple readings* demonstrates some of these cognitive strategies. Students are required to read a text and then critically analyse it, using the questions in Box 3.17b as a guide.

Box 3.17b: Discussion questions

Questions following the first reading	Questions following the second reading
• What people are mentioned in the text? • How does the author want the reader to feel, think or respond to the material in the text? • What view of the world is being constructed by the author? • Who benefits from the way the author presents the information in this text? • Who has the power in this situation?	• What people are not mentioned in the text? • What information has been omitted from the text? • What people do not have power in this situation? • What other ways could an author construct the information in this text?

Following a reading task, students, as 'Text analysts', are asked to detect beliefs, values, attitudes and then make judgements about a text.

In summary, *communication* in the classroom, *authenticity*, in terms of tasks and texts, *learner autonomy* and *critical thinking and analysis* are the principles underpinning the activities in this book.

The content of the activities

To facilitate access for the teacher, the activities have been organized into six chapters: *Speaking, Listening, Reading, Writing, Vocabulary development* and *Grammar*, but it is both desirable and inevitable that there will be an integration of skills and language systems (vocabulary and grammar) within most activities.

The content of each activity is summarized at the beginning of the activity. The information provided includes, variously, the language and skills which will be the focus of the activity, an outline of the activity and the suggested minimum level of English proficiency (* being least demanding and *** being most demanding). It is important to note that the text chosen by the teacher also determines the level of difficulty. A suggested time frame is also included for the activity. In my experience, activities may take a little longer when first introduced, but when the students are familiar with the activity type, they will complete such tasks more quickly. Guidance is also given on the preparation required for each activity, and at times I have added background information for the teacher. An example of this content information is given for Activity 4.17: *Joint construction*, which offers a model for the teacher and the students to construct a text jointly.

4.17   Joint construction

Skill	Establishing thematic progression
Outline	Through a series of prompt questions, the teacher and the class construct a text together.
Level	*
Time	20–30 minutes
Preparation	This activity could follow a brainstorming activity in which ideas for writing have been explored and recorded on the board. Write the topic of the writing task on the board. See Box 4.17a.
Background	The 'teacher talk' in Box 4.17b demonstrates how teachers can assist student writers to achieve cohesion in their written texts.

Materials and preparation

Communicative Activities for EAP provides activities which need very little preparation. Most activities require a board, and some activities call for photocopying. The activities are designed so that teachers can choose their own oral and written texts. However, should the teacher decide to use the texts and support materials from the book, these are included on a CD-ROM for convenient copying. Many activities also come with links to websites which act as a resource for the teacher and a learning tool for the students. These useful online resources have been listed at the end of the book. Answers, scaffolding and sample student responses are provided, and there are suggestions for follow-up at the end of each activity. This makes the book accessible to all teachers, whether they be language educators in an intensive language centre, ESL support teachers in a university, speakers of English as an additional language or relief teachers.

How to fit an activity into an overall scheme of work

Preparing to speak, listen, read and write

When addressing the four macro skills, teachers firstly prepare the class to speak, listen, read or write. For the productive skills of speaking and writing, students build the field by looking at new vocabulary and exploring the concepts to be discussed or written. These preparation lessons are also used to introduce new grammar and revise the structures and skills that will be needed in the larger task. For the receptive skills, teachers help students prepare by encouraging them to establish a purpose for listening or reading, creating expectations, predicting and exploring the concepts and vocabulary of the field. Chapters 5 and 6 (*Vocabulary development* and *Grammar*) provide ideas for this preparation phase of productive and receptive tasks.

In this preparation phase, the 'Code user' and 'Code breaker' activities contained in Chapters 1 to 4 also help to develop receptive and productive skills as well as specific language items. Activity 1.2: *Reading aloud*, for instance, could be used to prepare students for an oral presentation.

1.2   Reading aloud

Skill	Reading aloud with appropriate chunking, pausing and stress
Outline	Students work in pairs to first listen to and then analyse a quote, marking in chunking, pausing and stress symbols. They then read the quote aloud to the class.
Level	*
Time	10–15 minutes
Preparation	Write the quote on the board. Photocopy the same quote. See Box 1.2a. Students will need to choose another quote from an academic text.
Background	While students most often speak from a set of notes, they sometimes support a key point with a quote which they read aloud.

Following this activity, students prepare and present an oral presentation which includes quotes from reference material.

While speaking, listening, reading and writing

As teachers observe and work with their students, they can draw on the communicative activities to meet specific needs. For example, EAP students are required to conduct research and need specialized skills to choose suitable material. In a class where the research task has been set, a teacher could use reading Activity 3.6: *Book covers and contents tables* below to reinforce skills like predicting. Following the activity, students choose their own resources and continue with the research task.

3.6   Book covers and contents tables

Skill	Predicting
Outline	Students match the cover of a book and its table of contents to an extract.
Level	*
Time	20–25 minutes
Preparation	Each group chooses an academic reference book and photocopies its cover, the contents page and a short extract from the book. They make a poster by pasting the copy of the cover and the contents page onto one piece of paper. See Box 3.6a. If students prefer, they could access the academic textbook from online bookstores.

The teacher displays the book extracts around the classroom. Then the students' posters are handed out randomly. The groups predict the content of the book from the information on the poster, and then match their poster to an extract.

After speaking, listening, reading and writing

The post-phase of speaking and writing offers opportunities for learners to evaluate their productive skills, and this evaluation may lead to activities which address gaps in knowledge or usage. The post-phase for listening and reading also offers students a chance to evaluate their receptive skills. Activity 2.3: *Evaluating vocal features*, for example, encourages students to reflect on the effectiveness of vocal features during a discussion, i.e. a television panel discussion on an academic topic.

2.3 Evaluating vocal features

Skill	Identifying vocal features and evaluating their effectiveness
Outline	Students use an evaluation table to assess the effectiveness of vocal features.
Level	*
Time	25–30 minutes
Preparation	Access a recording of a panel discussion between two or three people. You could record a discussion from a TV programme, but take care to choose an academic topic, e.g. literature, science, technology. See the Websites section, pp. 309–10, for useful links.

After the students have focused on the vocal features of the panellists, they use this knowledge to shape their own vocal production.

Further reading

For teachers who are interested in following up on any of the ideas or themes from this book, a short list of reference works that I have found especially helpful while writing *Communicative Activities for EAP* is included at the back of the book.

1 Speaking

As speakers, 'Code users' draw on their knowledge of the sound system to communicate meanings through appropriate stress, intonation, pausing and chunking.

1.1 IT vocabulary rap

Skill	Exploring correct stress and rhythm
Outline	Students use vocabulary to create and perform a 'rap'.
Level	*
Time	20 minutes
Background	A 'rap' is a type of rhythmical poem, made famous by African-American youth culture.

Procedure

1 Explain to the class that using the correct stress and rhythm of words can facilitate effective communication in English. In this activity students will be asked to brainstorm vocabulary within a particular field and then use these words to create a rap. The example in Box 1.1 uses words within the field of Information Technology (IT).

2 Divide the class into small groups and give each group a blank piece of paper.

3 Ask the groups to appoint a scribe, and in one minute, students should write as many words connected to your topic as possible.

4 After one minute, groups pass their paper to the neighbouring group. They have a few moments to read the other group's vocabulary, then in one minute the groups contribute more vocabulary. Keep rotating the papers until they return to the original group.

5 Students can choose any words from their piece of paper to create a rap. Provide a sample rap to illustrate. See Box 1.1.

6 As they work on their raps, ask the groups to use stressed and unstressed syllables as well as pauses to create a rhythmic pattern. In Box 1.1, 'X'

represents a stressed syllable, 'x' is an unstressed syllable. '–' signifies a pause.

7   Students then practise their raps in preparation for a group performance. If students are not sure how to pronounce some of the words, you could refer them to an online source such as http://encarta.msn.com/ Using this online dictionary, students can enter their words and listen to how they are pronounced. They can also discover the stress patterns of the word along with a definition.

8   Finally, ask the groups to perform their raps for the class.

Box 1.1: IT rap

Multimedia (Xx – Xxx)

Cellular phone (Xxx – X)

Icon, Interface (Xx – Xxx)

HTML (Xxx – X)

Follow-up

- Students may be interested in a short video of a real rap performance. They could note the gestures which accompany the rap and incorporate these into their own raps.
- Groups teach their rap plus movements to the other groups.
- If you collect all the raps, these could be used in 'warm-up' activities.

1.2 Reading aloud

Skill	Reading aloud with appropriate chunking, pausing and stress
Outline	Students work in pairs to first listen to and then analyse a quote, marking in chunking, pausing, and stress symbols. They then read the quote aloud to the class.
Level	*
Time	10–15 minutes
Preparation	Write the quote on the board. Photocopy the same quote. See Box 1.2a. Students will need to choose another quote from an academic text.
Background	While students most often speak from a set of notes, they sometimes support a key point with a quote which they read aloud.

Procedure

1 Divide the class into pairs and appoint one student as A, and the other as B. Distribute the quote you have chosen for analysis.

2 The pairs read the quote and discuss the gist of the text. Encourage the students to share their understandings of the text and to ask questions in order to clarify unfamiliar vocabulary.

3 Introduce symbols which students can use to indicate how the text should be read aloud. Demonstrate these so that the students understand the function of the symbols. At this stage in the activity, focus only on chunking, pausing and stress. See Box 1.2b.

4 Refer to the quote on the board and read it aloud to the class. As you read, ask Student A to note the words that you grouped together, the places where you paused for a short time and for a longer time. Student B listens for the syllables which you stressed. They should mark their copy of the quote to demonstrate these features of spoken language.

5 Draw on their observations to mark the quote on the board and invite the class to join you in a chorus reading of this text. See Box 1.2c.

6 Ask the pairs to find another quote that they want to read out in support of a key point in a presentation. They now use similar symbols to mark this quote and practise reading it aloud. Offer feedback and support as they practise.

7 Finally, the pairs memorize their quote and together present it to the class. Allocate points for chunking, pausing and stress and have a small prize for the best performance.

Box 1.2a: Managing employees

Managers know that people make the critical difference between success and failure. The effectiveness with which organizations manage, develop, motivate, involve and engage the willing contribution of the people who work in them is a key determinant of how well those organizations perform.

© Institute of Personnel and Development 1997

From *Communicative Activities for EAP*

© Cambridge University Press 2011   PHOTOCOPIABLE

Box 1.2b: Symbols for oral pronunciation

Symbol	Meaning
Underline these words	Chunk these words together
/	Short pause
//	Long pause
ˇ	Rising pitch
ˆ	Falling pitch
Bold syllables	Stress these syllables

Box 1.2c: Analysed quote

Managers **know** / that **pe**ople make the **cri**tical **diff**erence // between suc**cess** ˇ / and **fail**ure ˆ. // The ef**fec**tiveness with which organizations **man**age, ˇ / develop ˇ, / **mo**tivate, ˇ / invol̲ve ˇ / and en**gage** the **will**ing contri**bu**tion / of the **pe**ople who **work** in them / is a **key** de**ter**minant / of how **well** those **or**gani**za**tions per**form** ˆ.

Follow-up

Choose a different quote and write it on the board. Ask the class to suggest the stressed and unstressed syllables, the places for pausing and the words that are grouped together. Mark these on the quote. Now read the quote aloud, and ask the students to note the rising and falling pitch of your voice.

Use symbols to mark these features on the quote. See Box 1.2b. Finally, invite the class to participate in a chorus reading of the quote.

1.3 Fish bowl

Skill	Inferring meanings from non-verbal communication
Outline	A small group of students are seated in a circle inside the 'fish bowl' and others sit on the outside of the circle looking into the 'fish bowl'. It is their job to make observations about what is going on in the 'fish bowl'.
Level	*
Time	30–40 minutes
Preparation	You will need a short video excerpt of a group of people discussing a topic (two or three minutes). Enter 'panel discussion' into an online search engine and choose a topic of interest to your class. You should also prepare a number of questions for small-group discussion. See Box 1.3a for suggestions.
Background	In all cultures, messages are communicated through non-verbal communication. The same body language may have different meanings in different cultures.

Procedure

1 Point out to the class that in spoken language, words communicate only a part of our message. Body language and tone of voice also contribute to our meaning. You could demonstrate this by saying something very complimentary to the class, but use body language and a tone of voice to signal that you are sad or angry. Then ask the students to name the body language and vocal signals that communicated your message. Did they believe your words or your non-verbal communication?

2 Introduce the short video excerpt by providing the topic for discussion and a little background about the speakers.

3 Show the video with the sound turned off. Ask the students to observe the body language of the participants. Then show the video with the sound. For both showings, use the questions in Box 1.3a as a guide for class discussion.

4 Divide the class into groups with four or five students in each group. You will need an even number of groups. Either provide a different discussion question for each group or invite the groups to determine their own question. See examples of questions in Box 1.3b. Group members could take on different roles, e.g. a group leader, an expert in the field, a

journalist, an academic. Allow time for the groups to decide on their roles and then to discuss the question briefly.

5 Next, ask the groups to practise 'discussing' without speaking. They should use body language to re-enact their discussion from Step 4.

6 Ask two groups to join. Firstly, the students inform each other of the questions to be discussed. Then Group 1 sits inside the 'fish bowl' facing each other in a small circle, while Group 2 sits around the outside, looking in. Now ask those in the 'fish bowl' to 'discuss' their question using body language only.

7 The students on the outside make observations about the body language of the speakers. They then report their observations to Group 1. See Box 1.3a for a list of observation questions.

8 Group 1 now conducts their discussion 'with the sound on'.

9 Allow a few minutes for the groups to discuss how accurate they were in interpreting the messages. Then ask the groups to swap positions in the 'fish bowl' and repeat the activity from Step 6. Complete the activity with another opportunity to discuss the accuracy of their interpretations.

Box 1.3a: Observing body language

Viewing without sound

- What do you think each participant is talking about?
- Who is influential in the group?
- Who are the leaders and who are the followers?
- What is the relationship between the participants?
- What body language sent you these messages?

Viewing with sound
- How did the speakers use body language to enhance their verbal messages?
- Were there any instances when the body language did not match the verbal message?

Box 1.3b: Discussion topics
- Why are some marketing campaigns successful and others not successful?
- What are the benefits/disadvantages of globalization?
- Should governments exercise more control over the banking system? Why? / Why not?
- To what extent is human activity responsible for global warming?
- What are the benefits/disadvantages of the jury system?

Follow-up
In multicultural classrooms, explore how different cultural groups use body language to communicate. For instance, how much personal space should be left between friends, colleagues, business partners, employer and employee, or strangers? How should a person in business greet a visiting business person? What are the taboos?

1.4 Connected speech

Language	Making statements
Skill	Connecting speech
Outline	Students ask and answer questions and reflect on techniques for connecting their speech through weak forms, liaison, elision and assimilation.
Level	*
Time	20–30 minutes
Preparation	Decide on a number of topics for a question and answer discussion and write these on the board. The example uses topics related to ethics. See Box 1.4a.

Procedure

1 Ask students to work individually. Refer them to the discussion topics on the board and ask them to choose one topic. Alternatively, they could choose a topic of personal interest.

2 The student has time to think about the topic and then decides on a personal position in relation to the topic. For instance, the student may feel strongly about abolishing/reinstating the death penalty.

3 The student then writes a short statement outlining his/her position. In the example in Box 1.4a, the student creates a position statement about 'academic integrity'.

4 Write a sample statement on the board and demonstrate how to connect the speech. (See the examples in Box 1.4b.) Read the text aloud and point to the sounds which are linked. Then invite the class to 'read along' with you. You could also ask individuals or pairs to read your sample text so that everyone understands what to do.

5 Still working alone, students analyse their position statements and mark the text where speech should be connected. Encourage the students to read their sentences aloud and offer assistance as needed.

6 Next, each student chooses a partner – not necessarily one who has chosen the same topic. They write out their position statement minus the markings and give this copy to their partner. The first student reads out his/her position statement, making sure to connect the speech as marked. Their partner listens and notes on their copy which words were linked.

7 The pairs compare the notes of the listener with those of the speaker. They then swap roles. As you observe, you could call on individuals who have mastered the skill to demonstrate to the class.

8 After both students have presented their position statements to their partner, provide an opportunity for the pairs to question and discuss the statements.

Box 1.4a: Ethics topics

Ethics topics		Sample statement: academic integrity
Abortion Academic integrity Animal rights Bioethics Computer/IT ethics The death penalty Punishment Environmental ethics Euthanasia	Gender and sexism Poverty and welfare Race, racism and ethnicity Sexual orientation War, peace and terrorism World hunger	All universities have an established ethical standard, but because of the explosion of information on the World Wide Web, ideas can easily be plagiarized. Universities should provide clear guidelines in the form of an academic code of ethics for all new students.

http://ethics.sandiego.edu/index.asp#PageCite

Box 1.4b: Techniques for linking speech

Example	Techniques for linking speech
an established ethical standard *ə-n əstabl əsh-teth əcəl stand əd* ideas and material *idea-s ən-material*	Weak forms (often pronounced as /ə/) Liaison (a sound is introduced at word boundaries)
academic code *academi-code*	Elision (the sound disappears)
World Wide Web *worl-wi-dweb*	Elision (the sound disappears) Assimilation (the sound is influenced by a neighbouring sound)

© Cambridge University Press 1997

Follow-up
Students record a small sample of authentic speech. They transcribe the speech and mark the text showing how the speaker has linked the words with weak forms, liaison, elision and assimilation.

TEXT MAKER

'Text makers' draw on their prior knowledge as well as their knowledge about genres to create texts, make intertextual links and express literal meanings.

1.5 Tips and advice

Language Outline	Generalizations
	This activity could provide a framework for group speaking tasks.
	(i) After providing a topic for discussion, groups decide on a number of sub-topics.
	(ii) Students discuss the sub-topics and make generalizations.
	(iii) The groups then support their generalization with examples.
Level	*
Time	10–15 minutes for preparation plus 5 minutes for each presentation
Preparation	On the board, write the generalization signal words from Box 1.5a.

Procedure

1   Divide the class into small groups.
2   Tell the class that you want them to prepare some tips or advice. Here are a few topics they could choose from: advice or tips for a hospital visit, advice about building a new home, tips for employers when meeting with employees or a union representative, or cultural advice to a foreign visitor. The activity would work well if students drew on their academic background and if each group had a different topic.
3   Firstly, the groups should brainstorm a number of subheadings. In the case of cultural tips, for example, these could be: food, customs, manners, traditions, language or family relationships. For hospital admission, subheadings could include: pre-admission appointments, health insurance, ward routines, facilities, catering, support for families of the patient or medical specialists' services.

4   Ask the groups to discuss their advice or tips. In expressing these tips, students are encouraged to generalize about common practices. Refer to the generalizations on the board. See Box 1.5a.

5   Next, ask the groups to elaborate on the tips with examples. See Box 1.5b.

6   Join two groups and ask each group to present to the other. The group members offer their advice in the form of a short presentation with each person speaking on one of the sub-topics.

7   Following each presentation, ask the 'listeners' to give feedback on which tips they considered to be the most enlightening or helpful.

Box 1.5a: Generalization signals

Generally
Generally speaking
Usually
Mostly
As a rule
It is usually expected that
By and large
Typically

Box 1.5b: Tips

Cultural tips	Hospital tips
Food: Eating in a restaurant	*Pre-admission appointment*
In restaurants, as a rule, each person orders individually. Generally, we do not start eating until everyone at the table has been served. Mostly, people do not talk with food in their mouths and when they do talk, it is typically loud enough for the others at the table to hear, but not loud enough to be heard at other tables in the restaurant. When we finish the meal, we usually place our knife and fork together on the plate. It is usually expected that the waiter will not take a plate from the table until they see the knife and fork together. By and large, diners decide to split the bill between them.	In hospitals, as a rule, patients are required to attend a pre-admission interview. The purpose of this interview is to ensure a hassle-free admission. Generally, patients are asked to bring documentation such as personal identification, medical insurance details and any X-rays or test results relevant to the hospital visit. It is usually expected that the staff will inform the patient about what to bring to hospital, for instance toiletries, chronic medication and sleepwear. Typically, staff strongly advise against bringing valuables and cellular phones.

Follow-up
- Students use the tips to make an information brochure, e.g. for a foreign visitor, for a hospital visit.
- Generalizations are often used in academic speaking and writing to introduce a topic. As the students read academic texts, ask them to be on the look out for other ways of expressing a generalization.

1.6   Text analysis

Language	Imperatives and generic structure of a procedure
Outline	Groups analyse the generic structure and language features of a procedure. They then use this model in a class presentation.
Level	*
Time	30 minutes for preparation plus 5–10 minutes for each presentation
Preparation	Photocopy a model of a procedural text. See Box 1.6a. On the board, write the headings for the generic structure of the text in a random order: Title, Background/Introduction, Equipment, Steps.

Procedure

1   For this activity you want the class to demonstrate a procedure. Divide the class into groups and give out a copy of the model text you have copied. Ask the students to match the generic structure headings on the board to sections of the text.

2   Next, ask the students to analyse the language features of the text. You should list these on the board and ask the students to match the language to examples in the text. In a procedure, for example, you could ask them to underline the imperative verbs, highlight the content-specific nouns and note the use of the definite article to talk about things in general.

3   In this step, groups use the model text as a guide for their oral presentations. Firstly, they decide on the procedure they wish to research. See a range of topics in Box 1.6b. Then allow time for the class to seek out information and prepare for their presentations. They may want to use the internet, reference books or information fact sheets. Some may want to interview an expert.

4   After rehearsing, the groups deliver their presentations to the class. Tell the students that as well as talking, you want them to use visual aids, such as a demonstration, pictures, charts or graphs, to support their talks. If it is possible, the others in the class could follow their instructions, e.g. in a first aid demonstration or a science experiment. Otherwise, the class could record the steps of the procedure.

Box 1.6a: First aid instructions

TEXT	Generic structure of a procedure
How to treat an ankle injury	
Ankle injuries are most likely to occur during physical exercise. It is very important to treat the injury immediately.	
To treat an ankle injury, you will need an ice pack and a compression bandage.	
Step 1: Rest the ankle immediately. Do not continue to walk on the ankle.	
Step 2: Apply ice to the swollen ankle.	
Step 3: Wrap a compression bandage around the affected area. Be careful not to bandage too tightly.	
Step 4: Elevate the ankle. This means you should raise the ankle above the level of the heart.	

Box 1.6b: Topics for procedural texts

Here are some other procedural topics that students may wish to demonstrate:
- How to test soil for nutrient content, composition or contaminants
- How to extract minerals from a mining site
- How to get bank finance for a business venture
- How to invest on the stock market
- How to stage an event, e.g. a festival, a product launch
- How to make a television advertisement
- How to install a computer program
- How to set up a website
- How to fireproof a new building
- How to restore/preserve ancient documents or pieces of art

Follow-up

Many first aid topics are described at http://www.videojug.com/ See examples in Box 1.6c. Students can either read or listen to someone talking about different first aid tips. They could also check their pronunciation while listening to the presenters on the website.

Box 1.6c: First aid topics

- How to bandage a hand
- How to treat an insect bite
- How to help with minor cuts
- How to treat a burn
- How to deal with heat exhaustion
- How to ice an injury
- How to deal with sunburn
- How to help someone who is feeling faint
- How to control bleeding from a cut
- How to remove a splinter

1.7 PowerPoint® presentations

Language	Grammar patterns: reporting research
Skill	Predicting content from a topic heading
Outline	Students predict the content of a PowerPoint talk from the title slide before each group delivers an oral presentation.
Level	*
Time	20–30 minutes for preparation plus 10 minutes for each presentation
Preparation	Create a speaking task based on a current class theme. The topic should be broad enough for students to explore a range of alternatives within a research field. Write the task on the board. See Box 1.7a. Also, write the language for reporting. See Box 1.7c.

Procedure

1 Refer the class to the task outline on the board. See Box 1.7a. The example asks students to reflect on advice about health from their childhood or from the popular media. Other areas for research could include medical breakthroughs, new technologies, alternatives to fossil fuels, or the latest developments in building materials.

2 Divide the class into groups and ask the students to decide on an aspect of the topic that they would like to present to the whole class. They should focus on areas of research that interest them within the broader topic. The example looks at research into health myths. However, if you choose 'alternatives to fossil fuels' for your broad topic, students could investigate the latest research into energy generated by solar, wind, nuclear, tidal, geothermal or hydropower as well as biomass, biogas or bio fuels.

3 The groups then collect information about their topic. This could be done in a class reading or listening lesson, in a computer lab or as a homework task.

4 Following their research, students should summarize their findings into main ideas, using bullet points in preparation for a number of PowerPoint slides. They should try to limit the words to 30 per slide. See Box 1.7b for examples of slides about a health myth. Topics for slides could include:

Slide 1: *Title plus research question*
Slide 2: *What is the research topic?*
Slide 3: *What are the research findings?*
Slide 4: *What are the recommendations?*

5   Allow time for the groups to practise their presentation. As they rehearse, refer the students to the language of reporting on the board and encourage them to use this language in their presentations. See Box 1.7c.

6   The first group shows Slide 1 and the next group predicts the content of this presentation.

7   Then each member of Group 1 takes a turn to speak about one of their PowerPoint slides, confirming or adding to the predictions of the previous group. They should try to speak about the topic, using the slides as a prompt, rather than read the information from a script. Continue this pattern of predicting and presenting until all the groups have had a turn.

Box 1.7a: Health myth task

Task
You have been asked to research the topic of health myths and then report your findings to the class. To support your presentation, create PowerPoint slides.

Box 1.7b: Health myth slides

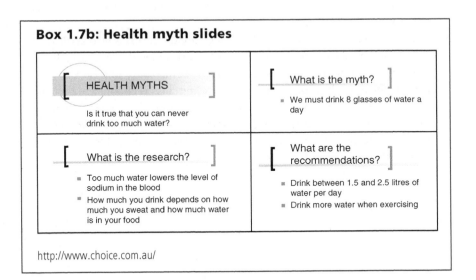

http://www.choice.com.au/

Box 1.7c: Reporting on research

- According to .... (a researcher, e.g. Dr J. Lewis, or a research organization, e.g. The World Health Organization)
- There is general agreement that ...
- Research suggests that ...
- Some studies have found ...
- Some studies indicate that ...
- Other studies draw mixed conclusions.
- Recent research based on the .... study (the name of a particular study, e.g. The International Obesity study) has found ...
- There's not enough evidence to be conclusive.
- Until a few years ago .... but now ....
- Critics argue that ...

Follow-up
- Allow time for a question and answer session following each presentation. This could lead to students engaging in further research as they follow their interests.
- Students could try PowerPoint Karaoke. Divide the class into groups and decide on the theme or topic. Each group is then presented with one random slide from the topic. Each speaker in the group takes a turn to speak to the points on the screen. The class is encouraged to call out suggestions and encouragement as the participants 'invent' their presentation on the spot. Award points for the most inventive teams. PowerPoint slides from a wide variety of topics are available at http://www.slidesharetoys.com/karaoke/

1.8 Group seminars

Skill	Presenting a well-structured seminar
Outline	Students research a topic, allocate subsections to members of their group, and present a seminar to the class. Following the seminars, students provide peer feedback for each group.
Level	**
Time	10–15 minutes for initial planning plus 10–15 minutes for each seminar
Preparation	Photocopy the structure of a seminar from Box 1.8a and the peer feedback form from Box 1.8b. Either choose a number of topics for the seminars, or ask the students to suggest topics they would like to talk about.
Background	A university subject is often divided up into key areas and sometimes lecturers allocate one of these areas per week as the subject of a group seminar. Students are required to read a number of journal articles and then present the main ideas of the articles to the class in a seminar presentation.

Procedure

1   Explain that in tertiary institutions, students are often required to present a group seminar. See Background above.

2   On the board, write a number of topics for seminar presentations and divide the class into small seminar groups. Ideas for seminars could be drawn from a range of topics as diverse as traditional medicine, colonialism, public relations, global migration or any other academic area of interest to your class. Allow time for the class to share briefly what they already know about these topics before allocating one topic per group.

3   Now hand out the *Structure of a seminar* presentation. See Box 1.8a. Ask each member of the group to take one section of the seminar. Ideally, one student introduces the topic, two or three students elaborate on the topic and one student concludes the seminar.

4   Once this planning stage is completed, the groups research their topic for the seminar presentation. This could be done in class or as a homework activity.

5   As groups present their seminar, ask the other students to record peer feedback. See Box 1.8b for prompts indicating how students could comment. When all the seminars are completed, the feedback sheets are handed to the groups. They then take time to consider the feedback.

Box 1.8a: Structure of a seminar

Structure	What do you do?
Introduction	• Capture the attention of your audience. You could start with some key facts or a quote which may surprise the audience. • Give a brief background to the topic. • Give an overview of the aims and sub-topics within your seminar. Your audience should know how many points you are going to make and the title of each sub-topic in the presentation. • Have your aims and key points in visual form, e.g. on the board, in a PowerPoint® presentation. • Make sure you look at your audience.
Body	• Introduce each segment clearly. Use discourse markers such as *to begin with, firstly, next, secondly, finally*. • Do not have too much information in each segment. Limit your points to three or four.
Conclusion	• Signal clearly to the audience that you are concluding the presentation. For example, say: *In conclusion* or *To conclude*, or *To sum up*. • Summarize and evaluate the main points of your presentation. • Present any recommendations.

Box 1.8b: Seminar – peer feedback

Criteria	Score			
	VG	G	S	U
The presenters spoke confidently.				
The presenters spoke fluently.				
The presenters used visual aids to support their seminar.				
The seminar ideas were presented in a logical order.				
Relevant material was selected.				
The speakers used accurate sentences in their presentation.				
Vocabulary was relevant and new terms were explained.				
The presentation was given at a comfortable speed, with appropriate pausing.				
Pronunciation was clear with appropriate stress and intonation.				

Note: VG = Very good; G = Good; S = Satisfactory; U = Unsatisfactory

From *Communicative Activities for EAP*

© Cambridge University Press 2011   PHOTOCOPIABLE

Follow-up

Following the seminars and the feedback session, ask the class to decide on their collective strengths and weaknesses. Together decide on how future lessons could help them to improve their seminar skills.

Note: The World Health Organization has produced fact sheets on a wide range of health topics which could be used as topics for seminars. These are available at http://www.who.int/mediacentre/factsheets/en

1.9 Literature review: palm cards

Skill	Tutorial presentation using palm cards
Outline	Students prepare a short analysis of a reference book. They then present a literature review in a tutorial, using scaffolded sentence stems.
Level	*
Time	30–40 minutes
Preparation	Write the tutorial task on the board. Do not include the prompt questions. See Box 1.9a. Ask each group to borrow a reference book from the library to be used in the tutorial task.
Background	Tutorials usually supplement a lecture. Students are required to do prior reading and to contribute to a discussion or present information from the readings. Tutorials are quite informal and tend to involve much more student interaction than the more formal lecture or seminar presentation.

Procedure

1   Introduce the students to the expectations of their role in tutorials. See Background above.
2   Refer the class to the tutorial task on the board. In the example, students are required to report on a review of a music history reference book about a composer. You could use reference books from other disciplines, e.g. art history, film history, dance history, opera. Or you could choose from completely different disciplines, such as architecture or law. Whatever discipline you choose, there needs to be a number of sub-topics. For instance, in the discipline of architecture, students could review reference books about classical, medieval, Romanesque, Gothic, Baroque, Greek or Victorian architecture.
3   In small groups, ask the students to break the task down into a number of key points. See Box 1.9a.
4   Then ask the groups to plan sentence stems that will introduce each section of their literature review. They should write these on a palm card and allocate one sentence stem to each group member. See Box 1.9b.
5   Allow students time to use their reference books to gather the information they need to participate in the tutorial.
6   Bring the whole class together to simulate a tutorial, keeping in mind the informal nature of tutorials. Call on the members of the small groups to present their literature review to the large tutorial group. See Box 1.9b.
7   Ask the class to decide which books they would find most helpful and give reasons for their selections.

Box 1.9a: Literature review task

Task: You have been allocated five minutes in a tutorial group to present a brief review of a reference book about an influential composer.

- Which composer have you chosen and which book have you decided to review?
- Describe the author and his/her credentials.
- What is the scope of the book?
- Would you recommend the book? Why? / Why not?

Box 1.9b: Tutorial presentation

Palm card	Extended presentation
• Today I'm going to review … • Although this book is relatively short, it covers … • *The Life of Bach* was written by … who is … • I'd strongly recommend this book because it not only … but it also … • I think this book makes an important contribution to our discussion because …	Today I'm going to review *The Life of Bach*. Although this is a relatively short book, it covers the life and work of Bach from his early years (1685–1703) right through to his final years in Leipzig and his death in 1750. *The Life of Bach* was written by Peter Williams, who is an eminent English musicologist, organist and harpsichordist. I'd strongly recommend this book because it not only presents the important facts about Bach's life and music, but it also links these to the philosophies of eighteenth-century Germany. I think this book makes an important contribution to our discussion because it challenges the reader to question the conventional understandings of the composer's life and work.

Follow-up

In small groups, ask the students the following questions:

- When you are deciding on which book to borrow from the library, what aspects of the book do you consider to be most useful: the cover, the index, the contents, information about the author, an abstract, the introduction?
- What sort of information do you look for?'

Invite the groups to share their ideas and experience with the class.

TEXT USER

'Text users' apply their understanding of context, audience and purpose to create a range of staged texts with appropriate vocabulary and grammar choices. They also adapt the register of their texts to suit the context, audience and purpose for speaking.

1.10 Rotating trios

Language	Coordination: continuing the same idea
Outline	Students are divided into groups of three, and each group has a different problem to consider. They brainstorm the factors which have contributed to their problem. Members of the trio then rotate and explain the causes of their problem to their new trio.
Level	*
Time	25–30 minutes plus time for research (optional)
Preparation	Create a number of 'problem' cards for discussion. This activity has examples about environmental problems. See Box 1.10a. Write the language of coordination on the board. See Box 1.10b.
Reference	This activity is based on an idea in M. Silberman (1996) *Active Learning: 101 Strategies to Teach Any Subject*. Boston: Allyn and Bacon.

Procedure

1 Divide the class into groups of three. Allocate a different problem card to each trio.
2 Allow about ten minutes for the trio to brainstorm and list the factors which have contributed to the problem. Students may need extra time to

research the causes of their problem by watching videos, reading books or articles, or doing an online search.

3   Refer to the language of coordination on the board. Tell the students that this language is used when a writer or speaker wants to list a number of factors. Ask the trios to use these signals as they practise listing the causes they have uncovered in their research. See Box 1.10b for an example.

4   Now each group member takes a number: 1, 2 or 3. Number 1 rotates one trio to the right and Number 2 rotates two trios to the right. Number 3 does not move. In the new trios, ask the students to take turns to describe their problem and list the causes.

5   Monitor the trios and provide assistance if needed. Where students have been particularly successful in linking and expressing ideas, ask them to demonstrate this to the class.

6   The trios rotate once more. See Step 4.

7   Invite the new trios to summarize all the factors contributing to the problems raised in their group. As they present these to the class, encourage the use of coordinating language.

Box 1.10a: Environmental problems

Environmental problems

Land pollution

Water pollution

Air pollution

Acid rain

Global warming

Rainforest destruction

Soil salination

Water shortages

Extinction of some species

Rising sea levels

For more information about environmental problems, visit
http://library.thinkquest.org/26026/index.php3

Box 1.10b: Using language of coordination

Language of coordination	Causes of acid rain
and in addition in addition to furthermore what's more besides this also another as well too equally similarly likewise	**There are a number of factors** contributing to the problem of acid rain. Industrial waste which pollutes the air is the primary cause of acid rain. This pollution consists of two chemicals: sulphur dioxide and nitrogen oxide. Sulphur dioxide comes mainly from coal-fired power plants, **and** nitrogen oxides are a result of car emissions. **Besides these** human factors, there are **also** non-human sources of nitrogen oxides. These include the pollution from fires **and** volcanos. **In addition**, lightning adds to the amount of nitrogen oxide in the environment. **Equally**, nitrogen oxide is released into the atmosphere through bacterial decomposition.

Follow-up
- Ask the trios to come up with a number of solutions to the problems they have discussed.
- Students could investigate other problems. For example, what are the causes of problems in:
  industrialized societies?
  developing countries?
  international relations?
  the world banking system?
  the education system?

1.11   Jigsaw

Language	Agreeing, disagreeing and comparing
Outline	Students work together to complete a task.
Level	**
Time	30–40 minutes
Preparation	Write the task on the board. There should be three elements in the task (e.g. passions, values, experience) to enable the jigsaw activity to work. See examples of tasks in Box 1.11a. Photocopy the language from Box 1.11b.

Procedure

1   Ask the class to read the task on the board and check that everyone understands that three elements should be considered in order to complete the task. See Box 1.11a.

2   Divide the class into three groups. Allocate one element of the task to each group.

3   Ask the groups to think about examples to illustrate these three elements. Encourage them to think of at least five ideas. See examples in Box 1.11a.

4   Hand out copies of the language of agreeing, disagreeing and comparison (see Box 1.11b) and encourage the students to use this language in the following discussion.

5   Drawing on their work in Step 3, ask the groups to rank their ideas from 1 to 5: 1 being the most important and 5 being the least important.

6   Create new groups, with three students in each group. The new groups contain one person from each of your original groups.

7   Ask the groups to synthesize their ideas to complete the task. Once more, the language from Box 1.11b should be used in these discussions.

8   Finally, the new groups present their completed task to the class. In doing so, they outline how they came to their decisions.

Box 1.11a: Problem-solving tasks

Task 1: You have been asked to design a computer game for senior citizens. You believe that your game should reflect the *passions*, *values* and *experience* of the elderly.

Examples from Task 1		
Passions	**Values**	**Experience**
Gardening	Family relationships	Retirement from paid
Bowls	Religious beliefs	employment
Golf	Caring for others	Financial independence
Religious affiliation	Hard work	Possible health issues
Charity work	Self-sufficiency	Grandparenthood
Politics	Community	Increased leisure time
Books	Friendships	to follow personal
	Financial security	interests such as travel

Other tasks with three elements:
- Design an advertising campaign for a product which targets parents, children and grandparents.
- Prepare a town plan for a new suburb which includes recreational facilities, public transport and affordable housing.
- Develop a political campaign using print, electronic and internet media resources.

Box 1.11b: Agreeing, disagreeing and comparison

Language of agreeing	Language of disagreeing	Language of comparison
That's a good point. It supports what I've been saying. (Agree + elaboration) I like that idea because … (Agree + reason) I think that would work. For instance … (Agree + example) I agree with what you are saying. I think that's a very valid argument.	I don't think that is a convincing argument and this is why I disagree. (Disagree + reason) Do you think so? I'm not sure that's the case. Wouldn't it be better to …? (Disagree + alternative) I can't agree with that idea. It's a bit out of character, don't you think? I'm not convinced that would work.	More appropriate than … A more fitting storyline might be … I'd rather include … than … Isn't … more suitable for this group? … is less important than … The most essential element is … … is the least important

From *Communicative Activities for EAP*
© Cambridge University Press 2011   PHOTOCOPIABLE

Follow-up

Ask the students to draw on their own academic discipline areas to create tasks which have three elements for consideration. They present these to the class and suggest how they would integrate the three elements to complete the task.

1.12   Hot potato

Skill	Developing fluency
Outline	An object, e.g. a ball, is tossed randomly around a circle, while students take turns to speak on a topic.
Level	*
Time	15–20 minutes
Preparation	Decide on a topic and a number of sub-topics to be discussed. Choose topics that allow students to draw on their background knowledge to elaborate on a point of view. In the example, the topic is 'Power in society'. See Box 1.12.

Procedure

1   Ask the students to sit in a large circle and then explain how the 'hot potato' game works. If you have a large class, you could have a number of circles.

2   Toss the ball to one class member and read out your first discussion question. When the student decides to finish, or when someone else wants to contribute, the speaker can toss the ball to another student who continues the discussion. The others must listen carefully so that, should they be next, they can add to what has already been said without repeating ideas.

3   If students run out of ideas, encourage them to elaborate on a point with examples from their own experience in order to maintain the flow of ideas.

4   When you feel that the class has exhausted the topic, read out a follow-up question. Alternatively, a student who receives the 'hot potato' may ask for a new topic.

5   At the end of the game, encourage the students to record the main points from the discussion. They could use these notes for future speaking or writing tasks.

Box 1.12: Questions – power in society

DISCUSSION QUESTIONS	Who or what has power in society? How do these individuals or organizations use their power?	What institutions or individuals have increased their power over recent times? What is the cause of this increase? What has been the result of these changes in power?	What institutions or individuals have had their power decreased in recent times? What is the cause of this decrease? What has been the result of these changes in power?
SAMPLE ANSWERS	Governments Police Parents Schools Religious leaders The media Men/women Employers Trade unions The military The wealthy The courts Example: The media uses its power to increase newspaper sales and TV and radio ratings. It achieves these increases by focusing on controversial issues.	The power of women has increased in recent times. Causes: • The feminist movement • Women can be financially independent • Equal opportunity legislation resulting in more women in the workforce • Scientific advances in birth control Results: • There are more women in positions of power in businesses and governments • Household duties and decisions are more likely to be shared between men and women • Women have more control over their fertility	The power of trade unions has decreased in recent times. Causes: • Individual work contracts • More part-time and casual work • Economic growth so that employees are able to change jobs easily if they are dissatisfied Results: • Falling membership of trade unions • Workers negotiate directly with employers • Fewer strikes

Follow-up

Here are some other topics for the 'hot potato' game:

- What are our basic human rights? How are they decided? How are they defended? Are there any human rights that should be excluded/included? Who does not experience human rights? Why? / Why not?

- What is 'social capital'? What are the elements which contribute to an interconnected society? How do communities benefit from a cohesive society? What are the roadblocks to community building? How does the financial world benefit from civic engagement?

1.13   Role play

Language	Clarification and back-channelling
Outline	This is a simulation activity where a student asks questions about a criteria sheet and a lecturer explains and addresses some of the student's concerns.
Level	*
Time	30–40 minutes
Preparation	For this activity you will need photocopies of a criteria sheet from an academic discipline. See Box 1.13b. On the board, write the speaking signals from Box 1.13a.

Procedure

1   Explain to the class that for students to fully understand the requirements of an assessment task, they need to be clear about the criteria for assessment. Sometimes a student will need to discuss these criteria with the lecturer.

2   Divide the class into pairs. Hand out the criteria sheet and allow time for the students to read it and decide on the meaning of the criteria. See Box 1.13b. They should discuss how the criteria for each grade differ. You could ask: 'What's the difference between an A and a B on this criteria sheet?' Go from pair to pair and answer any questions. If you are using a criteria sheet that is familiar to the class, then this step may not be necessary.

3   Tell the class that speakers use a number of signals to ask for clarification if they are unsure of a response. Speakers also use 'back-channelling' signals to respond during a conversation. These language signals let the

other person know that the listener is following the gist and participating in the conversation. Provide some examples of these signals and demonstrate the speaker's intonation and tone of voice. See Box 1.13a. Allow some time for the pairs to experiment with these signals.

4   Introduce the idea of a simulation where one person will play the part of the lecturer and the other will be the student. The setting could be in the lecturer's office. The student has made an appointment because he/she needs clarification on some of the items on the criteria sheet. Ask the pairs to decide which items on the criteria sheet need clarifying.

5   Now the pairs prepare to simulate a discussion between a student and a lecturer where they clarify some elements of an assessment criteria sheet. Students should use speaking signals to assist the flow of their communication.

6   Monitor the class as students experiment with the speaking signals. Then invite volunteers to perform their simulation for the class.

7   Finally, using the criteria sheet, lead a class discussion. Ask the class: 'What do you think the lecturer will be looking for when allocating a grade?' 'What do you think students could do to improve their grade?'

Box 1.13a: Speaking signals

Asking for clarification	Back-channelling
So you're saying …	*Right*
Am I supposed to …	*OK*
Is this what the question is asking?	*Hmmmm*
In what way?	*Aha*
What do you mean?	*Is that right!*
Why do you say that?	*I see*
In other words …	*Really!*

Box 1.13b: Art assignment – criteria sheet

Criterion	Standard A	Standard B	Standard C
Visual literacy	The student: • researches, develops and resolves individualized artworks, reflecting an evolved personal aesthetic • defines and solves complex problems relevant to concepts • uses visual language and contexts to construct and effectively communicate intended meanings	The student: • researches, develops and resolves individualized artworks, reflecting a personal aesthetic • defines and solves problems relevant to concepts • uses visual language and contexts to construct and communicate intended meanings	The student: • researches, develops and resolves individualized artworks • solves problems relevant to concepts • uses visual language to reproduce meanings
Application	The student: • applies knowledge and understanding when selecting, exploring and manipulating materials, techniques and processes	The student: • applies knowledge when selecting and using materials, techniques and processes	The student: • applies knowledge when selecting and using materials

From *Communicative Activities for EAP*

Follow-up
- Students could evaluate the criteria. You could ask: 'Are the criteria clear?' 'Will students know what to do in order to do well?' 'Would you reword the criteria?'
- Students could use these speaking signals in other simulations:
    Discussing an assignment with a peer
    Preparing for a group presentation
    Discussing a draft of a research proposal with a lecturer
    Discussing theories, authors or journal articles in a tutorial
    A question and answer session following a seminar presentation.

1.14 Videoed discussion

Language	Discourse markers which signal 'cause and effect'
Outline	This activity is a small-group discussion on the immediate, short-term and long-term consequences of a policy.
Level	**
Time	30–40 minutes plus time for video feedback
Preparation	Select a number of topics from an academic discipline and write each topic on a card. Choose topics which reflect a policy or decision with immediate, short-term and long-term consequences. It is preferable to have a different topic for each group. The example refers to economic policy. See Box 1.14b. Photocopy the turn-taking strategies from Box 1.14a. You will also need a video camera for this activity.

Procedure
1 Before you start, find out if the class has background knowledge of the topic you have chosen. If so, they will be equipped with the concepts for discussion, but if not, then this activity should be preceded by either a reading or listening activity where students have opportunities to explore the concepts before they talk.
2 Point out to the class the importance of being involved in group discussion in academic settings. Note, however, that all participants, and non-native speakers in particular, need strategies to assist their participation. Refer to the strategies on the handout and allow time for students to read and ask questions about the strategies. See Box 1.14a.

3   At this stage you could use the model discussion in Box 1.14b to illustrate the turn-taking strategies. Ask three students to read aloud from the model, and then invite the class to identify the turn-taking strategies as they occur.

4   Distribute your topic cards to the groups and allow time for them to discuss the immediate, short-term and long-term consequences.

5   Now ask the groups to rehearse their discussion and apply the turn-taking strategies from Box 1.14a. This is in preparation for a performance which you will video. Make sure that students do not simply take turns around the circle, but that they participate in an animated discussion. See an example in Box 1.14b.

6   Take note of the language of cause and effect which you observe going from group to group and write these language features on the board. Then ask the students to add to this list of discourse markers. See the words highlighted in bold in Box 1.14b. Encourage the use of this language as groups rehearse.

7   When the groups are ready, film their presentations with the class acting as an audience.

8   When the groups have completed their performances, you could play back the videoed material to demonstrate where groups were successful in achieving the aims of the activity and invite the class to make suggestions on how they could improve their communication. Another option would be for individual groups to play back their material and evaluate their own work in private.

Box 1.14a: Turn-taking strategies

Strategies for obtaining a turn	Strategies for retaining a turn	Strategies for relinquishing a turn	Strategies to shift the topic
• Respond to a question or statement • Expand on the current speaker's theme • Complete the speaker's sentence during a pause • Fill a silence • Use facial and body movements, e.g. leaning forward, maintaining direct eye contact	• Increase speed and volume • Pause within a sentence rather than at the end • Use markers like *firstly, on the one hand* to indicate that you have more to say • Disregard an interruption by returning to the topic with expressions like *that's a good point, but …*	• Direct a question to another participant • Use tag questions, e.g. *Don't you? Can't you?* • Slow your rate of delivery towards the end of a sentence and lower the pitch of your voice • Use body language, e.g. direct your eyes to another in the group	• Use introductory expressions: *There's another way of looking at this. That's one consequence, but what about …? Yes, and what about …? I'd like to make a comment at this point. We haven't considered …* • Intonation – the proceeding utterance begins on a very high pitch

© *TESOL in Context*, 10(1) 2000

From *Communicative Activities for EAP*
© Cambridge University Press 2011

Box 1.14b: Discussing economic policy

TOPICS	DISCUSSION: Removing tariffs on imports
What are the immediate, short-term and long-term consequences of the following?	
• Lowering/raising interest rates • Deregulating the currency • Deregulating/regulating the banking system • Removing/increasing tariffs on imports • Protecting local industries with government subsidies • Subsidizing housing • Increasing/decreasing personal income tax • Increasing/decreasing corporate tax • Introducing a goods and services tax • Privatizing utilities such as water, electricity, transport or telecommunications	A Let's start by looking at the immediate **effects** of lowering import tariffs. I think the first point to make is that when import tariffs are lowered or removed, **this leads to** lower prices throughout the economy. B That's right. And this decline in price **means that** there is an overall expansion in demand … A For these products. Right. And so the whole industry becomes much more competitive in the long term. C Yes, but what about employment? In the short term, workers in these industries are laid off as cheaper imports flood the market. B That's true, but perhaps these industries are less efficient and need to reform anyway. In the long term, governments are sending the message that they will no longer prop up inefficient industries. C That's one long-term **consequence**, but governments also potentially lose revenue by removing tariffs and what are the **effects** of this? B Well, one **result could be** that they increase personal income tax rates or even cut welfare spending.

Note: Performing in front of a camera is a challenge for everyone. For this activity to be successful, there needs to be a very supportive and collegial classroom environment.

Follow-up
- Following this activity, students could debate the effectiveness of the policies.
- In their discussions, students could explore the immediate, short-term and long-term consequences of government decisions in areas such as health, education, infrastructure, immigration and foreign policy.
- Notes from this discussion could form the basis of an analytical essay.

TEXT AGENT

'Text agents' use oral texts to influence others. They express values, judgements and attitudes within a social context. They also present alternative positions and points of view.

1.15   Circle of voices

Skill	Developing fluency
Outline	In small groups one member has uninterrupted time to speak. The next speaker should paraphrase what has been said and then express his/her own views on the same topic. This continues until everyone in the circle has spoken. Then the 'floor' is available for open discussion.
Level	* * *
Time	20–30 minutes
Preparation	Write a quote on the board which will promote discussion in the class. Choose a topic that enables students to draw on their personal experience or prior reading. See examples in Box 1.15.
Reference	This activity is based on an idea in S. D. Brookfield and S. Preskil (1999) *Discussion as a Way of Teaching: Tools and Techniques for Democratic Classrooms*. San Francisco: Jossey-Bass Publishers.

Procedure

1   Divide the class into groups of three and ask each group to form a small circle facing each other.
2   Refer the class to the quote on the board. Give students a few minutes to gather their thoughts, and then invite the first speaker to address the topic. There is usually a time limit of two or three minutes, depending on the confidence and ability of the class. During this time the others listen without interrupting. Encourage the speaker to include examples from his/her own experience or prior reading.

47

3 After the agreed time has expired, the next speaker paraphrases what has already been said and then adds his/her own thoughts.

4 When the set time limit has expired, the third speaker paraphrases what has been said already and then continues with his/her own contribution.

5 When everyone has spoken, the group is now free to have an open discussion on the topic.

6 At the end of the activity, the groups compare how they explored the topic.

Box 1.15: Quotes for discussion

Here are some quotes on the topic of intercultural communication:

- 'The intercultural speaker mediates between two or more cultural identifications.'
- 'Respect and tolerance for difference rather than conformity is the first and foremost factor for successful intercultural communication.'
- 'To deny their first language and cultural background is to deny [English language learners] what has made them cultural beings.'
- 'Intercultural competence is what the learners need [in order] to operate in the multicultural world today.'

© *EA Journal*, 22(1) November 2004

Follow-up

In all group speaking activities, finding different ways to group students adds interest to the task. Students of similar cultural background could be grouped together, or you could form groups with a mix of nationalities. Other ways to group students include random selection, i.e. number students 1, 2, 3, 4, etc. and then ask those with the same number to make a group. You could also have tasks where students select their own group members.

1.16 Defending a position

Language	Making suggestions, giving reasons and presenting arguments and counter-arguments.
Outline	In groups, students discuss ways to address a problem. They display their solutions in the classroom, and when questioned by others, defend their ideas. They then decide whether or not to revise their solutions.
Level	* * *
Time	30–40 minutes
Preparation	On the board, write a problem you would like the class to discuss. See an example in Box 1.16. Also, refer to Box 1.11b and display these examples of language for agreeing, disagreeing and comparison.

Procedure

1   Divide the class into groups and refer them to the problem on the board. Check that students understand the topic.

2   Explain the steps of the activity and then ask the groups to discuss the problem and suggest solutions. See Box 1.16. Go from group to group, encouraging students to expand on their ideas by providing reasons and examples.

3   Next, the groups choose five solutions and rank them according to how successful they are likely to be in solving the problem: 1 = the most effective; 5 = the least effective. They should discuss their reasons for these opinions.

4   The groups now display their ranked solutions around the classroom. They allocate one group member to remain with their work while the others investigate the opinions of the other groups.

5   The person who remains with the group display acts as a salesperson who tries to convince visitors to the display that these decisions are sound. The other group members will take notes as they listen to the defenders from each group. You could suggest that students take turns in remaining and defending. During this stage, students should draw on the language of argument and counter-argument from the language items on the board. See Box 1.11b. As you move about the room, monitor the students' use of this language.

6   Students now return to their original group, share their notes and decide whether or not to revise their list of solutions.

7   At the end of the activity, ask the groups to share whether or not they changed their original list and to give reasons for their decisions.

Box 1.16: 'Green' households

Discussion topic: The planet is facing challenges in terms of sustainability. How can households make a difference?

reduce
reuse
recycle
eat less meat
buy local produce
grow own fruit and
  vegetables
walk
ride bikes
use public transport
	switch off lights
	install solar power
	install a water tank
	limit water use
	use compact florescent
	  light bulbs
	use non-toxic cleaning
	  products
		compost food and
		  garden waste
		donate to green groups
		join a green group
		refuse plastic bags
		vote for 'green'
		  candidates
		lobby the local member
		  of parliament

Follow-up

- Other questions for discussion could include:

  What role should governments play in reducing our carbon footprint?
  How can the world's food production be sustained?
  How can the corporate world contribute to a sustainable future?
  In what ways can urban design be a factor in making our cities more environmentally friendly?

- This activity could be preparation for a 'Problem/Solution' essay.

1.17 Progressive debate

Skill	Presenting alternative points of view
Outline	Each group is given a card which describes their role and position statement in a debate. At the end of the activity, groups prepare a statement which accommodates all points of view.
Level	***
Time	30–40 minutes
Preparation	Decide on a situation or question for debate. Create cards which describe a number of roles and position statements for each group. See examples in Box 1.17.

Procedure

1 Explain to the class that in academic study being able to synthesize and incorporate a number of viewpoints is an essential skill.

2   Explain the situation for debate and outline the different positions of the participants. See an example in Box 1.17.

3   Divide the class into groups of three. Allocate one position statement card to each group. The example allows for a class of 18 (i.e. three students per group and six position statement cards – one for each group). For larger classes you will need extra cards.

4   Allocate some time for the groups to read their position statements and then to prepare to defend their position. For every group member, there should be one key argument.

5   The progressive debate begins. The first speaker has one minute to make the first point and then the other groups have one minute to question and challenge this position. The original speaker has the right to choose who will ask the questions from the other groups. During this time, anyone from the original group can rebut or answer their challengers.

6   Each interest group has a turn. The first speakers talk for one minute and then answer questions from the other groups. While the debate is going on, group members should be taking notes of the key arguments presented.

7   The progressive debate continues with the remaining two speakers adding extra arguments to their side of the debate.

8   When all speakers have had their turn, the groups have to come up with an outcomes statement which takes all the arguments into consideration. Allow some time for the students to formulate their final statement and then call on volunteers from each group to share this with the class.

9   Students should decide which outcomes statements best synthesizes the points of view in the progressive debate.

Box 1.17: Position statements

Situation: A new housing development is proposed in your area. Some properties will have to be bought back and a new road will be built close to the school. The local councillor chairs a meeting of interested parties.

POSITION STATEMENTS	**Councillor** The town needs the income from new residents as the council is struggling to maintain basic services.	**Architect** There are a number of low-cost, medium-density options available for elderly residents who are not able to maintain their own properties.
	School principal The new road will increase noise and air pollution in the classrooms. The school could also face difficulties accommodating extra children, and staffing could be a problem.	**Developer** The development provides economic opportunities for the town as younger families and entrepreneurs move into the district.
	Elderly residents The development will mean that many will have to move out of the houses that have been their homes for generations.	**Environmentalist** The development will have an impact on the natural environment because of land clearing and the subsequent destruction of wildlife habitat.

Follow-up

Students could devise a prop, such as a hat, a map, a walking stick, to symbolize the role they are taking in the debate. Here are two more scenarios for a progressive debate.

- *Medical breakthrough.* Scientists believe that they are on the brink of a medical breakthrough. However, they need to trial a drug on critically ill patients. They call a meeting of interested parties to discuss whether or not to proceed with the trial.

   Chair – Head of research   Patient's partner
   Lawyer   Politician
   Patient   Ethics expert

- *Rural bank closure.* A rural bank has been targeted for closure. The bankers argue that most people conduct their business online, but many residents are reluctant to do internet banking even though there are computers at the library. The bank manager chairs a meeting of interested parties:

Chair – Bank manager	Local politician
Resident	Farmer
Chamber of commerce representative	Librarian

Progressive debates could represent a brainstorming activity prior to writing. Students could use arguments and examples from the progressive debate in an argumentative essay.

1.18　Clarification continuum

Language	Persuasive speech
Outline	Students engage in a clarification exercise by placing themselves along a continuum.
Level	*
Time	20–30 minutes
Preparation	On the board write a question for debate. See an example in Box 1.18b. Write the persuasive expressions from Box 1.18a on the board.

Procedure

1　Introduce the topic for debate. Ask students to talk about examples from their personal experience or from prior reading or listening. This step is not meant to explore the pros and cons, but to allow the students to draw on their prior knowledge and experience of the topic before the debate begins.

2　Divide the class into small groups and ask the students to discuss the pros and cons of the issue.

3　Ask the students to stand up. Create an imaginary line from one end of the classroom to the other. Students are invited to place themselves along the imaginary line. At one end are the students who strongly agree and at the other end are the students who strongly disagree.

4　As students decide where they want to stand, encourage them to ask each other to give reasons for choosing to stand in a particular place along the continuum. They should give examples to back up their opinions. Some students may want to try to convince others to change their mind about where to stand. They will need to be quite persuasive to do this. Have some examples of persuasive speech on the board so that students can draw on these expressions during the activity. See Box 1.18a.

5　At the end of the exercise, ask the students to record the pros and cons in a table. See an example in Box 1.18b.

Box 1.18a: Persuasive speech

Well, what about ...?	*In my view ...*
Just think about ...	*Yes, but don't forget ...*
Have you thought about ...?	*Look at it this way ...*
That may be true, but ...	*I've thought about that but ...*
In my opinion ...	*Can't you see that ...?*

Box 1.18b: Pros and cons of blogging

Debate question: Does 'blogging' contribute positively to public discussion?

Pros	Cons
• Blogs create connection and communities of people with similar interests.	• Some bloggers are poor writers, so the quality of the text is inadequate.
• Blogs encourage a two-way interaction – unlike newspapers or other printed formats.	• Some bloggers use the internet to discriminate against others, e.g. racial vilification.
• Blogs allow people to be 'independent journalists'.	• Some bloggers can damage the reputation of people or companies, e.g. defamation.
• Only a small number of people have letters to the editor published in newspapers, but anyone can express an opinion in a blog.	• Bloggers may reveal company secrets.
• Bloggers generate the content of the blog: they have the freedom to say whatever they like.	• Bloggers are not held accountable for their contributions.
• Businesses can advertise and build their customer base through blogs.	• Some bloggers write about irrelevant and boring personal material.
• Political parties can explain their policies and reach a wider audience in a blog.	• Potential employers may access your blogs, and this could result in missing out on a job.
• Blogging is an instrument for democratic activity.	• A blogger's opinions are in the public arena for anyone to read. There is no control over who reads the blog.
• Travellers can communicate with friends and family at home through a blog.	• Blogs are easy to start and difficult to maintain.

Follow-up
- Other topics for this kind of debate could include:
    Are video games addictive?
    Should children have mobile phones?
    Should governments censor the internet?
    Should employers have access to employees' emails?
    Has television been replaced by online entertainment?
- The students' summary tables could be used as a basis for writing an argumentative essay on the topic.

1.19 A strategic plan

Language	Introducing, developing, transitioning and synthesizing ideas
Outline	A group of students develop a strategic plan. In doing so, they introduce an idea, develop the idea, explore other ideas, synthesize ideas and come up with a set of recommendations.
Level	**
Time	30–40 minutes
Preparation	On the board, write the strategic plan process from Box 1.19a. Also, write a problem for discussion. In choosing your topic, try to focus on a local issue. See examples in Box 1.19b.

Procedure

1 Begin by leading a class discussion about the problem on the board. From the discussion, list the factors which have contributed to the problem.

2 Divide the class into small groups and refer to the strategic plan process on the board. Ask the groups to brainstorm what language a speaker could use in each of these phases of the process. Record the students' suggestions on the board. See Box 1.19a for ideas to add to the list.

3 The groups now use the strategic plan process and the associated language to try to come up with a number of recommendations. Encourage the students to 'think outside the box' as they explore the problem.

4 Invite a spokesperson from each group to report on their strategic plan. Encourage debate about which ideas would work well in your area.

5 At the end of the class discussion, the groups should synthesize the ideas which arose in the discussion and decide on a 'whole-class' strategic plan to address the local problem.

Box 1.19a: Strategic plan

Process	Language
Introduce an idea	*I suggest …* *What if we …?* *The first thing to consider is …* *I think we should begin by looking at …* *My initial response is that …*
Develop an idea	*How can we build on this concept?* *We could also have …* *What would happen if …?* *What do you think of that idea, (Jane)?* *Can we assume that …?* *I'd also like to mention …*
Explore other ideas	*We haven't looked at … yet.* *Another thing to consider is …* *What about …?* *There's another way of looking at this.* *Has anyone got any other thoughts on this?*
Synthesize ideas	*Well, what have we decided so far?* *Would you say that we can agree on …?* *To sum up …* *The essence of what we're saying is that …* *Just to recap on what we have so far …*
Strategic plan: presenting recommendations	*The major outcomes of our discussion are that …* *Our consensus is that …* *We've come to the conclusion that …* *We recommend that …* *As a result of our discussion, we've agreed that …*

Box 1.19b: Local issues

- What can the city authorities do to alleviate traffic congestion?
- Some cities could be described as 'concrete jungles'. How can local authorities alter this perception?
- How can local governments address the problem of homelessness in cities?
- 'People space' is valued by city dwellers. How can urban planners meet this need in densely populated areas?
- How can local authorities reduce energy consumption?

Follow-up

If students have explored a 'real' problem, they could write to the local authority outlining their suggestions on how to improve the situation. They could also write letters to the editor of their local newspaper, or publish their views in an online discussion.

2 Listening

2.1 Numbers

Skill	Selective listening
Language	Percentages, numbers, language of increase and decrease
Outline	Partners listen for different details and then together use this information to create a visual summary.
Level	*
Time	20–25 minutes
Preparation	Photocopy a number of up-to-date stock market reports. These can be found in newspapers or on the website of your local stock exchange. Record a stock market report from the internet, radio or TV.

Procedure

1 Divide the class into pairs and then give an overview of the steps in the activity. Students should be aware that each partner will collect different details from the listening text and that they will then collaborate to complete a summary. The example used here is a stock market report. Alternatively, they could listen for trends reported in a research project.

2 Provide background reading material so that students are familiar with the content vocabulary in the listening activity. Then list the content words on the board, e.g. the names of companies in a stock market report. Ask the pairs to write these content words in their notebooks, allowing space for their note-taking in Step 3.

3 Now either read out the listening text or play a recording. See an example in Box 2.1b. The first time they listen, the pairs tick the content words as they appear.

4 The pairs now brainstorm language which indicates an increase or decrease in value. Write this language on the board. See examples in Box 2.1a.

5 The second time they listen, Student A uses up and down arrows to indicate the trend, e.g. the direction of the stock. Student B notes percentages and numbers, e.g. the current value of the stock. They write their notes next to the content words they have ticked in Step 3.

6 The pairs then create a visual summary of the information. See Box 2.1c. Summaries could also be recorded in a table or diagram, depending on the type of information given in Step 3.

7 Group together two or three pairs so that they can compare their visual summaries and thereby check their listening comprehension.

Box 2.1a: Stock market

Name of the company + value of the stock	Language of increase	Language of decrease	Neither increase nor decrease
Vodaphone $18.22	*rise/rose*	*tumbled*	*stabilize*
BHP $39.33	*jumped*	*contracted*	*stable*
Exxon Mobil $68.14	*up*	*dropped*	*steady*
Wal Mart stores $51.29	*bolster*	*lower/lowest*	*neutral*
Microsoft $18.83	*boost*	*plunged*	*flat*
General Electric $11.83	*increased*	*battered*	*firm*
Toyota $77.11	*growth/growing*	*fall/fell*	
Coca-Cola $45.03	*gains/gained*	*shrank*	
Google $379.52	*added*	*cut*	
McDonald's $53.93	*enjoyed*	*retreat*	
	upgraded	*damper*	
	outperformed	*lost*	
	high/higher/highest	*decline*	

Box 2.1b: Stock market report

Here is the market report for today. The energy sector jumped 2% with BHP the front runner for the oil producers. BHP shares are up 2.1% and Exxon Mobil also posted solid gains on the back of a positive lead overnight. Exon has added 1.5% since the start of trade to be $68.14 at lunchtime today. Elsewhere, retail stocks fell significantly for the first time this quarter. General Electric continued to be battered by the fall in overseas demand. The stock shrank 4.7% to $11.79, and Wal Mart didn't fare much better as it dropped by 5.6% to an all-time low of $48.29. Coca-Cola showed a decline of 1.9% to $44.03, while McDonald's is off by 1.25% to $51.93. Car manufacturers are also feeling the pinch as car production plunged by 51% last month. Toyota shares contracted 5.7% to $71.11.

Box 2.1c: Stock market chart

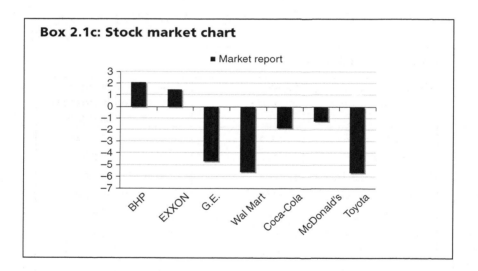

Follow-up
- Students can track the market trends online at http://www.economist.com/, http://www.ft.com/markets National Stock Markets also post daily market reports which can be used as texts for this type of activity.
- You could use tables or graphs from a research paper. One student has a chart or a graph describing the research data. They describe the trends to a partner who has to draw the graph from the description. To add a degree of difficulty to the task, there could be two or three charts, and as

one student reads the description, the other has to identify which graphic is being described.

- If students are enrolled in different subjects, they could challenge a partner to listen for room numbers, times and days in order to complete their partner's timetable. They could also listen for due dates for assignments, as well as for the contact phone number and email address of their partner's lecturer.

2.2 Using contextual clues

Skill	Deducing meaning of unfamiliar vocabulary
Outline	Students identify unfamiliar vocabulary and then listen for contextual clues.
Level	* *
Time	25–30 minutes
Preparation	Photocopy a short audio transcript. Choose a text that contains a small number of vocabulary items which may be unfamiliar to your students. See the Websites section, pp. 309–10, for links to audio transcripts. Copy the contextual clues in Box 2.2.

Procedure

1 Divide the class into small groups and give each group a copy of the transcript.
2 Allocate five minutes for the students to scan the transcript quickly and highlight unfamiliar vocabulary. A scribe writes these words for the group.
3 Now collect the transcripts. As the groups listen for the first time, they tick the words from their list as they hear them.
4 Allow a few minutes for the students to discuss possible meanings of these words.
5 Give out the summary of contextual clues and the model text in Box 2.2. Using the model text, some group members identify semantic clues, while others look for syntactic clues. Go from group to group and assist where needed.
6 As students listen to the original transcript for the second time, they identify contextual clues which may help them to comprehend unfamiliar vocabulary. (See Step 2.) They write these clues in note form as they listen.
7 The groups use their listening notes to discuss the meaning of unfamiliar vocabulary.

8 Return the transcripts. Students now decide on the meaning of the words they identified in Step 2. They also compare their listening notes with the contextual clues in the transcript.

Box 2.2: Contextual clues

Semantic clues	Syntactic clues	Example: from studies about the built environment
Is the word explained in the immediate context? Are examples provided to explain the meaning? Does the speaker use synonyms or antonyms, e.g. *connected/ isolated*? Can the meaning be deduced by looking for a lexical chain, e.g. *places visited, destinations*?	What can we learn about the word by analysing its root and its affixes? Does the ending of the word indicate its part of speech? For example, *-ity* in *connectivity* is a noun ending. Does the speaker signal comparison, cause/ effect or contrast, e.g. *as opposed to*?	*Connectivity* relates to how places are connected to each other to ensure that they are readily visited, *as opposed to* being isolated destinations.

From *Communicative Activities for EAP*
© Cambridge University Press 2011   PHOTOCOPIABLE

Follow-up
Students create an oral cloze activity: for homework (or in self-access / computer lab) students locate a transcript of a lecture that interests them. (See the Websites section, pp. 309–10, for useful links.) They copy a small excerpt and paste it into a Microsoft® Word document, making sure they use double line spacing. They create a cloze activity by deleting a number of vocabulary items, thus creating a gap in the text. In class, pairs of students read their transcript to a partner, who listens and fills in the gaps. If the text is on an unfamiliar topic, the students may include the missing words at the bottom of the page in a random order.

2.3 Evaluating vocal features

Skill	Identifying vocal features and evaluating their effectiveness
Outline	Students use an evaluation table to assess the effectiveness of vocal features.
Level	*
Time	25–30 minutes
Preparation	Access a recording of a panel discussion between two or three people. You could record a discussion from a TV programme, but take care to choose an academic topic, e.g. literature, science, technology. See the Websites section, pp. 309–10, for useful links.

Procedure

1 Tell the class the number of people who will participate in the recording of a panel discussion. They then create a table with one column for each participant. See Box 2.3.

2 Brainstorm the features of vocal production which contribute to clarity of communication, e.g. appropriate volume. Also, ask the students to name features which may detract from communicating effectively, e.g. hesitations. The students list these features in their table. See Box 2.3.

3 Divide the class into groups. Allocate one vocal feature to each group member.

4 Now play the recording and ask the students to rate the performance of each speaker by allocating A, B or C. (For the negative criterion 'repetition', an 'A' score means the speaker used very few repetitions.)

5 Create new groups so that students who evaluated the same feature are sitting together. Ask the students to compare their evaluations and give reasons for the scores they allocated.

6 Students return to their original groups and decide which speaker was the most effective communicator and why. Check if there is overall agreement across the whole class and explore any differences in opinion.

Box 2.3: Evaluation table

Features of oral production	Speaker 1	Speaker 2	Speaker 3
Volume			
Clarity			
Fluency			
Pausing			
Chunking			
Rhythm			
Pitch variety			
Speed			
Repetition			

Follow-up
- Effective speakers use a range of techniques and skills in order to communicate clearly. Following this activity, ask: 'What other elements of oral language played a part in effective communication (e.g. structuring of a contribution, supporting ideas with examples)? 'Which factors were the most important in this panel discussion?'
- Record a number of group discussions from your class. As each group plays their recording, ask the members to evaluate the speakers, using the table in Box 2.3. Ask the class to consider which elements of their own vocal production are effective and which require more attention.

TEXT PARTICIPANT

The listener as 'Text participant' comprehends texts by drawing on knowledge about genres and intertextual relationships, as well as prior knowledge of the subject matter. The Text participant identifies literal meanings, makes inferences, and interprets and evaluates spoken texts.

2.4 Listening comprehension

Skill	Enhancing listening comprehension by completing a sentence
Outline	Pairs ask and answer a variety of comprehension questions based on a transcript from a lecture or interview.
Level	*
Time	20–30 minutes
Preparation	Each pair will need a short excerpt from a lecture or interview. See Box 2.4a. (The *Philsopher's Zone* website offers audio and transcripts on a range of philosophical topics.) The pairs should all have a different excerpt. See also the Websites section, pp. 309–10, for links to a wide range of lectures and interviews (audio and transcripts). Copy the model text in Box 2.4a and the comprehension activities in Box 2.4b.

Procedure

1 Divide the class into pairs. Each pair will need a different excerpt from a lecture transcript. If your students are able find their own short transcripts, encourage them to do so and to bring their excerpt to class. They can choose from any academic discipline according to their interests. If you supply the transcripts, you could cut up one transcript into sections and give out a different section to each pair. See an example of an excerpt from a transcript in Box 2.4a.

2 The students should have a clear understanding of the contents of their transcript before the activity begins. They may have prior knowledge from their own field of academic study, or they could discuss the meaning with each other and gain extra assistance from you or from their dictionaries.

3 Each pair now has the task of designing three comprehension exercises from their transcript (you could use the text from Box 2.4a to illustrate):

　i A gist question which requires a yes/no answer.

　ii A (*who, what, when, where*) statement with up to three missing words at the end.

   iii   A (*why, how*) statement with up to three missing words at the
         end. If necessary, use the examples in Box 2.4b to demonstrate the
         construction of the comprehension exercises. Monitor the students'
         work as they write.

4   The students form new pairs with someone who has a different
     transcript. They give their set of comprehension exercises to their
     partner, who has a few minutes to read them.

5   The students take turns to read their transcript aloud while their partner,
     attempts to complete the activity. It could be that the listener asks for
     parts of the transcript to be read again before they decide on their answer.

6   The pairs provide feedback to each other and, if necessary, explain the
     answers to their partner.

Box 2.4a: Philosophy and politics

Hello, and welcome to *The Philosopher's Zone*. I'm Alan Saunders.

Raymond Geuss is a Professor in the Faculty of Philosophy at the University of Cambridge, and the author of *Philosophy and Real Politics*.

For Geuss, politics is a craft. It's about responding to situations, and it's not always about predictability and routine, however much we might like it to be.

Raymond Geuss: For most of human history, human life has been a terribly dangerous and unpredictable activity; disease struck people down unexpectedly, and so it's not at all surprising that as human beings we have a deep-seated need for regularity and predictability in our lives, and a desire to have a sense of having control over the world, and one of the ways in which we get control over the world is by having predictive mechanisms, and having reliable instruments for dealing with situations is a perfectly understandable human desire. And of course it isn't just understandable, it's a good thing we have that desire. But it doesn't follow that we can actually have that, and we ignore the fact that we can't actually have that, it seems to me, at our peril.

http://www.abc.net.au/rn/philosopherszone/default.htm

From *Communicative Activities for EAP*

Box 2.4b: Comprehension activities

Gist questions requiring a yes/no answer	A *who/what/when/where* question	A *why/how* question
Does the speaker believe that politics provides stability for communities? (No) *Does the speaker believe that predictability is unattainable through politics?* (Yes)	*What is the main goal of a political system?* (respond to situations) *What do human beings desire?* (regularity/ predictability/control)	*Why do human beings look for predictability in their lives?* (because human life is dangerous and unpredictable) *How do people develop a sense of control in their world?* (through predictive mechanisms, reliable instruments)

From *Communicative Activities for EAP*
© Cambridge University Press 2011   PHOTOCOPIABLE

Follow-up

This activity provides a useful preparation for a formal listening test, e.g. an IELTS test. Students could find other sorts of questions in a listening test (e.g. multiple choice), and then use these as a model to write more comprehension exercises.

2.5   True/false questions

Skill	Understanding conceptual meaning
Outline	Each group composes one true and one false statement from a section of a transcript before participating in a competition.
Level	*
Time	25–30 minutes
Preparation	Choose a lecture topic which will interest your class. Photocopy the transcript of the complete lecture and divide it into numbered sections. See Box 2.5. Write the topic of the lecture on the board. See the Websites section, pp. 309–10, for links to lectures and transcripts.

Procedure

1   Divide the class into groups and give each group one section of the lecture. Make sure that these sections are clearly numbered according to the sequence of the lecture.

2   Refer the students to the topic on the board and ask them to keep this topic in mind as they read the transcript and decide on the gist of their section. Students could refer to their dictionaries if the excerpt contains unfamiliar vocabulary.

3   After reading and discussing the gist of the transcript excerpt, ask the groups to use this text to write one true statement and one false statement. You could use the text and questions in Box 2.5 to illustrate this. Check their work and assist as needed. Their page should look something like this:

   Section 7:

   True statement: *False statement:*

4   Collect the statements and order them according to the sections of the lecture. Write one of the first statements on the board, i.e. either the true or the false statement.

5   The class reads the statement and listens to the first section of the lecture.

6   Each group discusses whether or not the statement is true or false. They should write T or F on their notebooks next to number 1.

7   The group that wrote the statement can now answer the question and explain why the answer is true or false. Groups get a point for each correct answer.

8   Continue this pattern with the remaining sections of the lecture. At the end of the activity, the groups tally their points. You could award a small prize for the winning group.

Box 2.5: Chinese vistas

Transcript	T/F STATEMENTS
Section 7 Now I'd like to turn to the period of Chinese history that covers the 17th century right up to the early 19th century – the period that we in the West often refer to as 'the opening up' of China. This was the time when British trade with China really blossomed, although it's important to point out that the relationship between the Western traders and the Chinese was by no means an easy one. What you may not realize is that along with the rush of traders from Western countries came early travellers and missionaries who were fascinated by their encounters with Chinese life. Many of these visitors wanted to communicate with those back in England about their experiences in this strange new world, so they put pen to paper in the form of memoirs. The travellers' stories reflected their observations of family life in China, politics and religion, and so we see that these fiction-like memoirs gave those at home quite an authentic peek into the daily life of the Chinese at this point in history.	TRUE STATEMENTS: 1 During the period between the 17th and 19th centuries, the relationship between the Chinese and the British was cautious and uncertain. 2 Early traders and missionaries wrote memoirs to inform those at home in England about Chinese life. FALSE STATEMENTS: 1 The memoirs of the early traders and missionaries were more like fiction than a true understanding of Chinese life. 2 From the 17th century to the 19th century, foreigners were indifferent to the politics and religion of the Chinese. 

From *Communicative Activities for EAP*
© Cambridge University Press 2011

Follow-up

Students create a third 'red herring' statement. This statement contains information which could possibly appear in the transcript but does not. Here is a statement which could be used with the transcript in Box 2.5: 'British traders faced a hostile reception from their Chinese counterparts.' Include some of these 'red herrings' with the true/false statements. If the students suspect a 'red herring', they could write NA (not applicable).

2.6 Dictogloss

Skill	Selecting, organizing and reviewing listening notes
Outline	Students write key words as they listen and then use their notes to construct meaningful sentences.
Level	*
Time	20–25 minutes
Preparation	Choose a short text which addresses an issue of interest to your class. In the example the issue is 'culture shock' (see Box 2.6). Photocopy the text.
Reference	For more information about dictogloss, see R. Wajnryb (1988) 'The Dictogloss method of language teaching: a text-based, communicative approach to grammar', *English Teaching Forum*, 26(3), pp. 35–8.

Procedure

1   Write the issue on the board and invite the class to define terms and, if appropriate, to share some of their experiences.
2   Firstly, divide the class into small groups. Tell them that you are going to read the text. At this stage, they do not write, but just listen to you read. You should read at a normal, steady pace.
3   Tell the class that you are going to read the text again, and this time you want them to write key words as they hear them. Tell them not to write words like *and, now*, etc. Rather, you want them to focus on content words, e.g. *culture shock*.
4   In their groups, the students reconstruct the essence of the text. Note that this is not a dictation, so you are not looking for a word-for-word answer. The aim of the dictogloss is for students to capture the main ideas of the text.
5   Encourage all group members to contribute the vocabulary from their notes. Also keep in mind that this is an opportunity for students to work together to create accurate sentences. All group members should

be monitoring their jointly constructed text for grammar and spelling accuracy.

6 Display the students' work around the classroom and invite the groups to compare their text with the others. If they have listened well, each text should reflect the gist of the original reading.

Box 2.6: Culture shock

Note: This is part of a welcoming speech to new students made by the director of studies at an English language college.

And now I want to speak briefly about 'culture shock'. Most people who live in a foreign country suffer from culture shock. Learners of English who study abroad have to adjust to different food, customs, manners and traditions. They also have to adapt to speaking and listening to English at college or university as well as in the community. This can be very draining, and you may find that you become quite tired. While we encourage you to speak English in the classroom, we also understand how necessary it is for you to gain support from friends who have the same language and cultural background as your own.

From *Communicative Activities for EAP*
© Cambridge University Press 2011   PHOTOCOPIABLE

Follow-up

You can choose any short text to use in a dictogloss activity. If you want to build the field of a particular topic, select a text which contains the concepts and vocabulary of this field. Alternatively, you may decide on a text which introduces a particular aspect of grammar or text organization as the focus of your dictogloss.

2.7 Symbols and abbreviations

Skill	Note-taking with symbols and abbreviations
Outline	Following the teacher's model of note-taking, pairs and then individuals take notes.
Level	* *
Time	20–30 minutes
Preparation	Choose a listening text which has clear headings for each section of the presentation. Photocopy the text. See Box 2.7. (The Videojug website has examples of practical explanations and demonstrations where speakers organize their presentations around subheadings.) Decide on suitable note-taking symbols and abbreviations for your class. Examples of symbols and abbreviations can be found under 'Study Skills: Note-Taking Tips' at http://english-zone.com/index.php

Procedure

1 Introduce the students to one or two symbols and abbreviations used in note-taking and ask them if they know of any others. Explore briefly how these symbols enable a listener to take meaningful and effective notes.

2 Introduce the topic for listening and allow time for students to share their knowledge of the topic.

3 Either play the first section of the recording or choose a couple of competent readers from the class to read from a transcript. In this step the students observe you taking notes on the board, using symbols and abbreviations.

4 Call on the class to reflect with you about the effectiveness of your notes. Is there anything you or they would change?

5 Divide the class into pairs. The students listen and use symbols and abbreviations to take notes on the second section of the listening text. The pairs then compare notes and make suggestions on how they could be improved.

6 For the final section of the listening text, individuals use symbols and abbreviations to take notes.

7 Then ask for a couple of volunteers to give an oral summary of this final section, using their notes as a guide. The other students check these oral summaries against their own notes and draw attention to any differences in interpretation.

Box 2.7: Description of PDAs

Transcript	Note-taking
What is a PDA?	**PDA?**
A personal digital assistant (PDA) is an electronic version of a daily planner. It allows you to capture thoughts to a memo pad, organize your address book and organize your calendar. Furthermore, using a PDA you can install third party applications such as expense management systems and car maintenance information programs which allow you to input information tailored to your specific needs.	PDA = personal digital assistant elec. daily plan Uses: 1 thoughts → memo pad 2 address bk 3 calendar 4 exp. man'ment syst. 5 car info. 6 own needs
How long will the battery last on my PDA?	**Battery?**
Batteries in most PDAs typically last the user between one to three days depending on how heavy your usage is. If you are using a device that has GPS, the more you use the GPS feature, the less your battery life will be. It's really dependent upon what features of the device you're currently using and how long it can accommodate those features.	1 → 3 days ↑GPS ↓battery life
Are all PDAs equipped to 'beam' information?	**Beam information?**
Not all PDAs are equipped to beam information. Most PDAs, however, have an infrared port because it is a standard that all the Palm devices have infrared ports. However, some other manufacturers that create PDAs don't always use the same technology and try to use different ways to interconnect different devices so they are not necessarily equipped to beam information.	Not all Most palm devs – infrared port Some PDAs – diff. interconnect devices ∴ no beam

http://.videojug.com/interview/pda-basics~what-is-a-personal-digital-assistant-pda

From *Communicative Activities for EAP*

Follow-up

Divide the class into a number of teams. Each team nominates one member to be the first to take notes on the board using abbreviations and symbols. Now play or read the first part of the listening text. There should be about four or five students taking simultaneous notes on the board, while the remainder of the class observe and listen. Ask the volunteers to explain why they used particular symbols and whether or not they would like to change any of their notes. As the whole class compares the notes on the board, lead a collegial discussion on which symbols were effective in conveying the main points of the presentation. As the students listen to the remaining sections of the presentation, the teams nominate different students to take notes on the board. Each time you stop to reflect, you would expect to see the skill of the note-takers improving.

2.8 Connecting ideas

Language	Phrases and sentences which add cohesion to an oral text
Outline	Groups decide on the function of cohesive language items in an oral text and generate examples of what could follow these words.
Level	* *
Time	20–25 minutes
Preparation	Scan through a lecture and make cards containing the phrases and sentences the speaker uses to guide the listener through the presentation. See Box 2.8. Each card should contain a different text. A wide range of transcripts on various topics is available at http://www.bbc.co.uk/radio4/reith2008/

Procedure

1 Divide the class into small groups and give each group a card containing cohesive language taken from a lecture. Everyone in the group copies the content of the card into their notebooks.

2 Allow some time for the students to discuss the function of these cohesive devices in an oral presentation. You may wish to give a few examples here.

3 Create new groups, each consisting of one representative from each of the original groups.

4 The students take turns to read out the phrases and sentences from their card. The others listen and then discuss the function of these words in connecting the ideas and topics in the lecture. The student with the card should manage this discussion and help the group come to a consensus.

5   Next, the groups discuss ideas for what might follow the words on the cards. The student with the card records these ideas.

6   When all the students have had a turn, write the words from the cards on the board. Invite individuals to explain the function of the cohesive devices and share the examples generated in their group.

Box 2.8: Cohesive language

Language used to guide the listener	The function of the cohesive language
In this lecture I'd like to ...	Introduces aim of a lecture
As we saw in my previous lecture ...	Recaps key points from previous lecture
In particular, what I'd like to do is raise the question ...	Signals a new focus
Now let me add a note of caution before I begin ...	Signals an exception or alternative point of view
Let me put it somewhat differently ...	Explains the idea, using a different explanation or example
And at first glance, you'd think that ... *Mind you, there are ...* *That seems quite reasonable. But what about ...?*	Signals a contrast
But obviously that can't be the whole story. *But that's not all there is to it.*	Elaboration and extra examples will be added
Actually, if you think about it ...	Signals an explanation will follow
What's the evidence for all this?	Examples to support an argument will follow
Well, what's that got to do with it?	An objection or challenge will be answered
It's a well-known fact that ...	Concrete evidence will be provided
In another equally striking example ...	An additional example will be given

From *Communicative Activities for EAP*

© Cambridge University Press 2011   PHOTOCOPIABLE

Follow-up

Ask the class to go back to their original groups in Step 1 above. Play the audio text from the lecture. Ask the students to listen for the words on their card and note what comes next. They then discuss whether or not the cohesive language on their card performed the function they expected.

2.9 Listening jigsaw

Skill	Listening for conceptual and vocabulary clues
Outline	Students listen to a lecture and order sections of the transcript as they listen.
Level	*
Time	20–30 minutes
Preparation	Choose two transcripts from lectures on similar topics. Copy one transcript and cut it into sections. (For this activity you will need enough copies for each pair to have the complete lecture transcript between them.) Copy two or three paragraphs from the other lecture. These will act as 'red herrings'. (The Reith Lectures consist of a series of five lectures on the same theme. Transcripts are available at www.bbc.co.uk/radio4/reith2008/)

Procedure

1 Divide the class into pairs and distribute the sections of the lecture. Each pair should have different sections but should have the complete transcript between them. Among their handouts, there should also be one or two 'red herrings' from a lecture on a related topic.
2 Allow time for the students to skim through their transcript sections and make some initial judgements about the order in which they may appear in the lecture.
3 The pairs now listen to the lecture and while doing so order their transcript sections.
4 At the end of the lecture, ask the pairs to read out the 'red herrings' that did not appear in the lecture.
5 Invite the pairs to reflect on the sorts of clues they found most helpful in deciding the order of the lecture.

Follow-up

The pairs evaluate their receptive skills by reflecting on the following questions:

- Did I understand the gist of the talk?
- Did I identify key vocabulary?
- Did I infer the meaning of words from the context?
- Did I recognize irrelevant information?
- What strategies helped me listen?

2.10 Pre-listening

Language	Cohesive devices
Skill	Drawing on background knowledge and dictionary skills
Outline	Students decide on the effectiveness of pre-listening activities.
Level	*
Time	25–30 minutes
Preparation	Using a transcript from a lecture, create five pre-listening activities. See Box 2.10a for some ideas. The excerpt in Box 2.10b comes from a series known as the Boyer Lectures. The website (http://www.abc. net.au/rn/boyerlectures/) contains both audio text and transcripts of a wide range of lectures.

Procedure

1 Briefly introduce the topic of the listening text.

2 Divide the class into five groups and allocate one pre-listening activity to each group. See Box 2.10a.

3 Allow between five and ten minutes for the students to complete the activity.

4 Make new groups consisting of one member from each of the original groups. This means that everyone in the new group has done a different pre-listening activity.

5 Students listen to the oral text and then discuss the gist of the text. They share their ideas with the class.

6 Finally, ask the groups to reflect on their listening experience. Ask: 'Did the pre-listening task have an effect on your ability to comprehend the lecture? How?' Call on individuals to share their experiences with the class.

Box 2.10a: Pre-listening activities

Pre-listening activities	Examples See the transcript in Box 2.10b
Background reading *Number the facts in this passage.*	Within the Westminster system, the government of the day introduces a bill to the parliament. The bill is debated and, if passed, becomes law. It is considered the role of the judicial system to independently investigate the truth in a court and then apply the parliamentary law. However, as judges face new situations and changing circumstances, or if the law is ambiguous or unclear, the court makes interpretations of the legislation. These interpretations and adaptations are often referred to in future cases, so in this sense, the Common Law is developed through the courts.
Vocabulary *Use your dictionaries to help you decide on the meaning of these words.*	*Parliament, the Executive, legalism, legitimacy, judicial function, mechanistic, preordained*
Topic *Share your background knowledge of this topic.*	Do judges make the laws?
Oratory techniques e.g. <u>allegory</u>, exemplification, rhetorical questions, sarcasm, humour *What oratory technique is the speaker using in order to get his/her message across?*	I want to start with a fairytale. It's a very popular fairytale. The public and especially newspaper editorialists hate to see it doubted. Once upon a time, Parliament made the law. The judges only interpreted and applied it. *continued*

Box 2.10a: (*cont.*)

Cohesive devices e.g. linking adjuncts, lexical repetition, <u>reference</u>, substitution, ellipsis *In the text, locate the referents for the underlined words.*	The Common Law was to be discovered in the bosom of the judges. Imagine the image that phrase conjured up in the mind of generations of young law students. The judge, faced by a difficult problem, was somehow to look downwards and <u>there</u>, lo and behold, in <u>his</u> bosom would be the pre-existing law just waiting to be discovered by <u>him</u>.

From *Communicative Activities for EAP*
© Cambridge University Press 2011

Box 2.10b: Judges and the Common Law

Note: The judge in this excerpt is reflecting on who makes the laws within the Westminster system.

Michael Kirby: I want to start with a fairytale. It's a very popular fairytale. The public and especially newspaper editorialists hate to see it doubted. Once upon a time, Parliament made the law. The judges only interpreted and applied it. The Executive enforced it. In this kingdom of strict and complete legalism, it was considered that the judge certainly never made new law himself, he had no democratic legitimacy to reform the law or to express views on what the law should be. These were tasks to be left to Members of Parliament, people elected to reform the law. Indeed, there was a quaint myth which I thought almost sexual when I first heard it. The Common Law was to be discovered in the bosom of the judges. Imagine the image that phrase conjured up in the mind of generations of young law students. The judge, faced by a difficult problem, was somehow to look downwards and there, lo and behold, in his bosom would be the pre-existing law just waiting to be discovered by him.

This view of the judicial function was faithfully held for hundreds of years, into our generation. In fact it's still held by many Australian judges, who feel distinctly uncomfortable in the notion that they're making law, new law, reformed law, not simply applying in a mechanistic way, the preordained rules of the system.

http://www.abc.net.au/rn/boyerlectures/

From *Communicative Activities for EAP*
© Cambridge University Press 2011

Follow-up

Here are some further ideas for pre-listening activities:

- Students build the field by brainstorming vocabulary connected to a topic.
- Given the topic, students determine their purpose for listening, e.g. answer questions, detect bias, identify key issues or arguments, distinguish between fact and opinion, or collect evidence to support particular claims.
- Given the topic, students predict how the text will be structured, e.g. will the speaker demonstrate a procedure? Will a number of items be compared? Will cause and effect relationships be explored?

TEXT USER

As 'Text users', listeners draw on their understanding of a range of texts and how these are placed within a variety of social contexts. They understand that people speak for a purpose and to a particular audience. They can interact with others about these spoken texts and adjust their listening strategies to suit the type of text and their purpose for listening.

2.11   Introducing top-level structures

Skill	Students identify a range of text organizations
Outline	Students create note-taking grids and then decide which grid is most suitable for a listening text.
Level	* *
Time	25–35 minutes
Preparation	Photocopy a transcript of a short oral text which is organized around a top-level structure, e.g. cause and effect. See the transcript in Box 2.11b. ABC's *Health Minutes* website (http://www.abc.net.au/health/minutes/) provides many transcripts of one-minute talks that use a 'cause/effect' structure which will enable students to take effective notes.
Reference	The top-level structures in this activity have been drawn from B. J. Bartlett (1978) 'Top-level structure as an organizational strategy for recall of classroom text', PhD dissertation, Arizona State University.

Procedure

1   Tell the class that when people speak and write well, they organize their ideas, often around a 'top-level structure'. There are four main structures:

- cause/effect
- compare/contrast
- problem/solution
- listing (factors, elements, pros and cons)

2   In pairs, ask the students to design a note-taking grid for each of these top-level structures. See Box 2.11a for examples.

3   Now introduce the topic of the listening task and encourage the class to draw on their own experience to talk about the topic.

4   Play your recording, read the text you have chosen or ask a colleague to prerecord it for you. Ask the students to listen in pairs. At this stage they do not write notes but try to identify the top-level structure of the text.

5   Lead a class discussion and establish the structure and the corresponding note-taking grid for this text. The students may wish to adapt one of their grids from Step 2 to accommodate the text.

6   This time, the pairs listen and take notes, with each person taking a different listening role. The sample text (see Box 2.11b) is organized around a cause/effect structure. In this instance, you could ask Student A to listen for what happened first, i.e. before the result was known (cause), and Student B will listen for what happened after, i.e. the result (effect).

7   After listening, the pairs compare notes. See Box 2.11c for an example of notes. Give out a copy of the text so that students can cross-check this with their listening notes.

Box 2.11a: Note-taking grids

(i) Cause/effect

Event	Cause: What happened first?	Effect: What happened after?

(ii) Comparison/contrast

Topics 1 & 2	How are they similar?	How are they different?

(iii) Problem/solution

Topic	Problem	Solution

(iv) Problem/solution + cause/effect

Topic	Problem	Cause of the problem	Effect of the problem	Solution

(v) Listing

Item to be classified, defined or described	
• A	features
• B	steps
• C	topics
• D	arguments
• E	attributes
• F	examples
• G	elements
	factors

Box 2.11b: The placebo effect

The placebo effect is a source of endless fascination. Just what is it about dummy treatments that can often have the same benefits as the so-called real treatment?

There are lots of theories, but what are the elements which make the placebo work?

A US study tested three things: the first was simply being assessed properly and followed up; the second was the sham treatment itself; and third was having the placebo from a supportive, warm and confident clinician.

This was done in a trial of acupuncture for irritable bowel syndrome – a common condition of troubled bowels and tummy pain.

Now you'd think that with something as potent as having a needle stuck into you, the sham treatment would be the most powerful part of any placebo effect. Well, certainly very few of those just being observed and followed up had any placebo improvement.

Next up the scale was indeed the sham acupuncture. But the combination of the pretend treatment with the warm confident practitioner actually doubled the rate of placebo improvement – to around 40 per cent.

If we harnessed this placebo effect properly, the nation's health could be improved at little cost – and what this shows is that the style that a doctor or other health professional brings to his or her relationship with patients may be the clincher.

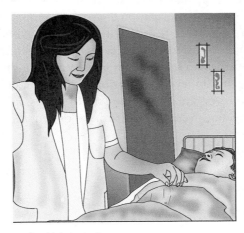

http://www.abc.net.au/health/minutes/

From *Communicative Activities for EAP*

Note: In the broadcast on the placebo effect, the effects of Test 2 may cause some difficulties. Students have to deduce that if Test 3 doubled the rate of the placebo treatment to 40%, then the actual placebo treatment must have a 20% rate improvement.

Box 2.11c: Cause/effect listening notes

Events	Cause: What happened first?	Effect: What happened after?
Test 1	Proper assessment and follow-up	Very few had improvement
Test 2	Sham/placebo treatment	20% improvement
Test 3	Placebo + supportive, warm and confident clinician	40% improvement

---

Follow-up

In an ideal world, oral texts are organized logically, but in reality some speakers may digress from their topics and then return to their theme, include asides or irrelevant information or go off on a tangent altogether. Some speakers may speak 'off the cuff' with little obvious overall organization to guide the listener. As students listen to lectures, discussions or interviews, invite them to refer to their note-taking grids from this activity in order to identify the top-level structure of the texts. Should they listen to texts which are poorly organized, ask the class to suggest how the speaker could have improved the overall structure of the presentation.

2.12   Applying top-level-structure knowledge

Skill	Identifying a range of text organizations within an extended lecture.
Outline	As students listen to a lecture, they identify the top-level structure of various sections of the oral text.
Level	✻ ✻ ✻
Time	25–30 minutes
Preparation	Choose a lecture with clear top-level-structure organization and print out the transcript. The text in Box 2.12a is an excellent example of four consecutive sections of a lecture, each with a different top-level structure. (The Reith Lectures consist of a series of five lectures on the same theme. Transcripts are available at http://www.bbc.co.uk/radio4/reith2008/)

Procedure

1   Divide the class into groups with four students in each group. Allocate one top-level structure to each student. If students are unfamiliar with these organizing structures, you may want to do the introductory activity (Activity 2.11: *Introducing top-level structures*) before your students attempt this more challenging activity.

2   As the students listen to the lecture, each group member identifies sections which are organized around their top-level structure. They do not need to listen for all the details but should be able to identify the gist of the section. For example, 'What was the problem?' 'What was the solution?'

3   As they listen for a second time, ask the students to identify the language which the speaker uses to organize the text within these top-level structures. See the words in bold in the transcript in Box 2.12b.

4   The students now talk to each other about the top-level structures they identified and provide examples of the language from the listening text to support their views.

5   Provide the groups with the transcript and ask the students to confirm their observations and identify any additional clues which indicate the top-level structure of the segment.

Box 2.12a: The triumph of technology – collaboration

Mind you, there are dangers in collaboration, especially in the security of ideas – patents can protect ideas but necessarily give away the details when they are published. Individuals have this dilemma. They need to be a part of the larger world and communicate with it, but the moment they reveal their ideas, they have to be ready to run fast or competitors will out-speed them. I will return to this question in my third lecture.

The process of collaboration has been vastly enhanced by modern communications. The World Wide Web, which Tim Berners-Lee originally developed to allow physicists to work together, now allows creators of technology in every corner of the earth to work together – or to compete. And it is amazing how the efforts of creative engineers lead to advances and novel concepts that could not have been imagined by those who carried out the original research.

Which brings me to the laser. Few now remember that the laser was an adaptation of the earlier maser. The maser, an acronym for Microwave Amplification by Stimulated Emission of Radiation, was a device devised by Charles Townes to meet the need for an electronic oscillator that would operate at very high radio frequencies. It was an electronic device. Townes proposed that a similar device should be possible that operated at optical frequencies and two years later Theodore Maiman demonstrated the first laser. The laser uses the same principles as the maser but operates at optical frequencies, hence the acronym Light Amplification by Stimulated Emission of Radiation.

It was predicted in 1960, when the laser was first demonstrated, that it would revolutionize optical imaging systems and make holograms feasible, but no one could have imagined the breadth of applications that were to emerge. No one could have foreseen that lasers would be used to transmit the majority of the world's telephone and television signals, or to record and play back sound and vision using plastic disks, let alone the plethora of other applications that now benefit everyone. These were subsequent accomplishments of technologists.

http://www.bbc.co.uk/radio4/reith2005/lecture2.shtml

From *Communicative Activities for EAP*
© Cambridge University Press 2011   PHOTOCOPIABLE

Box 2.12b: Analysis of text

Top-level structures	Transcript
Problem/solution Security of ideas/patents, act quickly	Mind you, there are **dangers** in collaboration, especially in the security of ideas – patents can protect ideas but necessarily give away the details when they are published. Individuals have this **dilemma**. They need to be a part of the larger world and communicate with it, but the moment they reveal their ideas, they have to be ready to run fast or competitors will out-speed them. I will return to this question in my third lecture.
Cause/effect WWW → physicists work together / novel concepts	The process of collaboration has been vastly enhanced by modern communications. The World Wide Web, which Tim Berners-Lee **originally** developed to allow physicists to work together, **now** allows creators of technology in every corner of the earth to work together – or to compete. And it is amazing how the efforts of creative engineers **lead to** advances and novel concepts that could not have been imagined by those who carried out the original research.
Compare/contrast Maser (high radio frequencies) / Laser (optical frequencies)	Which brings me to the laser. Few now remember that the laser was an adaptation of the earlier maser. The maser, an acronym for Microwave Amplification by Stimulated Emission of Radiation, was a device devised by Charles Townes to meet the need for an electronic oscillator that would operate at very high radio frequencies. It was an electronic device. Townes proposed that a **similar** device should be possible that operated at optical frequencies and two years later Theodore Maiman demonstrated the first laser. The laser uses **the same** principles as the maser **but** operates at optical frequencies, hence the acronym Light Amplification by Stimulated Emission of Radiation.

continued |

Box 2.12b: (*cont.*)

Listing	It was predicted in 1960, when the laser was
Laser applications:	first demonstrated, that it would revolutionize
• telephone	optical imaging systems and make holograms
• television	feasible, but no one could have imagined
• plastic disks	the **breadth of applications that were to emerge**. No one could have foreseen that lasers would be used to transmit the majority of the world's telephone **and** television signals, **or** to record and play back sound and vision using plastic disks, **let alone the plethora of other applications** that now benefit everyone. These were subsequent accomplishments of technologists.

http://www.bbc.co.uk/radio4/reith2005/lecture2.shtml

Follow-up
Students scan through transcripts of lectures and identify the signals that speakers use to create structure within their presentations. They use these as models for their own speaking.

2.13 Career questions

Language	Question forms
Skill	Predicting, listening for key words
Outline	Students prepare questions and predict answers before listening to a career presentation.
Level	*
Time	20–25 minutes to prepare plus 20–25 minutes for presentation and group summary
Preparation	Either invite a guest speaker to give a career talk or use a transcript of an interview.

Procedure

1   Divide the class into small groups according to their academic background.

2   Ask the students to decide on five or six career questions they would like to ask a visiting expert. These should be general questions rather than questions that are specific to one particular career. Point out the importance of asking open rather than closed questions. See Box 2.13a.

3   On the board, write a range of interview questions generated in the groups. At this stage, draw attention to the structure of each question. Some groups may wish to adapt their questions from Step 2. Students record their questions in a note-taking grid. See Box 2.13a.

4   This step involves students in a role play. In their groups, they nominate one member to be the first 'expert'. Another group member asks the first of their prepared questions. After the expert responds, the group notes the key words from the answer and writes these next to their question.

5   Another group member becomes the expert and the process continues until all the questions have been asked.

6   In this step, the class interviews a career expert. This could be a 'real' guest or you could read from an interview transcript or listen to a recording. See Box 2.13b. If you have students who are competent speakers, you could ask them to role play an interview from a transcript. As they listen, ask the students to write key words next to each question.

7   The students compare notes from the presentation and formulate a group answer to their career questions.

Box 2.13a: Interview questions

Interview questions	Key words Steps 4 & 5	Key words Step 6
1 What made you want to become a ....?		
2 What skills do you need to become a ....?		
3 How long does it take to become a ....?		
4 What qualifications do you need to become a ....?		
5 What is the most satisfying part of being a ....?		
6 What is the most difficult part of being a ....?		

Box 2.13b: Career interview

An interview with a General Practitioner

1   *What made you want to become a doctor?*

When I was nine years old, I shut my finger in a door, and I was missing the end of one of my fingers. I spent many weeks in the hospital having plastic surgery, and it was at that time I decided I wanted to become a doctor.

2   *What skills do you need to become a doctor?*

The skills you need to be a good doctor depend on the field of medicine in which you are practising. For me as a GP one of the most important things is to be able to talk to my patients and to be approachable. For other people, such as surgeons, they have to be good with their hands. Others need to have a very good scientific brain and be good with computers, so there is a very wide range of things you can do in order to be a good doctor.

3   *How long does it take to become a doctor?*

It takes either five or six years to become a doctor, depending on the type of course that you do. If you do a scientific degree in the middle, as I did, it takes six years. Otherwise, it takes five years, but that's just to get basically qualified. Once you have qualified, you then have to have a probationary year as a house officer before you can become fully registered with the General Medical Council.

4   *What additional qualifications do you need to become a GP?*

I don't think scientific ability is all there is to it. You also need to be able to relate to people. Medical schools increasingly are not just looking for the clever students, they are also looking for people who can talk to patients and have a humanitarian approach to other people.

5   *What is the most satisfying part of being a GP?*

To me, the most satisfying part of being a GP is to watch people get better, and to relieve their pain.

6   *What is the most difficult part of being a GP?*

For me, the most difficult part of being a GP is patients who are aggressive, who are rude to me, argue with me, and don't listen to what I say. They've just come in to demand what they think they need. Sometimes they're right, but quite often they're wrong. Trying to get that message across is very difficult.

http://www.videojug.com/interview/career-questions-2

From *Communicative Activities for EAP*

© Cambridge University Press 2011   PHOTOCOPIABLE

Follow-up
Your students may wish to interview you or another staff member, using their questions. If you video interviews with guest speakers, you can use these again with another group of students.

2.14 SWOT analysis

Skill	Listening for key features, e.g. strengths, weaknesses, opportunities or threats (SWOT)
Outline	Students listen for the key features of a product. They then conduct a survey before completing a SWOT analysis to evaluate the product.
Level	* *
Time	Steps 1–3: 15 minutes. Step 4: 15 minutes. Steps 5–6: 15 minutes
Preparation	Many short videos introducing products are available online. (See http://www.videojug.com) On the board, write the SWOT analysis information from Box 2.14a.

Procedure

1 In small groups, students decide on a product they would like to evaluate. These could range from products as diverse as motor vehicles, cosmetic products/procedures or pharmaceuticals. The example looks at mobile phones.

2 Students within the groups choose a partner and allocate one brand of the product to each pair, e.g. one type of mobile phone.

3 For the first part of the activity, students use online videos to listen to presentations about the different products. If they do not have access to a computer lab, they may have to do this as a homework task. Alternatively, students could read advertisements about the product or watch TV commercials advertising the product. Ask them to investigate the strengths and opportunities associated with the product. They should write notes on these points as part of their research.

4 Next, the pairs construct two or three survey questions in order to investigate the weaknesses and threats associated with the product. See Box 2.14b. They could conduct their survey within the classroom or in the wider community. They record the responses in note form.

5 The pairs now return to their group with their research. They use the SWOT analysis as a basis for their group analysis of the product. See an example in Box 2.14c.

6 At the conclusion of their deliberations, groups recommend a product to the class and justify their decision.

Box 2.14a: SWOT analysis

Strengths: What are the best features of the product? Why are these features better than those of their competitors?	**Weaknesses:** Does the product have any missing features? Is it likely to appeal to a wide customer base?
Opportunities: What is the future of the product? Who are the future consumers?	**Threats:** Is the product safe to use? Could there be any legal implications in the future?

Box 2.14b: Questionnaire: mobile phone

Questions	Responses
Have you ever heard of the .... phone?	
Does this phone appeal to you? Why? / Why not?	
Are there people who would not be attracted to this phone? Why not?	
What features should be added to the phone?	
What safety issues are connected to the use of this phone?	

Box 2.14c: SWOT analysis of a smartphone

Strengths: internet connected, portable, email, web browsing, touch screen, GPS, pocket-sized	**Weaknesses:** small screen; difficult to write emails and text messages with small touch pad
Opportunities: faster networks; target new markets in addition to those in the professions or business, e.g. students, older citizens	**Threats:** viruses; security of confidential information

Follow-up

When students have taken listening notes, they could use the following techniques to help them organize their work and thereby make the notes more accessible in speaking and writing tasks:

- Use different coloured highlighter pens to identify similar information.
- Write key vocabulary on sticky notes next to examples.
- Draw boxes around important information.
- Underline the main point in one colour and the example in another colour.
- Number the key points.
- Use question marks if they need to follow up on something.

Students write up their SWOT analysis discussion in the form of a formal report.

2.15   KWL: Know/Want/Learned

Skill	Scanning for specific details
Outline	Students identify gaps in their knowledge of a topic, then listen for these details.
Level	*
Time	30–40 minutes
Preparation	From a podcast, select a lecture which would interest your class. See the Websites section, pp. 309–10, for links.

Procedure

1   Briefly introduce the topic of the lecture before dividing the class into small groups.
2   Ask the students to discuss what they already know about the topic and then to record this information in bullet points in a research table. See Box 2.15.
3   Next, say to the groups: 'What would you like to know about this topic?' Ask them to list these ideas as questions in the research table.
4   The groups then listen to the lecture, keeping their specific questions in mind. They note any answers that occur in the lecture.
5   The groups discuss and record their answers, confirming what they have learned from listening to the lecture. See Box 2.15.
6   They now note which of their questions remain as a focus for future listening or reading.

Box 2.15: Research table

What do you know?	What do you want to know?	What have you learned?
•	•	•
•	•	•
•	•	•

Follow-up

After listening, ask the students to reflect on the information they thought to be irrelevant in terms of their listening goals. Invite them to share these opinions with the class.

TEXT ANALYST

As they listen, 'Text analysts' identify ideological meanings. They detect the values, beliefs, attitudes and judgements of the speaker and recognize how the speaker uses vocabulary, grammar and text organization to achieve a purpose. Text analysts also accept, reject or challenge the position of the speaker.

2.16 Critical response

Skill	Establishing a critical response to a stated position
Outline	Students listen for a speaker's point of view and then respond with an alternative position.
Level	* * *
Time	20–30 minutes
Preparation	Choose a recording of a discussion, interview or lecture in which strong points of view are presented. See Box 2.16a for ideas about topics. Write the topic on the board. A sample text appears in Box 2.16b. This modified transcript comes from a radio programme called *All in the Mind*, which focuses on psychology, mental health and brain function. The website (http://www.abc.net.au/rn/allinthe mind/) contains both transcripts and online audio text.

Procedure

1   Explain to the class that in academic settings, students are often asked to listen to discussions in which a range of information is put forward and

differing views are expressed, challenged and defended. A key listening strategy is to identify points of view and then respond with alternative positions.

2　Divide the class into small groups and ask them to discuss what they already know about the topic of the recording.

3　Students listen to the first part of the oral text and then together list the points of view of the speaker/s.

4　Play the next section of the recording and then invite the groups to add to or adapt their list from Step 3.

5　The groups now formulate alternatives to the views expressed in the oral text.

6　Each group presents their alternative points of view to the class.

7　Class members decide which of these views they agree with.

Box 2.16a: Topics for discussion

- The economy
- Green issues
- Politics
- Science
- Technology
- Culture

Note: The FORA.tv Inc. website (http://fora.tv/) contains many mini-lectures on a wide range of controversial topics within the above fields.

Box 2.16b: Music therapy transcript

Interviewer: I suppose some of the scepticism about music therapy is engendered by ... you hear these quick fixes, listen to Mozart for ten minutes a day and you'll get 20% smarter. What's your stance on these sorts of claims for music therapy?

Music therapist: Well, I think that there's been a real populist application and it's not really a scientific application at all and it's certainly no part of music therapy.

Interviewer: One of the criticisms about music therapy is that maybe it is that personal attention and relationship that's what the patients are responding to, rather than the music itself.

Music therapist: Sure, and that is one of the things that the research will explore further, but we can draw upon some of the music psychology literature that indicates very clearly the use of prerecorded music and how it can promote change in people.

Interviewer: How do you assess the efficacy of the music therapy work that you do?

Music therapist: In my PhD research, I invited patients who experienced music therapy – staff, patients who overheard music therapy on the wards, visitors – to write anonymously: 'What did they think of the music therapy program?' And I collected over 250 response sheets and I analysed all of this data using qualitative research.

Interviewer: So when you evaluated these 200-odd surveys, what did you find?

Music therapist: What I found was that the patients were saying it helped take them to another space, another imagined space.

http://www.abc.net.au/rn/allinthemind/

From *Communicative Activities for EAP*
© Cambridge University Press 2011   PHOTOCOPIABLE

Follow-up

Ask the students to identify the strategies a speaker uses to validate their point of view. In the sample text, for example, the interviewer uses the following strategies:

- Rebuffs/refutes: 'it's certainly no part of music therapy'
- Names the criticism: 'populist'

- Refers to other sources: music psychology literature
- Refers to the academic context: the research, PhD, qualitative research

Academic discussions may refer to the methodology used in the research. Your class could be interested in exploring the differences between 'qualitative' and 'quantitative' research.

2.17 Accept, reject or challenge?

Skill	Critical listening
Outline	Students respond to a controversial topic by deciding whether to accept, reject or challenge a proposition.
Level	* * *
Time	30–40 minutes
Preparation	Choose a lecture which addresses a controversial topic and write the topic on the board. See Box 2.17a for examples. See Box 2.17c for an excerpt from a lecture from the series known as the Boyer Lectures. The website (http://www.abc.net.au/rn/boyerlectures/) contains both audio text and transcripts of a wide range of lectures. See also the Websites section, pp. 309–10, for links to other lectures. On the board, write the note-taking grid from Box 2.17b.

Procedure

1 Divide the class into groups of three and ask the students to brainstorm the issues related to the topic on the board. They should record these ideas in the form of a series of statements.

2 Invite representatives from the groups to write their statements on the board.

3 Refer to the note-taking grid in Box 2.17b. Say to the groups: 'Which of these ideas would you accept, reject or challenge?' Allow about ten minutes for the groups to discuss this question.

4 Note students' responses on the board. You could count votes, for example, and record the numbers of students who accept, reject or challenge each statement.

5 Now play the lecture for the first time. Students listen but do not write anything. They identify whether or not the points they have raised previously are contained in the lecture. They share their findings with the group and add any extra points made by the speaker in the lecture.

6 As students listen for a second time, they identify whether or not the speaker accepted, rejected or challenged the statements on the board.

7 The groups now write a short summary outlining the position of the speaker.

Box 2.17a: Controversial topics

- Cultural property housed in museums should be returned to its country of origin.
- Globalization has undermined the sovereignty of nations.
- Business plays a pivotal role in delivering a sustainable future.
- Professional performance and standards in public life are undermined by excessive regulation.
- The role of the court system is to punish offenders.
- Technology will determine the future of the human race.
- Above all, physicians must respect the rights of their patients to make decisions about their own treatments.
- Genetically modified crops will secure the future food supply for the world.

Box 2.17b: Note-taking grid

Accept the proposition	Reject the proposition	Challenge or question the proposition
• Key point • Example	• Key point • Example	• Key point • Example

---

Box 2.17c: Crime and punishment

Note: The role of punishment in criminal law differs from country to country. This lecture was given by a judge who canvasses various perceptions of the role of punishment.

Roma Mitchell: The consequence of a conviction for crime is the imposition of a penalty. In earlier times a convicted person was likely to be hanged or mutilated, flogged or transported and retribution was a substantial purpose of sentencing.

So it was said we should punish not simply to prevent crime but to show our hatred of crime. While execution, corporal punishment or transportation was the lot of the convicted person, the prison was primarily a place in which he was detained until the penalty could be carried out.

In the 19th century, more humane ideas of treating prisoners began to prevail in British countries, and imprisonment itself was frequently the penalty imposed for an offence. Imprisonment is now the ultimate penalty imposed for serious crime and while there may be an element of retribution in the sentence pronounced by the court, questions of deterrence of the prisoner himself and of others from committing the like crime, and of rehabilitation of the prisoner, loom larger in the determination of the sentence.

I say that retribution and general and particular deterrence continue to be among the aims of sentencing. No one doubts today that the main aim should be the rehabilitation of the offender, not only for his sake but also for the sake of the community into which he must at some time return to live, and in which he must take his place. There are those, however, who say that this aim should be effected by treatment of the offender and that the law should renounce all ideas of punishment as such. It has become fashionable to refer to the treatment rather than the punishment of offenders.

http://www.abc.net.au/rn/boyerlectures/

From *Communicative Activities for EAP*
© Cambridge University Press 2011   PHOTOCOPIABLE

Follow-up
- Organize opinions according to degrees of support for the opinion, e.g. strongly hold this view → could be persuaded to change our mind about this opinion.
- Here are some topics within the field of justice which your students may wish to explore:
  Utilitarianism: punishment is meant to achieve a future social benefit.
  Retributive justice: punishment is fully deserved, e.g. 'an eye for an eye'.
  Restorative justice: the goal of the justice system is to re-integrate the offender into society.

2.18   Fact or opinion?

Skill	Discriminating between facts and opinions
Outline	Students decide which ideas are factual and which ideas are the opinions of the speaker.
Level	**
Time	30–40 minutes
Preparation	The lecture you choose should contain both facts and opinions. See the Websites section, pp. 309–10, for links to lectures.

Procedure

1   Tell the students that lectures could be constructed in the following ways:
   a) The lecture is based mainly around facts but includes opinions of the speaker or other experts. These tend to be within the science fields.
   b) The lecture is focused mainly on expert opinion but also includes facts to support these opinions. Topics related to different theories are suitable here.
2   In small groups, ask the students to suggest one topic for a factual lecture and one topic for a lecture based around opinion. Encourage the students to draw on their own academic backgrounds here. See Box 2.18 for examples.
3   Next, the groups brainstorm facts and opinions connected with these two topics.
4   Invite the groups to share their thoughts with the whole class.

5 Now write the topic of your listening text on the board and ask the groups to decide whether the lecture will be constructed mainly around facts or opinions.
6 Ask the students to draw a line down a page in their notebook and write 'Facts' on one side and 'Opinions' on the other. They use this structure to take notes while they listen to the lecture.
7 The groups use their notes to reflect on their ideas in Step 5. They then compare notes and discuss any differences regarding whether or not ideas are facts or opinions. They should use evidence from the lecture to support their views.

Box 2.18: Lecture topics

Types of lecture	Lecture topics	Facts	Opinions
a) The lecture is based mainly around facts but includes opinions of the speaker or other experts	The diffusion and dispersal of chemicals	Which chemicals are routinely released into the environment?	Options for problem solving in the diffusion of chemicals in the environment: atmosphere, water, land
	Mental illness	Numbers of mentally ill patients; causes of mental illness	Treatment options: pharmacology/ therapy/ counselling
b) The lecture is focused mainly on expert opinion but also includes facts to support these opinions	World financial markets	The fluctuation in world stock markets	Different economic theories explain changes in world financial markets
	Television advertising	TV ratings data; sales figures	Theories about why people respond to TV advertising

Follow-up

Well-presented lectures make clear distinctions between facts and opinions, but in some instances, information may be presented as factual which, in reality, is the opinion of the speaker. After listening to a lecture, ask students to reflect on whether or not the speaker has selected points to conform with his/her opinion while ignoring other facts. This kind of critical thinking is highly valued in Western academic institutions.

2.19   Synthesizing ideas

Skill	Synthesizing ideas
Outline	Students participate in a listen → summarize → question activity in order to synthesize ideas.
Level	* * *
Time	30–40 minutes
Preparation	For this activity you will need a lecture with a clear structure and one which raises ethical or ideological questions. See Box 2.19. On the board, write an open-ended question. For example, 'Should museums return cultural property?' See the Websites section, pp. 309–10, for links to other lectures.

Procedure

1   Divide the class into small groups and allow a few minutes for the students to make an initial response to the open-ended question on the board.

2   Now play or read the introduction to the lecture. From the introduction, the groups should be able to identify the overall structure of the listening text. Ask the students to record this structure as a framework for their note-taking.

3   The students listen to the first section of the lecture and take notes. (See Activity 2.7 on p. 72 for a guide to note-taking.) They then use their notes to discuss the gist and prepare a summary of the section. Call on volunteers to read out their first summary.

4   Next, the groups prepare questions which arise from their listening so far. Write these questions on the board.

5   The students then follow the listen → summarize → question pattern for each section of the lecture.

6   At the end of the lecture, invite the groups to discuss the open-ended question once more. Call on representatives from the groups to report their answers to the class.

Box 2.19: Egyptian cultural objects

Note: Many museums hold relics including human remains which were taken from their place of origin. Here is an open-ended question based on this practice:

Should modern museums return cultural property?

In this modified transcript, the headings in bold should not be read out. These have been added as a guide to the teacher.

Piotr Bienowski, acting director at Manchester Museum: Thanks, David, good evening, I'm going to kick off with ancient Egypt, how and why Egyptian objects were collected, the modern Egyptian antiquities law. Then I want to look at the principles of repatriation and finish off with some comments on fundamental moral and ethical issues that these topics raise.

[How and why Egyptian objects were collected]

Now the core of this museum's Egyptian collection and that of all major museums was acquired in the nineteenth century when for the first time Egypt was opened up to western visitors. In 1798 Napoleon Bonaparte led a military expedition to Egypt. His purpose was to dominate the eastern Mediterranean and to directly threaten British power in India. Accompanying his campaign was a team of 150 scholars who studied and recorded all aspects of Egypt. Now the collectors tended to employ agents who literally robbed and destroyed tombs in order to get at the antiquities quickly.

[The modern Egyptian antiquities law]

Today the Supreme Council of Antiquities of Egypt's role is to monitor archaeological work in Egypt, to give permits for excavations to run the museums. It also has to give formal permission for the export of any antiquities from Egypt. Prior to 1928, however, it was perfectly legal to plunder Egyptian graves. Now this 1928 law is very significant for museums outside Egypt. In seeking to acquire Egyptian objects, museums must check if they left Egypt before 1928, in which case they left Egypt legally, or perhaps more accurately not illegally, or if there is evidence that they left Egypt after 1928, in which case they must be accompanied by an official export permit.

[The principles of repatriation]

But the principles of repatriation now I want to set aside purely legal considerations and look at this from a different perspective in terms of the principles of repatriation. If the Egyptian government did make a request for repatriation, what sort of grounds would they have in principle?

continued

Box 2.19: (*cont.*)

In the case with, for example Aboriginal human remains and associated material in western museums which can be linked with still living relatives and communities in Australia, here it seems to me that most western museums are very willing to discuss repatriation and it becomes a question of finding out who is the appropriate authority to deal with in the country of origin, in this case Australia. But it seems to me that there is a difference between Aboriginal cultures in Australia on the one hand and ancient cultures such as Egypt or Greece or Mesopotamia on the other hand in so far as it is impossible with those ancient cultures to identify living relatives here, and these are cultures and communities which no longer exist, they are historical. These more ancient items cannot be linked to any living indigenous communities and so if it is the sensitivities and opinions of living communities that are the paramount consideration there is no obvious ethical imperative to repatriate them.

[Fundamental moral and ethical issues]

Now I think there is something common to these different nineteenth- and twenty-first-century attitudes to Egyptian objects. Inevitably both see the ancient Egyptian past in light of their own present values: both attitudes have in them a sense of somehow owning the past, linking the past to present needs, identities and political and cultural realities and structures. Well, let's just consider that, museums are certainly changing in their attitudes to the objects they hold and their ownership and use and increasingly they consult with communities, they negotiate, they build relationships, surely therefore our attitude to the ancient people we study and whose objects we collect should reflect our attitude towards human beings in general. Is it ethical to use them as pawns in our own modern games, to relate them to structures they could have had no knowledge of? What does this mean in practical terms? Two years ago there was a government-sponsored report on human remains in museums in this country, and in this report the working group conceded that, and I quote, 'the ancient Egyptians would have disapproved strongly of the opening up and investigation of mummies. The question therefore arises as to whether and to what extent museums owe a responsibility to respect the views of original individuals and communities irrespective of the absence of any contemporary concern by living persons or extant of groups.'

http://www.liverpoolmuseums.org.uk/ism/resources/stealing_history_2005.aspx

From *Communicative Activities in EAP*
© Cambridge University Press 2011   PHOTOCOPIABLE

Follow-up
- Hand out the transcript so that students can check their listening notes.
- There is always a range of views when addressing ethical questions. Following this activity, ask the students to explore the views that were not represented in the lecture.
- Lectures and discussions about other ethical questions can be found at http://ethics.sandiego.edu/video/index.asp Here are some of the topics available:
  Stem-cell ethics
  Medical ethics and the humanities in end-of-life care
  Why ethics is so crucial in artificial intelligence
  Workplace surveillance
  Fundamental tensions in bioethics
  War and peace

3 Reading

CODE BREAKER

As 'Code breaker', the reader identifies phonological patterns and sound/letter relationships. The reader uses grammar, familiar words and context to confirm predictions about a text.

3.1 Recording references

Skill	Identifying key information in order to record a reference
Outline	In pairs, students record references using both the APA system and the Harvard system.
Level	*
Time	25–30 minutes
Preparation	Students will need either textbooks or access to an online catalogue, e.g. http://cambridge.org/uk. See Box 3.1b. Copy the text in Box 3.1a.
Background	In all academic study, students are required to provide reference lists to support their assignments. It is also essential that they accurately reference ideas throughout their work. The two systems of referencing used in this activity are the APA (American Psychology Association) system and the Harvard system (*Chicago Manual of Style*).

Procedure

1 In pairs, ask the students to find a reference book related to their field of study. They could choose a textbook, borrow a book from the library or use an online catalogue. See Box 3.1b.
2 Give the pairs a copy of the references in Box 3.1a and ask them to observe the similarities and differences between the two. Students may need to be referred to the punctuation used.
3 Ask one person in the pair to use the APA system to write the reference for their book and the other to use the Harvard system, using the models from Box 3.1a.

4 Next, the students read information about their book on either the front or the back cover or in the description given in the online catalogue. See Box 3.1b.

5 Using the model in Box 3.1a, the pairs jointly construct a short statement which incorporates the central theme of the book. They should include the author and the date of publication, as they would in an internal reference in an assignment. They should also write the information in their own words rather than copy directly from the book.

6 The pairs then display their work in the classroom.

Box 3.1a: References

APA

Barger, R. N. (2008). *Computer Ethics: A Case-based Approach*, Cambridge: Cambridge University Press.

Harvard

Barger, R. N. 2008. *Computer Ethics: A Case-based Approach*. Cambridge: Cambridge University Press.

Internal referencing for both systems:

Barger (2008) proposes taking a philosophical rather than a legal approach to explain ethical dilemmas in the field of computing. He elaborates on this theory by drawing on case studies from computer professionals.

From *Communicative Activities for EAP*
© Cambridge University Press 2011   PHOTOCOPIABLE

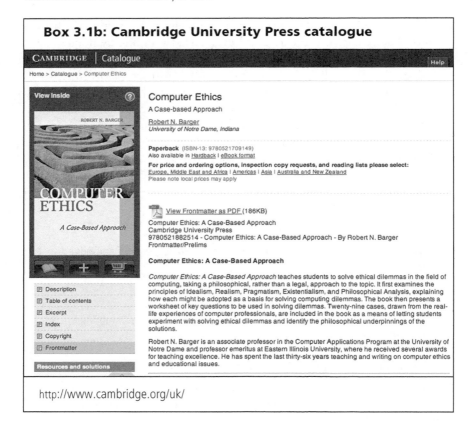

Box 3.1b: Cambridge University Press catalogue

CAMBRIDGE | Catalogue   Help

Home > Catalogue > Computer Ethics

View Inside ⑦

ROBERT N. BARGER

COMPUTER ETHICS

A Case-Based Approach

📖 ➕ 🎛️

▤ Description
▤ Table of contents
▤ Excerpt
▤ Index
▤ Copyright
▤ Frontmatter

Resources and solutions

Computer Ethics
A Case-based Approach

Robert N. Barger
University of Notre Dame, Indiana

Paperback (ISBN-13: 9780521709149)
Also available in Hardback I eBook format
For price and ordering options, inspection copy requests, and reading lists please select:
Europe, Middle East and Africa I Americas I Asia I Australia and New Zealand
Please note local prices may apply

📄 View Frontmatter as PDF (186KB)
Computer Ethics: A Case-Based Approach
Cambridge University Press
9780521882514 - Computer Ethics: A Case-Based Approach - By Robert N. Barger
Frontmatter/Prelims

Computer Ethics: A Case-Based Approach

Computer Ethics: A Case-Based Approach teaches students to solve ethical dilemmas in the field of computing, taking a philosophical, rather than a legal, approach to the topic. It first examines the principles of Idealism, Realism, Pragmatism, Existentialism, and Philosophical Analysis, explaining how each might be adopted as a basis for solving computing dilemmas. The book then presents a worksheet of key questions to be used in solving dilemmas. Twenty-nine cases, drawn from the real-life experiences of computer professionals, are included in the book as a means of letting students experiment with solving ethical dilemmas and identify the philosophical underpinnings of the solutions.

Robert N. Barger is an associate professor in the Computer Applications Program at the University of Notre Dame and professor emeritus at Eastern Illinois University, where he received several awards for teaching excellence. He has spent the last thirty-six years teaching and writing on computer ethics and educational issues.

http://www.cambridge.org/uk/

Follow-up

- As students conduct further research, encourage them to use a systematic method of recording their references. See Box 3.1c for an example.
- Students record references for books with two or more authors and journal articles. Advice and models for these sorts of references are available online. These can be found by using an internet search engine and entering either APA referencing system or Harvard referencing system.

Box 3.1c: Recording references

Bibliographical data for journal articles	Bibliographical data for books
Author's name and initials	Author's name and initials
Year of publication	Year of publication
Title of article	Chapter title
Title of journal	Editor's name
Volume and issue number	Title of the book
Page numbers	Page numbers
Classification number	City of publication
Website and date accessed	Name of publisher
Online journal	Classification number

© Pearson Education Australia 2007

3.2 Semantic and syntactic clues

Skill	Using semantic and syntactic clues to infer the meaning of words
Outline	Students create texts with 'nonsense' words and challenge others to infer the meaning of these words.
Level	*
Time	25–30 minutes
Preparation	Using reference books or journal articles, pairs of students select a short text to bring to the lesson. On the board, write the text from Box 3.2.

Procedure

1   For homework, ask pairs of students to select a short academic text to bring to class. The text should come from a familiar academic field and contain at least one vocabulary item which is repeated throughout in varying forms. See the example in Box 3.2.
2   Use the text in Box 3.2 to demonstrate how to replace a vocabulary item with a nonsense word. Ask the class to guess the meaning of the word *glog*. They should do this by drawing on the words around it and by using word order and word formations to establish the part of speech.

3   The pairs write out their text and replace a recurring word with a nonsense word, adapting it to reflect its part of speech in the text, e.g. plural *-s* or past tense *-ed*.
4   Each pair joins with another pair. They challenge each other to work out the meaning of the word.
5   Check which pairs were successful. If the pairs choose an alternative word which makes sense in the text, they should count this as a success.
6   Ask for volunteers to explain to the class how they determined the meaning of the nonsense word.

Box 3.2: Nonsense words

Note: The article below addresses such questions as: 'How accessible is the internet? Can disabled, poor or socially disadvantaged people in society access the internet?

The internet nowadays provides many tele-services (tele-work, tele-teaching, tele-care, etc.) that, in many cases, substitute or complement traditionally delivered services. In this situation, people that cannot **glog** computer networks may experience social exclusion.

Glogability is one of the key challenges that the internet must currently face to guarantee universal inclusion. **Glogable** Web design requires knowledge and experience from the designer, who can be assisted by the use of broadly accepted guidelines. Nevertheless, guideline application may not be obvious, and many designers may lack experience to use them.

Answer: *glog* = 'access'

http://www.springerlink.com/content/r31k865algm7e38h/

Follow-up
Students choose a text and identify a lexical chain. They could look for synonyms, antonyms or words within a particular academic field. 'Computer, networks, the internet, Web' is an example of a lexical chain in the text in Box 3.2. Students create a cloze activity by replacing these vocabulary items with a gap. They list the deleted words at the bottom of the page in a random order and then challenge a partner to fill in the blanks.

3.3 Suffixes

Language	Suffixes which form nouns, verbs and adjectives
Outline	Pairs play an information-gap card game.
Level	**
Time	20–30 minutes
Preparation	Each student will need their own short academic text. They could choose different pages from a textbook or photocopy their own text from an area of academic interest. They will also need a blank piece of card or paper.

Procedure

1   Initially students work alone. They read through their text and identify the nouns. You want them to focus on words with a suffix ending. See the words in bold in Box 3.3a.

2   Students choose one word and, using their dictionaries, identify its definition and the meaning of the suffix.

3   They then use an online source such as http://www.wordinfo.info/words/index/ info/list to find other words with a similar suffix. If they do not have access to a networked computer, they could refer to a grammar textbook. Most grammar books list suffixes, their meanings and sample words.

4   On the board, demonstrate some of the categories which could be used to make a master card. See Box 3.3b.

5   Each student then creates two cards from their blank piece of card or paper. One card is the master card and the other is a blank grid. While the vocabulary item is recorded in Square 5, it is important that the other categories on the master cards are recorded in a random fashion.

6   In pairs, the students play the card game. Student A asks for a number and then fills in the blank square on their card, e.g.

    Student A: *What goes in Square 6?*
    Student B: *The suffix '-acy'.*

7   The next student has a turn to pick a number. The winner is the first person to guess the word. This is recorded in Square 5.

Box 3.3a: Non-governmental organizations

My aim in this study is to investigate the present legal status of non-governmental **organizations** (NGOs) in international law, and to discuss this status in relation to the **functioning and legitimacy** of the international legal system. The seemingly technical issue of international legal status is closely related to broader questions about **participation and representation** of different groups on the international plane and the legitimacy of international law. The overall perspective chosen here is therefore a systemic one, which sees questions about the role of NGOs as legal actors as issues of how international law functions, and ought to function, as a system.

© Cambridge University Press 2006

Box 3.3b: Guess the word

Master card

1 **Meaning of suffix** state of being /quality	2 **First letter** L	3 **Part of speech** noun
4 **Definition** the state of conforming to recognized principles	5 **LEGITIMACY**	6 **Suffix** -acy
7 **Other word with same ending** privacy	8 **Field** law	9 **Other forms of the word** legitimate

Blank card

1	2	3
4	5	6
7	8	9

Follow-up
Play a similar game using verbs and adjectives. If you collect the master cards, you can build up a bank of cards for future classes.

TEXT PARTICIPANT

The reader as 'Text participant' comprehends texts by drawing on knowledge about genres and intertextual relationships as well as prior knowledge of the subject matter. The text participant identifies literal meanings, makes inferences, and interprets and evaluates written texts.

3.4 Library reading task

Skill	Skimming
Outline	Within a limited time frame, students survey the cover and contents pages of a number of library books.
Level	*
Time	20–30 minutes
Preparation	After deciding on an essay topic in small groups, each student in the group selects an academic reference book to bring to class. Alternatively, you could do this activity in the library.

Procedure

1 Group the students according to their academic interests. Ask the group to decide on an essay topic they would like to write about.

2 Each student in the group selects a reference book related to their essay topic. They could do this during the lesson if the class is located in the library. Alternatively, they could borrow a book and bring it to class.

3 At this stage, they all place their books face down on the table. Set a time limit in which students in the group quickly turn over all the books on the table and review the cover and contents pages.

4 Then using this information, ask the groups to decide which books would be most helpful in their writing task. They may choose a number of different books as references for various points they want to make in the essay.

5 The groups now report to the class. They talk about the books they have chosen and give reasons for their selections.

Follow-up

If students have access to a networked computer, members of each group could find one website or one online journal that would assist them to write their essay. The group then chooses three or four suitable resources for their writing task. Students use the table in Box 3.1c on p. 111 to record their references.

3.5 Note-making

Skill	Writing and interpreting symbols and abbreviations
Outline	Students create and interpret notes from a text.
Level	*
Time	30–40 minutes
Preparation	Provide one short text for each group and two blank pieces of paper per group. Each group should have a different text.

Procedure

1 Divide the students into groups and allocate a number to each group, i.e. Group 1, Group 2, etc. Each group will need a short academic text and two blank pieces of paper. You could supply the texts, or you could ask the groups to bring a text that interests them.

2 On the board, write notes from a short text that you have selected, using symbols and abbreviations. See an example in Box 3.5. You could also introduce other useful symbols and abbreviations such as the following:

    e.g. (for example)

    n.b. (note well)

    i.e. (that is)

    ~ (approximately)

    ≠ (does not equal; differs from)

    ∴ (therefore)

3 Ask members of the class to make suggestions about the gist of the text, using the notes on the board.

4 Next, you read aloud from the text, drawing attention to the connection between the symbols on the board and the meaning of the text.

5   In their groups, the students construct notes from their text, using symbols and abbreviations. The groups should number their page, i.e. Group 1 writes number 1 on the page.

6   Rotate the notes from group to group, allocating a reasonable time frame for them to discuss the notes and then write a short summary on a separate page. They should record the page number of the notes next to their summary.

7   A volunteer from each group now reads out their original text. Check the summaries of the groups and allocate points for each correct answer, keeping in mind that the aim is to write the gist rather than a word-for-word representation.

Box 3.5: Severe sepsis

Text	Notes
Approximately 150,000 persons die annually in Europe from severe sepsis and more than 200,000 die annually in the United States. Certain populations, such as the elderly, neutropenic patients and infants (especially low-birth-weight newborns), have higher attack and mortality rates. The incidence of sepsis is higher in men and non-white persons, as compared with women and white persons, respectively, for unclear reasons.	**Severe sepsis** Europe ~ 150 000 die annually US ↑ 200 000 ann. Populations w/ ↑mortality rates: • elderly • neutropenic patients • infants (low bth wt) Incidence of sepsis • men › women • non-white › white ? – unclear

---

Follow-up

Write notes on the board that represent the ideas in a short academic text. Add a few notes that act as 'red herrings', i.e. these ideas could be in the text but are not. Either read the text aloud, or give out a photocopy and ask the students to identify the 'red herrings'.

3.6   Book covers and contents tables

Skill	Predicting
Outline	Students match the cover of a book and its table of contents to an extract.
Level	*
Time	20–25 minutes
Preparation	Each group chooses an academic reference book and photocopies its cover, the contents page and a short extract from the book. They make a poster by pasting the copy of the cover and the contents page onto one piece of paper. See Box 3.6a. If students prefer, they could access the academic textbook from online bookstores.

Procedure

1   For this activity the class has already been divided into groups. See Preparation. Collect the book posters and distribute them randomly to the groups. Make sure a group does not receive its own poster. You should also collect the extracts that the groups have copied.

2   The students read the cover and the contents page and make predictions about the focus of the book.

3   Display the extracts in the classroom. The groups move around the room, reading them until they match their poster with the correct extract. They should attach the poster to the extract.

4   There could be an instance when two groups claim the same extract. Take this opportunity to challenge all groups to check their posters and extracts. Encourage lively discussion as the class engages in this problem-solving activity.

Box 3.6a: Textbook poster

The book	
	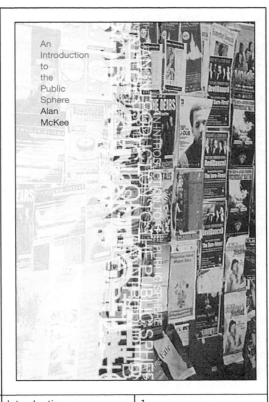 An Introduction to the Public Sphere Alan McKee
Contents	Introduction 1 1 Trivialization 32 2 Commercialization 66 3 Spectacle 105 4 Fragmentation 140 5 Apathy 172 Conclusion 204

Box 3.6b: Extract from textbook

Note: This extract comes from the introduction to a sociology textbook. The author draws on many examples from the contemporary media to examine the ways we communicate in the 'public sphere'.

There are five major themes common to popular and academic concerns about the public sphere in Western countries at the start of the twenty-first century: that it's too *trivialized*; that it's too *commercialized*; that it relies too much on *spectacle* rather than rational argumentation; that it's too *fragmented*; and that it has caused citizens to become too *apathetic* about important public issues.

'Personalities and individual behaviour dominate the presentation of contemporary politics. As public life has become emptied of its content, private and personal preoccupations have been projected into the public sphere. ... [The] tabloid media ... either *trivialise* significant events and give unbalanced and populist treatment of important themes or provide disproportionate coverage to frivolous subjects.'

© Cambridge University Press 2005

Follow-up

Use this follow-up activity to emphasize the use of the context in determining the meaning of unfamiliar vocabulary. Divide the class into groups and provide one reference book per group. Alternatively, students could bring their own texts. Ask the students to choose vocabulary items from the contents and cover that they all agree are unfamiliar. They then browse through the index to find extracts including these words. They use the extracts to hazard their guesses as to what the words mean. The extract in Box 3.6b illustrates how 'trivialized' is explained in an extract.

3.7   Comprehension challenge

Skill	Comprehending at different levels
Outline	Students compete in a reading comprehension game.
Level	* *
Time	30–40 minutes or two 20-minute lessons
Preparation	Set an academic article for reading homework or use a text from a recent reading test. Using the levels in Box 3.7b, compose a comprehension question for each level. If you use a text from a reading test, e.g. an IELTS passage, you could select comprehension questions from the test. On the board, write the key words for each comprehension level.

Procedure

1   Introduce the levels of comprehension from Box 3.7b. Using the selected text, provide one sample comprehension question for each level on the board. See Box 3.7b.

2   As a class, invite individual students to answer the questions and to use the passage to explain their answers.

3   Divide the class into groups so that the students can work together to clarify any questions they may have about the meaning of the text. Go from group to group and assist where needed.

4   The groups now compose three additional comprehension questions: one for each level. You will need to check these carefully to make sure they are well-constructed questions and to ensure that the group knows the answers.

5   Collect the students' questions.

6   Explain how the game works, i.e. each group takes a turn at answering a question which you will read out. Groups can choose the level of question and are allocated different points depending on the level, e.g. Level 1: 10 points; Level 2: 20 points; Level 3: 30 points.

7   Now play the Comprehension challenge game. Where students have written the question, get them to provide the answers. Keep a record of the points on the board. You could award a small prize for the winning group.

Box 3.7a: The crisis in antibiotic resistance

The synthesis of large numbers of antibiotics over the past three decades has caused complacency about the threat of bacterial resistance. Bacteria have become resistant to antimicrobial agents as a result of chromosomal changes or the exchange of genetic material via plasmids and transposons. *Streptococcus pneumoniae, Streptococcus pyogenes*, and *staphylococci*, organisms that cause respiratory and cutaneous infections, and members of the *Enterobacteriaceae* and *Pseudomonas families*, organisms that cause diarrhoea, urinary infection, and sepsis, are now resistant to virtually all of the older antibiotics. The extensive use of antibiotics in the community and hospitals has fuelled this crisis. Mechanisms such as antibiotic control programs, better hygiene, and synthesis of agents with improved antimicrobial activity need to be adopted in order to limit bacterial resistance.

http://www.sciencemag.org/cgi/content/abstract/257/5073/1064

Box 3.7b: Comprehension questions

Level 1: Recall Key words: *who, what, when, where, define, list, retell, give examples, details*	How long have antibiotics been used? What is resistant to older antibiotics? Where are antibiotics mainly used?
Level 2: Interpret relationships within the text Key words: *compare, contrast, generalize, explain, cause, effect, purpose, main idea, how*	Explain the cause of the current crisis. What causes diarrhoea, urinary infection and sepsis? How can bacterial resistance be limited?
Level 3: Evaluate Key words: *judge, analyse, interpret, recommend, verify, prove, justify, evidence, bias, to what extent, why*	Why have bacteria become resistant to antimicrobial agents? Justify why there is complacency about the threat of bacterial resistance.

Follow-up
If you have a computer in the classroom, you may want to look at the
template for constructing an electronic version of the game which is
available online at http://www.elainefitzgerald.com/jeopardy.htm

3.8 Reciprocal teaching

Skill	Reading comprehension (reciprocal teaching)
Outline	Students summarize, ask questions, clarify and predict in order to comprehend a text.
Level	*
Time	25–30 minutes
Preparation	Choose a text that can easily be divided into sections and make photocopies for each student. See Box 3.8a.

Procedure

1   Divide the class into pairs and distribute a copy of Part A of the text to
    each pair. They read the text and summarize the main ideas. They may
    not fully comprehend the text, but they summarize the concepts they
    have understood thus far. See Box 3.8b.

2   The pairs create three or four questions about Part A. See Box 3.8b.
    Note that the question could ask for clarification about an unfamiliar
    vocabulary item.

3   Two pairs make a group of four and swap questions. The partners decide
    on their answers and then discuss these with the other pair. They then
    hypothesize about what might come next in the text.

4   The 'reciprocal teaching' cycle (outlined in Steps 1 to 3) starts again. Give
    the original pairs Part B of the text. Firstly, they check their predictions
    from Step 3 and then summarize this section. They create questions,
    clarify answers with another pair and predict what will follow.

5   Continue this pattern until the students have read the complete text. At
    the end of the activity, check if there are any unanswered questions and
    fill in the comprehension gaps.

Box 3.8a: The cinema of Hong Kong

Part A

Since its inception in the 1900s, the cinema of Hong Kong has been a significant part of Chinese film, which encompasses a multiplicity of cinematic sites and traditions. This connection was marked as much by artistic and financial interactions as by business rivalries. Movie producers, directors, actors, and technicians constantly traveled between Hong Kong and Shanghai, then 'Hollywood of the East,' to make films. For example, the giant Lianhau (United China) Productions, cofounded in Shanghai in 1931 ... had production studios and distribution offices in both cities. Tianyi (First) Film Company, on the other hand, moved its production arm to the colony in 1932 in the wake of the Japanese attack on Shanghai. After the outbreak of World War II in China in 1937, the whole company relocated to Hong Kong under the name of Nanyang (South Sea) Studio ... The industry has a complex history of contestation among various political and ideological-linguistic positions and aesthetic orientations ... Until the 1970s [Hong Kong] was too small to sustain a film industry; it was almost exclusively export oriented, but its products appealed mainly to the Cantonese-speaking communities along the southern coast of China and in Vietnam, the Philippines, Singapore, and the Americas.

Part B

Since the 1930s, Mandarin-language films have also been made in Hong Kong by Shanghai émigrés, but these filmmakers aimed – particularly after the founding of the People's Republic of China, which effectively closed the Chinese film market – to appeal to diasporic Chinese throughout the world (including, especially, Taiwan). The often cut-throat business competition, cultural conflicts, and artistic interflow between Cantonese-speaking and Mandarin-speaking filmmaking created an especially rich and complex tradition in Hong Kong cinema.

© Cambridge University Press 2000

From *Communicative Activities in EAP*
© Cambridge University Press 2011   PHOTOCOPIABLE

Box 3.8b: Reciprocal teaching responses

Summarize	Ask questions	Clarify	Predict
From the 1900s, both Shanghai and Hong Kong were the main centres of the Chinese film industry.	Who was the audience for the films? What language was used in the films? What were the films about? What are 'ideological-linguistic positions'?	Cantonese-language films were exported to the southern coast of China, Vietnam, the Philippines, Singapore and the Americas. The films were about different views in the fields of politics, ideologies and aesthetics. Perhaps 'ideological-linguistic positions' relates to the role language plays in describing an ideology.	The article may go on to talk about films in Mandarin; the effect of the formation of the People's Republic of China on the film industry; the Chinese martial arts films; the influence of Hollywood.

http://condor.admin.ccny.cuny.edu/~group3/Robert%20Villetto/ReciprocalTeaching Paper.doc

Follow-up

Once students are familiar with 'reciprocal teaching', this process could be used as preparation for a reading comprehension test. Select the article to be used in the practice test and set a time limit for the reciprocal teaching activity. The students then do the test. It would be a useful exercise to lead a class discussion on the effectiveness of the activity in preparing for a reading test.

3.9   Spot the referent

Skill	Identifying the referent
Outline	Students use arrows and underline sections of text to connect words to their referent.
Level	*
Time	25–30 minutes
Preparation	Write a sample text on the board, prepare an overhead transparency (OHT) or create an electronic version of the text. The text should include instances where the author uses the referent. See an example in Box 3.9b. Copy a different academic text for each group. On the board, write the referring expressions from Box 3.9a. (*Note:* References which operate within a text can either refer back to something in the text (anaphoric reference) or refer forward to something that comes later (cataphoric reference). Those which refer to something outside the text (e.g. 'the future') are called exophoric references. Highlighter pens and coloured pens would be useful in this activity.

Procedure

1   Read the sample text together and check that the students understand the vocabulary and gist.

2   Direct the class to the referring expressions on the board. Using the sample text, invite volunteers from the class to draw arrows from the referring expressions to the referents. They should also underline the referents. See Box 3.9c.

3   Call on volunteers to explain each section of text in their own words, drawing on the analysis in Step 2.

4   Group the students and hand out one text per group. If your students are able to find their own texts, encourage them to bring these to class. Together, ask the groups to locate the referring expressions in the text and highlight these.

5   The groups then use arrows to demonstrate the connections between the referring expressions and their referents.

6   Ask the groups to summarize the main ideas of their text as they did in Step 3.

7   Each group now displays their text around the classroom. They take turns at staying with the display and visiting other displays. The students who remain with the text explain the connection between the referring expressions and the referents to the visitors at their display.

Box 3.9a: Referring expressions

Pronouns	*he, she, it, mine, yours, this, that, these, those, some, none*
Determiners	*the, this, that, these, those*
Adverbs	*here, there, then*
Fixed expressions	*the foregoing, the previous, below, the following, as follows, the former, the latter*
Longer reference	*this is why, which is why, such is (the risk of this procedure)*

© Cambridge University Press 2006

Box 3.9b: Data, information, knowledge and wisdom

There is probably no segment of activity in the world attracting as much attention at present as **that** of knowledge management. Yet as I entered **this** arena of activity I quickly found there didn't seem to be a wealth of sources that seemed to make sense in terms of defining what knowledge actually was, and how was **it** differentiated from data, information, and wisdom. **What follows** is the current level of understanding I have been able to piece together regarding data, information, knowledge, and wisdom. I figured to understand **one of them** I had to understand **all of them**.

According to Russell Ackoff, a systems theorist and professor of organizational change, the content of the human mind can be classified into five categories:

1 **Data**: symbols

2 **Information**: data that are processed to be useful; provides answers to 'who', 'what', 'where', and 'when' questions

3 **Knowledge**: application of data and information; answers 'how' questions

4 **Understanding**: appreciation of 'why'

5 **Wisdom**: evaluated understanding.

Ackoff indicates that **the first four** categories relate to the past; **they** deal with what has been or what is known. Only **the fifth** category, wisdom, deals with the future because **it** incorporates vision and design. With wisdom, people can create the future rather than just grasp the present and past. But achieving wisdom isn't easy; people must move successively through the other categories.

A further elaboration of Ackoff's definitions **follows**:

http://www.systems-thinking.org/dikw/dikw.htm

From *Communicative Activities for EAP*

© Cambridge University Press 2011

PHOTOCOPIABLE

Box 3.9c: Locating the referent

Data, information, knowledge and wisdom

There is probably no segment of activity in the world attracting as much attention at present as **that** of knowledge management. Yet as I entered **this** arena of activity I quickly found there didn't seem to be a wealth of sources that seemed to make sense in terms of defining what knowledge actually was, and how was **it** differentiated from data, information, and wisdom. **What follows** is the current level of understanding I have been able to piece together regarding data, information, knowledge, and wisdom. I figured to understand **one of them** I had to understand **all of them**.

According to Russell Ackoff, a systems theorist and professor of organizational change, the content of the human mind can be classified into five categories:

1. **Data**: symbols
2. **Information**: data that are processed to be useful; provides answers to 'who', 'what' 'where', and 'when' questions
3. **Knowledge**: application of data and information; answers 'how' questions
4. **Understanding**: appreciation of 'why'
5. **Wisdom**: evaluated understanding.

Ackoff indicates that **the first four** categories relate to the past; **they** deal with what has been or what is known. Only **the fifth** category, wisdom, deals with the future because **it** incorporates vision and design. With wisdom, people can create the future rather than just grasp the present and past. But achieving wisdom isn't easy; people must move successively through the other categories.

A further elaboration of Ackoff's definitions **follows**:

http://www.systems-thinking.org/dikw/dikw.htm

Follow-up

Groups create comprehension questions based on their understanding of the role of the referent. Using the text in Box 3.9c, questions could include:

- What categories deal with the past?
- What area of activity is attracting world attention at present?
- What incorporates vision and design?
- What does the author need to understand?

TEXT USER

As 'Text users', readers draw on their understanding of a range of texts and how these are placed within a variety of social contexts. They understand that people write for a purpose and to a particular audience. They can interact with others about these written texts and adjust their reading strategies to suit the type of text and their purpose for reading.

3.10 Compare/contrast

Skill	Summarizing
Outline	Students take notes using a top-level-structure framework and then write a short summary.
Level	**
Time	25–30 minutes
Preparation	Photocopy a text which compares or contrasts two ideas or theories. See Box 3.10a. On the board, write the language of comparison and contrast from Box 3.10c.

Procedure

1 Introduce the topic of your text and invite students to share their knowledge of the subject matter.

2 Divide the class into pairs and ask the students to read the text. Check that they have grasped the gist by asking: 'What is this text about? What are the main ideas of the text?'

3 As concepts in this text are compared and contrasted, ask the students to identify the two ideas or theories being compared and then scan for similarities and differences.

4   The pairs now record notes in a note-taking grid, with each partner focusing on a different concept or theory. See Box 3.10b.
5   The pairs then jointly construct a short summary of the text from their notes, using the compare/contrast language on the board.
6   Ask some of the pairs to write their summaries on the board. Invite the class to comment on why these summaries are effective. They could also comment on how to improve the summaries.

Box 3.10a: Modern architectural theory

Architectural thought in France at the start of the seventeenth century, like that in Italy and Spain, was predicated on the notion that the art of architecture participated in a divinely sanctioned cosmology or natural order: a stable grammar of eternally valid forms, numbers, and proportional relations transmitted to the present from ancient times. Jean Bautista Villalpanda, in his 1604 commentary on the prophet Ezekiel and Solomon's Temple, attempted to prove that these numbers and proportions not only were compatible with the Vitruvian tradition but were given to Solomon directly by God himself. Within a few years, this tenet, more broadly considered, would meet philosophical resistance in the person of René Descartes (1596–1650). In his *Rules for the Direction of the Mind*, written sometime before 1628, Descartes noted: 'Concerning objects proposed for study, we ought to investigate what we can clearly and evidently intuit or deduce with certainty, and not what other people have thought or what we ourselves conjecture.' In this clash of two different systems of values – inherited tradition and the confident power of human reason – resounds the first stirrings of modern theory.

© Cambridge University Press 2009

From *Communicative Activities for EAP*
© Cambridge University Press 2011   PHOTOCOPIABLE

Box 3.10b: Architectural values

Architecture: inherited tradition	Architecture: human reason	Summary
Jean Bautista Villalpanda, 1604 Divinely sanctioned natural order Eternally valid forms Transmitted from ancient times	René Descartes (1596–1650) Investigate Evidence Certainty Not human conjecture	The view of architectural theory changed during the seventeenth century. Initially, architectural theory was based on the notion of the natural order in which divine values were transmitted from ancient times. In contrast, René Descartes argued against human conjecture and supported an evidence-based approach to architecture instead.

Box 3.10c: Compare/contrast language

Language of comparison	Language of contrast
The theories of … and … are similar because they both … … and … both agree that … … argues that … and … supports this theory.	Initially … / In contrast / However / On the other hand … While some theorists argued …, others … … differs from … in that … … argued against … … instead

Follow-up
- For information about other top-level structures, see Activity 2.11 on p. 80.
- In groups, ask the students to review their summaries. They should remove as many words as they can without losing the essence of the original text. Groups should aim at a coherent summary with the least number of words.

3.11   Tables

Skill	Interpreting tables
Outline	Students draw on their interpretation of research data to write a summary.
Level	*
Time	25–30 minutes
Preparation	Provide a number of tables from a research paper.

Procedure

1   Give the class some background to the research topic so that they can analyse the tables within a context. See 'Note' in Box 3.11a.
2   Divide the class into groups according to the number of tables you have copied.
3   Draw their attention to the title of each table and ask the students to decide on the type of information which is represented in their table.
4   Now ask each group to prepare a short oral summary describing the figures in their table.
5   Create new groups so that students who studied each table are represented.
6   The groups now draw on their previous discussions to create a written summary of the data in all the tables. Where the data does not go into specific details, e.g. 'Miscellaneous' in Table 6, ask the students to invent plausible examples.
7   A spokesperson from each group presents their summaries to the class. See Box 3.11b.

Box 3.11a: Research tables

Note: These tables come from a research paper on the topic of EAP writing courses. Table 3 refers to preparation courses, while Tables 4 to 6 refer to writing within an academic subject (content courses).

TABLE 3					
Preparation quality reported for ESL writing courses (%)					
Not well at all	**Not very well**	**Adequately**	**Well**	**Very well**	**Unknown**
4	13	29	39	9	6

TABLE 4			
Degree of success reported in content-course writing tasks (%)			
Very successful	**Successful**	**Only a little successful**	**Not successful**
24	55	20	1

TABLE 5					
Grades earned in content course (%)					
A	**B**	**C**	**D**	**Satisfactory**	**Unknown**
20	47	14	1	4	10

TABLE 6	
Reported requirement(s) for good grade on content-course writing task (%)	
Content	44
Rhetorical skills	22
Language proficiency	16
Thinking skills	14
Miscellaneous	4

http://biblioteca.uqroo.mx/hemeroteca/tesol_quartely/1967_2002_fulltext/Vol_28_1.pdf

From *Communicative Activities for EAP*

Box 3.11b: Summary of research findings

Table 3 shows that 48% felt the course had prepared them well or very well; 29% felt adequately prepared, while 17% felt that the course had prepared them either not well or not well at all. Taken as a whole, these results indicate that, by and large, ESL students were quite satisfied with the training they received in writing classes. Furthermore, they tended to rate their performance on their writing tasks across the curriculum as generally successful (Table 4), and their final grades (Table 5) in these courses support that perception. When asked what they had to do to get a good grade in the course (the results are shown in Table 6), 44% of the responses had to do with controlling the course content. Next, according to 22% of the responses, professors looked for rhetorical skill – including the ability to organize writing and to write clearly. Third, 16% of the responses indicated that language proficiency was important. Fourth, 14% of the responses had to do with the importance of thinking skills – the ability to think critically and analytically. The remaining category, miscellaneous, included responses about neatness and length of papers.

http://biblioteca.uqroo.mx/hemeroteca/tesol_quartely/1967_2002_fulltext/Vol_28_1.pdf

From *Communicative Activities for EAP*
© Cambridge University Press 2011   PHOTOCOPIABLE

Follow-up
You could use a range of other pictorial representations for this activity, e.g. graphs, diagrams, timelines, concept maps, pie charts or flow charts.

3.12   Reading strategies

Skill	Reading strategically
Outline	As students reflect on a number of reading strategies, they devise questions based on an academic text.
Level	* *
Time	20–30 minutes
Preparation	Select your text and make one copy for each student. On the board, write the reading strategies and explanations from Box 3.12a.

Procedure

1 Divide the class into two large groups and form smaller groups within the large groups.
2 Refer to the reading strategies and explanations on the board. Provide examples or extra explanations if necessary.
3 Allocate one reading strategy to each large group and ask the small groups to devise questions or tasks which allow the reader to apply this reading strategy.
4 Create pairs consisting of one person from each of the large groups. Each person completes their partner's questions or tasks. They check each other's answers.
5 Call on volunteers to share their work with the whole class.
6 Lead a class discussion where the students reflect on the differences between the reading strategies. Ask: 'In what circumstances would you skim or scan?' The students then share their views with the whole class.

Box 3.12a: Reading strategies

Strategy	Explanation	Questions and tasks
Skimming	Students look quickly over the text to identify the main ideas.	1 Read through the text and underline groups of words which should be read together in a group, e.g. *an overview of public health issues.* 2 Here are two words from the text: *prevention, trends.* Find the other words that should be grouped with these words. 3 Who would be likely to choose this course? 4 Draw boxes to represent each segment of this text. Write a heading in each box to describe the function of the section.
Scanning	Students look quickly over the text to locate answers to specific questions.	1 Who are the lecturers? 2 What is the assessment? 3 Can you do the course externally? 4 What is the textbook? 5 Does the unit take a practical or a theoretical approach?

Box 3.12b: Unit description – obesity and disease prevention

Unit of Study: PUBH5021 – Global Obesity and Disease Prevention

This unit of study provides an overview of public health issues related to obesity and chronic disease prevention in developed and developing countries. It examines the epidemiology of obesity in children and adults, including measurement and population-level trends. Causes of the global obesity epidemic, including behavioural, social and environmental causes, as well as current knowledge regarding effective preventive interventions and solutions are explored. The course will develop students' skills in analysing international and national prevention programs and policies related to the development of obesity. Energy imbalance, increased physical inactivity and increased food consumption, is discussed. Students will develop and apply knowledge to designing public health surveillance systems to monitor obesity, and to develop interventions in diverse social, cultural and community contexts. The course will reflect the roles of government and NGOs in obesity prevention. The context of obesity in non-communicable disease prevention will utilise international health perspectives, including the WHO 2004 Global Strategy on Diet, Physical Activity and Health. The links with non-communicable disease (diabetes, metabolic and cardiovascular health) are emphasised. A cross-disciplinary approach will be taken, with input from urban and transport planning, food industry and regulation, public health law, economics, and the media.

Unit coordinator: Professor Adrian Bauman, Ms Lesley King

Classes: 1 × 2 day intensive workshop, plus weekly online lectures and facilitated web-based classroom discussion and online student postings every week, for 10 weeks

Assessment: 1 × 1000 wd short assignment (25%), 1 × 2500 wd assignment (50%), participation in online discussion (15%), participation in workshop (10%)

Textbooks: Course notes will be provided.

University of Sydney website (http://www.health.usyd.edu.au). Used with permission.

From *Communicative Activities for EAP*
© Cambridge University Press 2011   PHOTOCOPIABLE

Follow-up

Below are some other reading strategies which contribute to effective reading:

- Have a clear idea of what you are looking for.
- Link new information to what you already know.

- Ask yourself questions as you read.
- Disregard material that does not meet your purpose.

Following a reading activity, write these strategies on the board. In pairs, ask the students to reflect on the strategies they use regularly and those they would like to try in the future.

3.13 Topics and examples

Skill	Matching the general to the particular
Outline	Students match headings to illustrative sentences.
Level	*
Time	30–40 minutes or over two 20-minute lessons
Preparation	Each group has a copy of a different academic text which is organized under a series of headings. They will also need scissors, glue or sticky tape and two blank pieces of paper. Each group's blank pages should be a different colour. Alternatively, if students can access a computer lab, they could 'cut and paste' the sections of text electronically.

Procedure

1   Divide the class into groups. Provide each group with a different academic text, or alternatively, ask groups to bring a copy of a suitable text to the class. The text should be organized around distinct headings.

2   Each group creates a puzzle for their peers. They cut off the paragraph headings and paste them in order onto a coloured blank page. Each paragraph heading should then be numbered.

3   The students select one sentence from each paragraph and glue or write these onto another blank page of the same colour. The sentences should be an illustration of the paragraph heading but, if possible, should not contain the exact words of the heading. See Box 3.13.

4   The pages from Step 3 are then cut up into sentence strips which are numbered in a random order. The groups should keep a record of which paragraph heading matches which sentence strip.

5   The puzzles are rotated around all the groups. The students first record the colour of the puzzle and then match the paragraph heading numbers to the sentence strip numbers (e.g. BLUE: Heading 1 / Sentence Strip 4).

6   When the puzzles are completed, invite the groups to read out their sequence of numbers. The authors of the puzzle adjudicate on the answers. Students tally their points to find the winning group.

Box 3.13: Economic development

Paragraph headings	Illustrative sentences
1 Inequality between the world's rich & poor	Calculations based on national accounts and income distribution indicate that about 700–1000 million (10–15 percent) of the world's 6.5 billion people (5.3 billion in developing countries) are poor or living on no more than $1 a day.
2 A North American family	They live in a comfortable apartment or suburban home with three bedrooms, a living room, kitchen, and numerous electrical appliances and consumer goods.
3 Indian farm families	Under a complex division of labor, the family receives consumption shares from the patron (or landlord) in return for agricultural work – plowing, transplanting, threshing, stacking, and so on.
4 Congestion, poverty & affluence in India's cities	There are few proper footpaths for pedestrians or separation of fast-moving vehicles from slower ones; the flow of traffic consists of the juxtaposition of buses, automobiles, taxis, trucks, jeeps, motorcycles, motor scooters, powered cycles, bicycles, human-drawn and motorized rickshaws, oxcarts, handcarts, cattle, dogs, and pedestrians walking or carrying head loads.
5 Globalization, outsourcing & information technology	Furthermore, as Anthony P. D'Costa (2003: 212) notes, India's incomes are uneven so that 'You have fiber optic lines running parallel with bullock carts.'
6 India's & Asia's Golden Age of development	The relative income of Asian elites (top 10 percent of income earners) increased from 43 percent in 1980 to 60 percent in 2000.
7 Asia's competition & American protests	Globalized firms, in their search for lower costs, are hiring Indians (and Chinese, Bangladeshis, and Malaysians) to do their work in place of middle-class Americans, Britons, Swedes, or Dutch; and in some instances, as noted earlier, Asians are subsequently establishing enterprises that compete globally.

Follow-up
- This could be a homework activity in preparation for a reading exam. Students make an electronic version of the puzzle. They create an individual challenge by emailing these to their classmates.
- Students cut off the paragraph headings. They glue the remaining text onto a blank page and these are rotated around the groups. Groups invent possible headings for each paragraph. These are then recorded on the board and compared with the original heading.

3.14 Audience, purpose and context

Skill	Identifying the context, purpose and audience of a text
Outline	In a jigsaw activity, students predict the audience, purpose and context of a range of academic texts.
Level	**
Time	25–30 minutes
Preparation	You will need a different text type per group and a copy of the text for each group member. Select from a range of texts and excerpts. See the following examples: an introduction to a journal article (Box 3.16b); a report (Box 3.14); an excerpt from a textbook (Boxes 3.8a, 3.10a); an abstract from a journal article (Box 3.7a); research data from a journal article (Box 3.11a); a Unit description (Box 3.12b).

Procedure
1 Lead a brainstorming session where you list a range of academic texts on the board. See examples in Preparation above.
2 Divide the class into groups and provide copies of one short text per group. The texts should reflect a range of academic literature.
3 Allow students a few minutes to read the text and clarify the gist and any unfamiliar vocabulary with each other. Address any of their comprehension questions at this point.
4 Write the following discussion questions on the board and ask the groups to discuss their texts in relation to them:
   - Where would you expect to find this text published?
   - Describe the author of this text.
   - Why do you think the author wrote this text?
   - Who is the audience for the text?
   Monitor students' discussions and assist with prompt questions if needed. For example: 'How do you know this?' 'Are there any other possibilities?' 'What was the author trying to achieve?' Encourage the

students to explore the questions thoroughly rather than settling for one-word answers. See an example of answers in Box 3.14.

5   Create new groups consisting of one representative of each of the original groups. The students now take turns to introduce their text and talk to the others about the text's audience, purpose and context.

Box 3.14: A report

Excerpt	Questions and responses
Obtaining a diploma or equivalency certificate after dropping out of secondary school was uncommon among youth with disabilities. As shown in Figure 3.3, only 3% of youth with disabilities as a whole had obtained such degrees 3 to 5 years after dropping out of secondary school. The likelihood of obtaining a diploma or certificate after dropping out did not differ significantly by disability classification (Figure 3.3) or by gender or ethnic background (Figure 3.4).	**• Where would you expect to find this text published?** The text appears to come from a formal report. It could be published in an education journal or it could be a specially commissioned report for a government education department. **• Describe the author of this text.** The author could be a teacher in a school, a university scholar/professor or an educational consultant. **• Why do you think the author wrote this text?** The aim is to investigate participation in post-secondary education for youth with disabilities. The results could be used to guide future policy decisions. **• Who is the audience for the text?** The audience could consist of secondary school principals and teachers, education departmental heads and academics and students who read education journals.

© SRI International 1992

From *Communicative Activities for EAP*
© Cambridge University Press 2011   PHOTOCOPIABLE

Follow-up

The jigsaw groups discuss the circumstances under which they might read these academic texts. They decide on the strategies they would use. For example, would they skim the text for gist or would they scan for specific information?

TEXT ANALYST

As they read, 'Text analysts' identify ideological meanings. They detect the values, beliefs, attitudes and judgements of the writer and recognize how the author uses vocabulary, grammar and text organization to achieve a purpose. Text analysts also accept, reject or challenge the position of the writer.

3.15 Author's values, beliefs, opinions and attitudes

Skill	Reading critically
Outline	Students ask questions about a text to determine the author's values, beliefs, opinions and attitudes.
Level	* * *
Time	25–30 minutes
Preparation	Photocopy a text which overtly reflects the author's values, beliefs, opinions or attitudes. See Box 3.15a for an example. On the board, write the questions from Box 3.15b and the group roles from Box 3.15c.

Procedure

1 Divide the class into groups of four. Ask students in each group to choose a role from the positions in Box 3.15c.

2 Give out copies of the text to be analysed. Explain to the class that reading can be much more than understanding the surface facts. Good readers 'dig deeper' into the text to understand the values, beliefs, opinions and attitudes of the author.

3 Refer to the questions from Box 3.15b. Ask the groups to read the text and discuss their answers to these questions.

4 Next, the students identify the language in the text that pointed them to their answers.

5 Invite the students to distinguish between the facts and opinions in the text in the light of their in-depth reading.

6 The reporters now present an overview of the group's discussion to the class.

Box 3.15a: Human-centred game design

Although rigorous project management is an essential part of game development, as for game design, it seems that games are often regarded as 'art'. A strong responsibility is given to the game designer, whose status equals the one of an artist or movie director. Game designers prefer to tap into their (self-perceived) unlimited creativity and come up with their own ideas, referred to as the I-methodology. This self-centred design process often results in hard-core gamers designing for hard-core gamers, or to put it in other words: 'boys' designing for 'boys'. As the game sector is looking to gain maturity and a larger target group there is a clear need for a more inclusive, more mature approach. However, combining the I-methodology with the fact that the game industry is mainly populated by male designers, the difficulties are obvious when trying to develop games aimed at a wider audience. As a result, a widespread critique is prevailing that there is little innovation in gameplay and that the game industry has difficulties in addressing non-traditional player groups.

Conference on Human Factors in Computing Systems CHI 2006

From *Communicative Activities for EAP*

© Cambridge University Press 2011   PHOTOCOPIABLE

Box 3.15b: Analysing a text

Questions for critical reading	Answers from the text in Box 3.15a	Language features from the text in Box 3.15a
What is the context for this text?	An oral presentation at a conference	*conference on human factors in computing systems*
Who is the audience for this text?	The participants at the conference	*conference*
What is the purpose of this text?	To convince the listeners that: 1 Game designs are not inclusive 2 Games are very similar	 *difficulties in addressing non-traditional player groups* *little innovation in gameplay*
What are the values and beliefs of the authors?	Games should be available for a larger target audience	*the difficulties are obvious when trying to develop games aimed at a wider audience*
What attitudes and judgements do the authors incorporate into the text?	Current games designers: 1 are immature 2 have an inflated opinion of their position and talent 3 come from a male-dominated industry	 *looking to gain maturity more mature approach self-centred hard-core gamers* *status equals the one of an artist or movie director (self-perceived) unlimited creativity* *'boys' designing for 'boys' mainly populated by male designers*
Whose opinions are not represented in the text?	Those of male games designers Those of regular games players	

Box 3.15c: Group roles

1   Group leader – takes the initiative in directing the discussion.

2   Scribe/secretary – keeps a written record of the discussion.

3   Clarifier – checks that everyone understands as the discussion progresses.

4   Reporter – summarizes the key findings of the discussion.

Follow-up

Ask the students to rewrite the article so that the tenor sounds more objective. They could also include the views of participants who have not been represented in the article. Invite the class to accept, reject or challenge the position of the writer and provide reasons for their views.

3.16   Six Thinking Hats®

Skill	Responding to a text; reading for different purposes
Outline	Students respond to a text using Edward de Bono's Six Thinking Hats®
Level	**
Time	30–40 minutes
Preparation	On the board, write the 'Six Thinking Hats' and the questions which accompany each 'hat'. See Box 3.16a. Copy an academic text and prepare a focus question or a problem or task for group discussion following the reading. See Box 3.16b.
Background	Edward de Bono's system of thinking, known as the 'Six Thinking Hats' (see http://www.debono.org) provides a framework for group discussion. In this activity, each 'hat' is a metaphor for the different ways a reader may approach a text.

Procedure

1   Divide the class into groups of six. Hand out the reading text and give students a few minutes to read silently.

2   The groups check their reading comprehension by briefly discussing the gist of the text and asking for help, or using their dictionaries to clarify any uncertainties.

3   Introduce the 'Six Thinking Hats'. Refer to the questions in Box 3.16a to illustrate the function of the 'hats'. Then ask the students in the groups to choose one hat each.

4 The students read the text again. This time each student will be 'wearing a different hat'. They should use the questions on the board to guide their reading.

5 The groups now discuss the focus question on the board. It is important that students do not digress from the function of their hat during this discussion.

6 Ask the wearers of the Blue Hats to report the group's conclusions to the whole class.

Box 3.16a: Six Thinking Hats

Thinking Hats	Questions
White Hat: Facts	What are the facts? What information do we need? How will we get missing information?
Yellow Hat: Positives	What are the pros / good points / strengths / benefits / potential opportunities? Give reasons. How can this help us?
Red Hat: Feelings	How do we feel about this idea? What are our emotions and hunches telling us? What is our initial reaction to this idea?
Black Hat: Negatives	What are the disadvantages / weaknesses / barriers / challenges / risks? What could go wrong? What should we be cautious about?
Green Hat: Creative thinking	What are the possibilities / alternatives? How can we solve this? Let's brainstorm ideas and solutions.
Blue Hat: Managing the thinking	What are our goals? Where do we start? What have we learnt so far? Where do we go next? What have we concluded?

http://www.debono.org/

Box 3.16b: Recycled water debate

Discussion task: Should governments introduce recycled water to supplement a declining water supply? Let's each wear a different 'thinking hat' so that when we discuss this question, we generate a range of views.

1 Introduction

Water resources are limited in both quantity and quality. The global water cycle is a closed system with water molecules being continuously taken in and excreted by living organisms (1). In this continuum of recycling takes place an interesting debate regarding the acceptance and suitability of water recycling. Water recycling is the treatment of municipal wastewater for the replenishment of available freshwater resources and consumption. Water recycling hence closes the water cycle on a more local level with the possibility of closing water cycles for individual households, buildings, factories, towns or regions. The motivation for this activity is mostly the realization that human water consumption has increased beyond sustainable levels, resulting in extended periods of 'drought', depletion of environmental flows in natural water systems and the decrease in healthy levels in drinking water reservoirs, including groundwater systems.

While wastewater treatment is available, to achieve recycled water qualities often superior to current potable water standards (2,3), the notion of drinking wastewater is not a concept that benefits from unconditional public support. In fact the public often vehemently reject water recycling activities and several public consultation studies have been carried out to explore reasons for this resistance and how to gain community support. As a result recycled water is available in countries with severe water restrictions, but clients for this recycled water often cannot be found. To blame are lacking infrastructure to supply such recycled water, a highly subsidized and very cheap potable water resource, and possibly a lacking community awareness of the limitations of such freshwater resources, in particular in urban areas. This requires new problem solving approaches to water supply (4).

http://ro.uow.edu.au/cgi/viewcontent.cgi?article=1145&context=commpapers

From *Communicative Activities for EAP*

Follow-up

The 'Six Thinking Hats' can be used in any activity requiring brainstorming or critical thinking skills. Once students are familiar with the 'hats', they can use these thinking skills in group discussions or to understand and interpret assessment tasks.

3.17 Multiple readings

Skill	Identifying the dominant discourse in a text and suggesting alternative readings
Outline	After reading a text and identifying the dominant discourse, students explore alternative readings.
Level	***
Time	30–40 minutes
Preparation	Provide copies of a short academic text which offers opportunities for multiple readings. The example is an administrative text. See Box 3.17a. Texts with a strong persuasive function would also be suitable. Copy the discussion questions from Box 3.17b.
Background	No text has a stable meaning. Texts and readings privilege some views of the world over others. In this activity the ideas of power and competing discourses are explored.

Procedure

1 Introduce the activity by providing some background to the idea of multiple readings. See Background.
2 Divide the class into small groups and allow a few minutes for students to read the text.
3 Refer to the questions on the board. Ask the students to discuss the 'first reading' questions in relation to the text.
4 Invite volunteers to summarize their discussion for the class.
5 The groups read the text again and discuss the 'second reading' questions.
6 Individuals share their ideas with the whole class.
7 Lead a class discussion on the value of a critical approach to reading academic texts.

Box 3.17a: Changing subjects

Scenario	Text for analysis: email to the student
The subject CKL066 has had to be cancelled because of low enrolment numbers. Some students have enrolled in this subject because it is a small class and offers a practical perspective in their area of study. The university administration wants students from this subject to enrol in a similar subject, but one which takes a more theoretical approach (CKL065). The new class will be quite large because it is a combination of two smaller classes.	Dear Student We are writing to inform you that the subject CKL066 is no longer being offered by the university this semester. We note that you have enrolled in this subject. As an alternative, we are pleased to offer you a place in CKL065, a subject which explores both a practical and theoretical approach. Please change your enrolment details online before the end of the week to confirm your place in this class. Should you have any questions, contact this office immediately. Yours sincerely

From *Communicative Activities for EAP*
© Cambridge University Press 2011   PHOTOCOPIABLE

3.17b: Discussion questions

Questions following the first reading	Questions following the second reading
• What people are mentioned in the text? • How does the author want the reader to feel, think or respond to the material in the text? • What view of the world is being constructed by the author? • Who benefits from the way the author presents the information in this text? • Who has the power in this situation?	• What people are not mentioned in the text? • What information has been omitted from the text? • What people do not have power in this situation? • What other ways could an author construct the information in this text?

From *Communicative Activities for EAP*
© Cambridge University Press 2011   PHOTOCOPIABLE

Follow-up
In small groups, students rewrite the text so that an alternative view is represented.

3.18   Exploring ideologies

Skill	Identifying and questioning ideologies
Outline	After exploring a range of ideologies, students discuss the dominant ideology of a text.
Level	* * *
Time	30–40 minutes
Preparation	Copy the summary of ideologies in Box 3.18a. Choose a text which reflects one or more of these ideologies. See Box 3.18b.

Procedure

1   Divide the class into small groups and provide each group with a copy of the descriptions in Box 3.18a.
2   After they have read these brief summaries, the students draw on their own experience and reading to expand on and explain these ideologies. The depth of this discussion will depend on the prior learning of the students in the class.
3   Hand out the reading text and allow a few minutes for the students to read and clarify the gist. See Box 3.18b.
4   The groups decide on the dominant ideology which is embedded in the text and share their views with the class.
5   Ask the groups to draw on their knowledge of ideologies to suggest alternative ways of reading this text. See examples in Box 3.18c.

Box 3.18a: Ideologies

Conservatism	Liberalism	Socialism	Post-modernism	Feminism
Traditional values are paramount. There is an emphasis on authority drawn from institutions such as religious organizations, the government and the courts.	Individual rights, liberty, choice and creativity are valued. The main role of institutions is to protect the rights of the individual.	Society has been constructed around social class, and institutions maintain the power of the ruling class.	Knowledge is relative – there is no objective truth. There is an emphasis on scepticism, especially concerning social morals and societal norms.	Feminism supports equality of both sexes. It advocates equal rights and legal protection for women in all aspects of public and private life.

From *Communicative Activities for EAP*
© Cambridge University Press 2011   PHOTOCOPIABLE

Box 3.18b: Social capital

The challenge of volatility

Nothing endures but change. – *Heraclitus* The software industry offers a striking example of volatility in organizations. Silicon Valley companies lure bright young software designers away from one another with the bait of higher salaries and juicier stock options. Today's hot new product may be hotter tomorrow, or forgotten. Some firms double or triple in size in months and are swallowed by one of the technology giants. Others run through their venture capital and disappear, their ex-employees snapped up by growing companies hungry for more talent. Fortunes are made and lost. Job hopping is expected and seen (with some justification) as part of the creative ferment of the region. A recent *New York Times* article pegged the typical annual turnover rate of Silicon Valley companies at well over 20 percent.

http://portal.acm.org/citation.cfm?id=358979

From *Communicative Activities for EAP*
© Cambridge University Press 2011   PHOTOCOPIABLE

Box 3.18c: Multiple readings

Liberalism: Do individuals have choice and freedom in such a volatile industry?

Socialism: Who has the power in this work environment: workers or employers?

Feminism: Are both male and female workers advantaged equally?

Follow-up

As students discuss a topic of academic interest, conduct a simulation discussion in which each of the ideologies in Box 3.18a is represented.

CODE USER

As writers, 'Code users' create meaning through words, phrases and sentences with appropriate punctuation and spelling.

4.1 Embedded quotes

Language	Word order in a sentence
Skill	Using punctuation conventions
Outline	Students arrange words and punctuation marks in order.
Level	*
Time	10–15 minutes
Preparation	Select a quote which has been embedded into a sentence and create word cards: one for each word or chunk of language in the quote. See Boxes 4.1a and 4.1c. Create punctuation cards: one for each item of punctuation in the quote. See Box 4.1b. In creating the cards, remove capitalization and punctuation marks.

Procedure

1 Hand out the word cards to volunteers and ask them to come to the front of the class. They should display their cards so that the 'audience' can see the word groups.

2 The first task is for the students to arrange themselves in a line in order to create a complete sentence with their word cards. The text should run from left to right. Their colleagues can call out directions to assist where necessary.

3 Now hand out the punctuation cards. Invite these students to place themselves 'into' the sentence where appropriate. Again, encourage the 'audience' to participate enthusiastically as they offer their advice and directions.

4 When the class is happy with the arrangement of students at the front, write the correctly punctuated sentence on the board.

Box 4.1a: Word cards

similarly
noël carroll argues that
film theorizing
should be dialectical
adding
by that I mean that
a major way in which
film theorizing progresses
is by criticizing
already existing theory

Box 4.1b: Missing punctuation cards

Capital letter
Capital letter
Capital letter
Capital letter
, Comma
, Comma
' Quotation marks
' Quotation marks
' Quotation marks
' Quotation marks
: Colon
. Full stop

Box 4.1c: Film theory quote

Similarly, Noël Carroll argues that 'film theorizing should be dialectical', adding:
'By that I mean that a major way in which film theorizing progresses is by
criticizing already existing theory.'

© Cambridge University Press 2000

Follow-up

Each student creates a pack of word cards and punctuation cards drawn
from some of their own writing. They should choose a sentence which
incorporates a quote. In pairs, they challenge each other to arrange the
words and add the punctuation marks to complete the sentence. More
information about punctuation rules is available at http://esl.about.com/lr/
punctuation/4257/4/ and http://grammarbook.com/

4.2 Scrabble

Skill	Spelling
Outline	Groups choose letters to make words.
Level	*
Time	15–20 minutes
Preparation	On the board, write or project the points table from Box 4.2. Students should have access to academic word lists. See http://www.victoria.ac.nz/lals/staff/averil-coxhead/awl

Procedure

1 Divide the class into groups and explain how this game of scrabble
works. Each group will have a budget of $1,000 to 'buy' letters. The aim
is to create words from the academic register and to score as many points
as possible without running out of money.

2 The first group chooses a letter. Cross this letter off the table (see
Box 4.2). For example, if 'B' is chosen, then no other group can choose
'B'; but if 'E' is chosen, then there are still five more 'E's available.

3 Keep a record on the board of each group's points and expenditure.

4 Students continue to choose letters until they can form a word. Check the
words and confirm that they are part of the academic register.

5   When all the teams have exhausted their funds for buying letters, tally up
    the points and announce the winning team.
6   Invite the groups to write their words on the board.

Box 4.2: Points table

Points	Letters	Dollars
0 points	☐ ☐ (2 blank squares): can represent any letter	$100
1 point	**E E E E E E** (×6) **A A A A A** (×5) **I I I I I** (×5) **O O O O** (×4) **N N N** (×3) **R R R** (×3) **T T T** (×3) **L L** (×2) **S S** (×2) **U U** (×2)	$70
2 points	**D D** (×2) **G** (×1)	$50
3 points	**B** (×1) **C** (×1) **M** (×1) **P** (×1)	$40
4 points	**F** (×1) **H** (×1) **V** (×1) **W** (×1) **Y** (×1)	$30
5 points	**K** (×1)	$20
8 points	**J** (×1) **X** (×1)	$10
10 points	**Q** (×1) **Z** (×1)	$5

Follow-up

The game can be made more complex by allowing only certain categories of words, e.g. nouns or verbs. You could also limit the words to key direction words used in exams, e.g. *define, describe, justify*.

4.3 Word relay

Skill	Making word associations
Outline	Following a brainstorming session, students group words according to key concepts.
Level	*
Time	15–20 minutes
Preparation	On the board, write the question or topic of a writing task. The example uses a topic from the built environment. See Box 4.3. This activity presupposes that students have done prior reading or listening to explore the concepts of the topic.

Procedure

1 Divide the class into three or four teams and refer the students to the writing topic on the board.

2 Give the teams a marker pen, which will act as a 'baton' in the relay. Each team's pen should be the same colour, e.g. black. On the board, the first team members write words that can be connected to the topic. During this phase of the activity, all members of the team can make suggestions to the participant.

3 The first writer returns to the team and hands the pen to the next member, who scans the words on the board and adds a new word. This continues until the board is full of words within the field of the chosen topic and each team member has had a turn. In small classes, the students could have more than one turn.

4 Look over the words and select a number of vocabulary items which represent key concepts within the field. You could expect to find three or four concept words. See Box 4.3. Underline each of these words in a different colour, e.g. blue, red, green and orange.

5 Allocate one concept to each team. Supply the first team members with a coloured pen to match the underlined words on the board.

6 The teams then circle vocabulary which could be associated with their concept. After each word is circled, the team member passes the pen to the next person in their team. Continue until all the students have had a

turn and all the words have been circled. If words have not been circled, discuss whether or not they belong with the overall topic.

7   At the end of the activity, students copy the words in lists under the concept words. See Box 4.3. These become a reference for when they write on this topic.

Box 4.3: Responsive environments

Topic	One goal of landscape architects is to make environments responsive to the needs of the users. What principles or guidelines should inform their designs?			
Concepts	Permeability	Variety	Robustness	Richness
Vocabulary	move	activities	multiple uses	sensory
	paths	people	configuration	sight
	objects	building	temporal aspects	smell
	space	meanings	specific times	touch
	physical properties	options	social space	sound
	appearance	view	meeting place	emotion
	unused	sense of place	channelling	visual sense
	private	visit	controlling	awareness
	public	location	movement	experience
	access	range	change	effect

http://www.psychnology.org/File/PSYCHNOLOGY_JOURNAL_3_1_MCCALL.pdf

---

Follow-up
Allocate one concept to each team. Students then use their word lists to jointly construct a paragraph about the concept.

TEXT MAKER

'Text makers' draw on their prior knowledge as well as their knowledge about genres to create texts, make intertextual links and express literal meanings.

4.4 Matching topic sentences

Skill	Matching topic sentences with their paragraphs
Outline	Groups match a topic sentence to a paragraph.
Level	*
Time	15–20 minutes
Preparation	Choose a published academic text or use samples from students' writing. Each group will need one paragraph, minus its topic sentence. Create an overhead transparency (OHT) or a digital representation of each topic sentence.

Procedure

1 For students who are not familiar with the concept of a topic sentence, briefly explain that topic sentences spell out the main idea of the paragraph. The remaining sentences support this idea in the form of examples and elaboration.

2 Divide the class into groups and distribute one paragraph to each group.

3 Students read their paragraph and check the gist with each other. They may want to use dictionaries for unfamiliar vocabulary.

4 The students then discuss and decide on the main idea conveyed in their paragraph.

5 Display the topic sentences on the screen or write them on the board. Allow a few minutes for the groups to read the sentences. Go from group to group, helping with comprehension where needed.

6 Ask each group to match one topic sentence from the board with their paragraph.

7 The activity ends when all the topic sentences have been successfully claimed.

Follow-up

Remove the topic sentences from a number of paragraphs. Give one paragraph to each group and ask the students to jointly construct the topic sentence. They then compare this to the original topic sentence.

4.5   Introductions to essays

Skill	Identifying the structure and language features of an introduction
Outline	Groups use a model introduction to an academic essay to identify the overall structure and the language features.
Level	*
Time	20–30 minutes
Preparation	Photocopy one model of an introduction to an academic essay – one copy for each student in the class. Copy other samples of introductions – a different one for each group. See Box 4.5a.

Procedure

1   Provide copies of a model introduction to an academic essay. Allow about five minutes for the class to read the text and to clarify concepts or familiarize themselves with new vocabulary.

2   Divide the class into six groups and allocate one task to each group. The tasks are to identify the following features of the model introduction (see Box 4.5b):
   • the overall structure
   • useful sentence stems
   • general academic vocabulary
   • grammar: verb tense, voice and modality
   • grammar: nouns and nominal groups
   • cohesion: linking words, lexical chains

3   Create new groups consisting of one member of each of the original groups. The students take turns to explain what they know about the structure and language features of the sample introduction.

4   Go from group to group and monitor their discussions. Should you find that important aspects of the text have not been identified by the students, then draw the attention of the whole class to these points.

5   Now hand out the other samples of introductions. Each group should have a different sample. Ask the groups to read it and then compare it to their original text. They should pay attention to the six areas they examined in Step 2.

6   Bring the class together for a discussion on the generic structure and language features of the introductions they have studied.

Box 4.5a: Model introduction

Topic: Should metacognitive strategies be taught to help EFL learners develop their learner autonomy to improve Second Language Acquisition (SLA) of reading?

Introductory paragraph

The purpose of this paper is to analyse the argument that an awareness of metacognitive strategies promotes learner autonomy and, as such, should be an essential element of a reading comprehension program for second language learners. To investigate the question, various definitions will be provided and a range of taxonomies of metacognitive learning will be presented. A number of research studies will then be examined to investigate the correlation between metacognitive learning strategies, learner autonomy and second language acquisition of reading comprehension strategies. Finally, several teaching implications will be explored. The paper will conclude by acknowledging that providing students with effective metacognitive strategies will equip them with the tools to become independent and strategic readers.

Kai Lian (Lillian) 2008. Unpublished paper. Used with permission.

From *Communicative Activities for EAP*

© Cambridge University Press 2011   PHOTOCOPIABLE

Box 4.5b: Analysis of an introduction

Structure	Sentence stems	Academic vocabulary	Grammar	Cohesion
The purpose of the paper/ essay How will the essay explore the question? What conclusions will the author make?	The purpose of this paper is to analyse … To investigate the question … … will then be examined Finally, … will be explored. The paper will conclude by …	*analyse* *essential* *element* *investigate* *provided* *presented* *examined* *correlation* *implications* *explored* *acknowledging* *effective*	**Tense + Voice + Modality** Simple Present tense Simple Future tense Passive voice Modal verbs **Nominal groups** Nominalization Noun phrases Gerunds	**Linking words** *then* *finally* **Lexical chain** (vocabulary from a common field) *metacognitive strategy;* *learner/ learning autonomy;* *comprehension;* *second language acquisition;* *teaching;* *reading*

Follow-up

From a current class theme, students use the results of the class discussion in Step 6 to write an introduction to an essay.

4.6 Concluding an essay

Skill	Identifying the structure of a conclusion
Outline	Pairs use a number of essay conclusions to identify the overall structure and the language features of a conclusion to an academic essay.
Level	*
Time	15–20 minutes
Preparation	Photocopy at least two models of a conclusion to an academic essay. See Box 4.6a.

Procedure

1 Divide the class into pairs and distribute the model conclusions. Allow a few minutes for the students to read the text. Clarify any of their comprehension questions.

2 Ask the pairs to work together to identify the structure of the conclusion. You could assist by asking: 'What sort of information goes in the first sentence?' 'What is the function or role of the first sentence?' 'What comes next?' 'What details should be included in the conclusion?' 'How do writers finish a conclusion?' 'What is the purpose of the last sentence?'

3 As students answer these questions, make sure they are not focusing on the content of the paragraph, but rather on the function or purpose of each sentence in the conclusion.

4 When they have decided on their answers, ask the pairs to write out a formula for a concluding paragraph. See Box 4.6b.

5 A number of volunteers now write their formulas on the board. Together, decide on a formula which suits your class.

Box 4.6a: Conclusions to essays

Topic: Developing students' intercultural competence through raising cultural awareness in the TESOL classroom: a Chinese teacher's perspective	Topic: Errors in senior secondary school students' writing
From this research, it is evident that in the field of the TESOL classroom, raising students' sensitivity towards target language culture will help them become successful and independent cross-cultural communicators. This is particularly important in the TESOL context in China, where the culture is significantly different from that in English-speaking countries. Therefore, while teaching language in China, an EFL teacher needs to be sensitive to the cultural influence on Chinese students' progress, as well as various methods of teaching culture suitable for the Chinese EFL classroom. However, as cultural learning itself is wondrous and complicated, and learners' intercultural competence is deeply related to other factors, the approaches EFL teachers employ to instruct cultural ability most effectively require further research and discussion in the future.	The findings in this study show that ESL writers have problems defining the semantic boundaries that separate lexical items. As a result, they failed to observe the rule of restrictions on the co-occurrence of lexical items. The implication of this is that ESL learners will find it difficult to produce coherent and meaningful texts as long as their learning of these lexical relations is imperfect. A clearer understanding of these relations can provide greater precision in guiding students towards meaning and in helping them to define boundaries that separate lexical items. Teachers should also sensitize their pupils to the difficulties involved in collocation by teaching types of collocations with which learners have the greatest difficulties. Teachers should also encourage their pupils to read widely in English, since collocations are better acquired through reading.
Kai Lian (Lillian) 2008. Unpublished paper. Used with permission.	http://www.njas.helsinki.fi/pdf-files/ vol10num3taiwo.pdf

---

Box 4.6b: Structure of a conclusion

1   Restate the thesis / controlling idea of the whole essay.

2   Summarize the key arguments of the essay.

3   Make recommendations.

Follow-up

The students use their formula when they write their next essay.

4.7   Conclusions as summaries

Skill	Identifying the content from the conclusion
Outline	Pairs use a number of essay conclusions to identify the content of essays.
Level	*
Time	20–30 minutes
Preparation	Photocopy at least two models of a conclusion to an academic essay. Photocopy the abstracts which accompany these essays or the complete essays, if possible.

Procedure

1   Ask the students to form pairs. Allocate each pair one concluding paragraph from a number of essays or academic articles.

2   Ask the students to predict the key points that the author of the text may have made in the body of the essay or article.

3   Join two pairs who have analysed the same paragraph so that they can compare their answers.

4   Then make new groups of four where each pair has looked at a different conclusion. The students then share their findings from Step 3 with each other.

5   Reinforce with the class the role of conclusions in summarizing the content of an essay or article.

6   Distribute copies of the abstracts (or complete essays) so that students can then check their predictions in Step 2.

Follow-up

Repeat this activity, but this time use introductions to essays or journal articles. From the introductions, the pairs predict what will follow.

4.8 Jumbled sentences

Skill	Creating cohesive texts
Outline	Students rewrite a set of jumbled sentences in the correct order.
Level	*
Time	20–30 minutes
Preparation	Choose a sample of cohesive student writing. The sample should demonstrate cohesion through linkers and the use of referents. Jumble the sentences and copy these for each group. See Box 4.8a.

Procedure

1 Divide the class into small groups. On the board, write the topic of the text to be analysed and invite the students to share their knowledge of this topic.

2 Hand out the jumbled sentences and allow students a few minutes to read them silently. See Box 4.8a.

3 The groups then work together to sort and then rewrite the sentences to form a cohesive text.

4 Go from group to group, asking the students to identify the words or phrases which helped them to order the sentences.

5 Draw up a table on the board and call on the groups to classify the cohesive devices used in the text. Record their work in the table. See Box 4.8b.

Box 4.8a: Bullying in the workplace

Jumbled sentences

1 If rumours or gossip are spread about a person, then this is a form of indirect bullying.

2 For example, if a manager threatens a worker's job security or chances for promotion, this is direct bullying.

3 Both these forms of bullying tend to lead to absenteeism and a high staff turnover.

4 It may also take the form of mental abuse when a person is insulted or humiliated.

5 Direct bullying could be defined as aggressive or intimidating behaviour.

6 Indirect bullying, on the other hand, is more subtle and is not always obvious.

7 Inappropriate sexual comments can also cause tension and stress at work.

 -

continued

Box 4.8a: (*cont.*)

Complete text

Direct bullying could be defined as aggressive or intimidating behaviour. For example, if a manager threatens a worker's job security or chances for promotion, this is direct bullying. It may also take the form of mental abuse, for example when a person is insulted or humiliated. Indirect bullying, on the other hand, is more subtle and is not always obvious. If rumours or gossip are spread about a person, then this is a form of indirect bullying. Inappropriate sexual comments can also cause tension and stress at work. Both these forms of bullying tend to lead to absenteeism and a high staff turnover.

From *Communicative Activities for EAP*
© Cambridge University Press 2011   PHOTOCOPIABLE

Box 4.8b: Cohesive devices

Classify the linkers	
Exemplification	*for example*
Addition	*also*
Contrast	*on the other hand*
Identify the referents	
this	*if a manager threatens a worker's job security or chances for promotion*
it	*direct bullying*
these	*direct and indirect bullying*

Follow-up
Divide the class into pairs. They swap a sample of homework writing. Using highlighter pens, the students identify cohesive devices in each other's work. As they read the piece, they note if the cohesion of the text could be improved and then feed this information back to their partner.

4.9 Add missing sentences

Skill	Creating cohesive texts
Outline	Students add two sentences to complete a text.
Level	＊＊
Time	20–30 minutes
Preparation	Choose a familiar paragraph from a textbook or previous reading class. Remove two sentences and write these at the bottom of the text. Write or project the paragraph and the missing sentences on the board. See Box 4.9a.
Reference	Thanks to Scott Thornbury for the ideas in this activity.

Procedure

1 Invite the students to recall the content of the familiar text.
2 Divide the class into small groups and display the paragraph and missing sentences.
3 After the students have read the texts, ask them, in their groups, to rewrite the paragraph and insert the missing sentences.
4 When the students have completed the task, ask them to discuss how they came to make their decisions. See Box 4.9b.
5 Call on volunteers to identify where the sentences belong in the text and then share their reasons for coming to these decisions.

Box 4.9a: Culture, economics and the arts

Text with two missing sentences

(1) Debate about the relationship between cultural and economic value has been carried on in philosophy since Plato and Aristotle. (2) Ancient thought claimed the attainability of a supreme value through the experience of bliss or divine pleasure; the experience of art played only a minor role in attaining that goal, and commercial action ranked even lower, being associated with the merely practical arts. (3) It was due to a series of English authors that included prominently the Earl of Shaftesbury, Francis Hutcheson, David Hume, and Adam Smith. (4) All of them saw a distinction between value arising from the disinterested experience of beauty and value from objects that serve the self-love of individuals. (5) The former was seen as clearly superior since it related to a contemplation of the Divine. (6) While morally inferior, the attainment of the greatest amount of utility became a legitimate and relevant goal of private consumption and of public action.

continued

Box 4.9a: (*cont.*)

Missing sentences:

A   But it was not until the seventeenth and eighteenth centuries that a major strand of modern aesthetic and economic thought was established.

B   Economic value, its complement, related to the pleasure derived from personal gratification.

Complete text

(1) Debate about the relationship between cultural and economic value has been carried on in philosophy since Plato and Aristotle. (2) Ancient thought claimed the attainability of a supreme value through the experience of bliss or divine pleasure; the experience of art played only a minor role in attaining that goal, and commercial action ranked even lower, being associated with the merely practical arts. **(A) But it was not until the seventeenth and eighteenth centuries that a major strand of modern aesthetic and economic thought was established.** (3) It was due to a series of English authors that included prominently the Earl of Shaftesbury, Francis Hutcheson, David Hume, and Adam Smith. (4) All of them saw a distinction between value arising from the disinterested experience of beauty and value from objects that serve the self-love of individuals. (5) The former was seen as clearly superior since it related to a contemplation of the Divine. **(B) Economic value, its complement, related to the pleasure derived from personal gratification.** (6) While morally inferior, the attainment of the greatest amount of utility became a legitimate and relevant goal of private consumption and of public action.

© Cambridge University Press 2008

From *Communicative Activities for EAP*
© Cambridge University Press 2011   PHOTOCOPIABLE

Box 4.9b: Justifications

Justification

Sentence A. This sentence follows the historical theme: Plato and Aristotle → Ancient thought → seventeenth and eighteenth centuries. It then introduces a new theme: modern aesthetic and economic thought. This contrast is signalled by the word 'but'.

Justification

Sentence B. In the previous sentence, 'the former' signals that two things are going to be discussed. The first idea is 'contemplation of the Divine'. The words 'its complement' signal that this is the second idea – 'personal gratification'.

Follow-up

Insert two 'rogue' sentences into the paragraph. Students specify the 'rogue' sentences and discuss their reasons for choosing them. Here are two 'rogue' sentences that could be inserted into the text in Box 4.9a (see Box 4.9c).

- Plato, Aristotle and Socrates are the founding fathers of Western philosophy. (Insert after Sentence 1.)
- The seventh Earl of Shaftesbury was a prominent politician and social reformer. (Insert after Sentence 4.)

Box 4.9c: Text with two 'rogue' sentences

Debate about the relationship between cultural and economic value has been carried on in philosophy since Plato and Aristotle. Plato, Aristotle and Socrates are the founding fathers of Western philosophy. Ancient thought claimed the attainability of a supreme value through the experience of bliss or divine pleasure; the experience of art played only a minor role in attaining that goal, and commercial action ranked even lower, being associated with the merely practical arts. But it was not until the seventeenth and eighteenth centuries that a major strand of modern aesthetic and economic thought was established. It was due to a series of English authors that included prominently the Earl of Shaftesbury, Francis Hutcheson, David Hume, and Adam Smith. The seventh Earl of Shaftesbury was a prominent politician and social reformer. All of them saw a distinction between value arising from the disinterested experience of beauty and value from objects

continued

Box 4.9c: (*cont.*)

that serve the self-love of individuals. The former was seen as clearly superior since it related to a contemplation of the Divine. Economic value, its complement, related to the pleasure derived from personal gratification. While morally inferior, the attainment of the greatest amount of utility became a legitimate and relevant goal of private consumption and of public action.

© Macmillan 2005

From *Communicative Activities for EAP*
© Cambridge University Press 2011   PHOTOCOPIABLE

4.10 Linking ideas

Skill	Creating cohesive texts
Outline	Students use a set of statements and a variety of cohesive devices to write a cohesive text.
Level	* *
Time	20–30 minutes
Preparation	On the board, write a number of statements based on an academic text. The statements should be in the order these ideas appear in the original text. See Box 4.10a. On the board, list the categories of cohesion that have been explored previously in class, e.g. lexical chains, reference and linkers. See Box 4.10b.

Procedure

1   Divide the class into small groups and ask the students to read the statements on the board. See Box 4.10a.

2   Ask a few clarifying questions to check that they have understood these statements, e.g. 'Why are Bangalore, Guadalajara and Daka mentioned in the text?'

3   Refer to the cohesive devices on the board. Provide a few examples to remind the students of how these devices function to link ideas in a text. See Box 4.10b.

4   The groups jointly construct a cohesive paragraph drawing on the statements on the board and their understanding of cohesive devices. Each group member should copy the paragraph into their notebooks.

5   Mix the groups so that students can share their work with their colleagues. In this step they could explore the following questions:

- How did each group create cohesion?
- Can we improve on any of these student texts?
- What elements of cohesion seem to be most effective in this text?

6 Invite the groups to report on their discussion to the whole class.

Box 4.10a: E-commerce and development report, 2001

Original text

The emergence of electronic commerce over the past decade has radically transformed the economic landscape. For developing countries, the digital revolution offers unprecedented opportunities for economic growth and development, as entrepreneurs from Bangalore to Guadalajara to Dakar will testify. On the other hand, countries that lag behind in technological innovations risk being bypassed by the competitive edge of those using the new technologies.

Original text broken down into statements

- Electronic commerce has emerged over the past decade.
- Electronic commerce has radically transformed the economic landscape.
- The digital revolution offers unprecedented opportunities for economic growth and development.
- Developing countries are benefiting from the digital revolution.
- Entrepreneurs from Bangalore to Guadalajara to Daka testify to the current opportunities for economic growth and development.
- Countries that lag behind in technological innovations risk being bypassed by countries which take on new technologies.

http://www.unctad.org/ecommerce/

Box 4.10b: Cohesive devices

Lexical chains (words from the same field)	Lexical chains (synonyms + repetitions)	Reference	Linkers
commerce economic development entrepreneurs competitive edge	digital revolution technological innovations new technologies economic (repetition)	those (determiner/ pronoun reference)	On the other hand (contrast)

Follow-up
Provide copies of the original text so that the groups can compare it with
their paragraphs.

4.11   Identifying lexical cohesion

Skill	Creating cohesion through vocabulary
Outline	Students highlight lexical chains and then complete a cloze activity.
Level	*
Time	20–30 minutes
Preparation	Photocopy a short familiar academic text which demonstrates lexical cohesion. Type the same text and remove these lexical chains. See Box 4.11. Pairs will need highlighter pens and dictionaries for this activity.

Procedure

1   Divide the class into pairs and ask them to read the photocopied text
    silently.
2   Identify the 'topical theme' in the first sentence and ask the pairs to
    highlight this, using a coloured marker. See Box 4.11.
3   The students then use their dictionaries to find other words which are
    directly related to this topical theme throughout the text. They use the
    same colour to mark these words and phrases.
4   Collect the students' work and then hand out the cloze activity. The pairs
    now complete the sentences, creating a cohesive piece of text.
5   Create groups of four so that the pairs can compare their work. Some
    pairs may have different answers, but accept all versions provided that
    the words make sense in the text.
6   Redistribute the original text for comparison.

Box 4.11: Responsive environments

Permeability is a property of how easy it is to **move** through an environment and depends heavily upon the **paths** and **objects** placed within the **space**. Two types of **permeability** include: **physical** properties (e.g. **a path**) and **visual** appearance. For example, although **a path** may exist in some environments, if it is not visually obvious it may remain unused. This in turn affects the sense of **place** people experience in the environment. **Permeability** is also influenced by the nature of **spaces**, for example whether they permit private or public **access**.

✂ --

Cloze activity

Permeability is a property of how easy it is to .... through an environment and depends heavily upon the .... and ....
placed within the .... Two types of .... include:
.... properties (e.g. ....) and ....
appearance. For example, although .... may exist in some environments, if it is not visually obvious it may remain unused. This in turn affects the sense of .... people experience in the environment.
.... is also influenced by the nature of .... , for example whether they permit private or public ....

http://www.psychnology.org/File/PSYCHNOLOGY_JOURNAL_3_1_MCCALL.pdf

From *Communicative Activities for EAP*
© Cambridge University Press 2011   PHOTOCOPIABLE

Follow-up
Students use longer academic texts to trace the progression of multiple topical themes throughout the paper or journal article.

4.12 Identifying patterns

Skill	Creating cohesion through patterns
Outline	Students identify 'zigzag' patterning.
Level	* * *
Time	20–30 minutes
Preparation	On the board, write or project a short academic text which illustrates a zigzag cohesive pattern. See Box 4.12. Photocopy another academic text for analysis, e.g. a section of a journal article or textbook.
Background	Texts can follow a number of patterns. One type of patterning is when a 'topical theme' is continued throughout the text. See Box 4.13c. Another pattern is the 'zigzag' pattern. It has a theme which contains given information and this is usually followed by a 'rheme' (i.e. a comment on the given information). In the zigzag pattern, the rheme of the preceding clause is picked up as theme in the next. See the example in Box 4.12.
Reference	L. Gerot (1995) *Making Sense of Text*. Cammeray, NSW: Antipodean Educational Enterprises.

Procedure

1   Together, read the text on the board and check that the students understand it. Explain any unfamiliar vocabulary and invite students to draw on their background knowledge to illustrate it. From the sample text, for instance, students may know of examples of the 'informal' economy.

2   Use a coloured marker to highlight the topical theme in the first sentence. See Box 4.12.

3   Next, underline the main parts of the rheme, i.e. important information about the theme. See Box 4.12.

4   Use arrows to demonstrate how the author sometimes picks up on the rheme of the preceding clause and turns this into the theme of the new sentence. In your explanation, you could use the 'zigzag' metaphor and point out that this also contributes to the cohesion of the text. See Box 4.12 and Background.

5   Divide the class into pairs so that the students can work together to analyse another published academic text. The students follow your analysis in Steps 2–4 and use coloured pens and arrows to identify topical themes and zigzag patterns.

6   As you move about the class, reinforce how this sort of patterning creates cohesion in written texts.

7   Two pairs now share their analysis with each other. Assist the groups if required.

Box 4.12: Zigzag patterns

Text to analyse

In assessing a country's standard of living or comparing the standards of living of different countries, it is common practice to use statistics of the Gross Domestic Product (GDP). The GDP measures incomes earned, and the goods and services produced, in the official 'formal' economy. But this tends not to account for the mass of productive activity outside the formal economy, which may well not be reflected in the indicators of GDP. And since the balance between the shadow and formal economy varies from country to country, comparisons on the basis of GDP may be quite misleading.

Theme (given information)	Rheme (new information or comment)
In **assessing a country's standard of living** or comparing the standards of living of different countries, it (Theme 1) —————▶	is common practice to use statistics of the Gross Domestic Product (GDP). (Rheme 1)
The GDP (Theme 2) —————▶	measures incomes earned, and the goods and services produced, in the official 'formal' economy. (Rheme 2)
But **this (formal economy)** (Theme 3) —————————▶	tends not to account for the mass of productive activity outside the formal economy, which may well not be reflected in the indicators of GDP. (Rheme 3)
And since **the balance between the shadow and formal economy** (Theme 4) —————▶	varies from country to country, comparisons on the basis of GDP may be quite misleading. (Return to Theme 2)

© Oxford University Press 1997

From *Communicative Activities for EAP*

Follow-up

In pairs, students analyse samples of their own writing in a similar way. Use this editing activity as an opportunity to promote text organization as a means of achieving cohesive and coherent writing.

4.13 Comparing two texts

Skill	Creating cohesion and coherence
Outline	Students compare two genres: a 'biography' and a 'process'.
Level	***
Time	25–30 minutes
Preparation	For this activity you will need two types of text: a biography and a description of a process. For both these genres, choose two examples: one simplified version for demonstration to the class and one sample from an academic text. On the board, write or project the simplified versions. See Box 4.13a. Photocopy the two short academic texts. See Box 4.13b. This activity presupposes that students have been introduced to the terms 'theme' and 'rheme'. See Activity 4.12.

Procedure

1   On the board, write 'Theme' and 'Rheme' and invite the students to explain these terms. For alternative terminology, see Activity 4.12.

2   Divide the class into two groups – Group A and Group B. Refer to the two texts on the board and allocate a different text to each group.

3   In pairs, ask the students: 'What do you notice about the patterns of themes and rhemes in your text?' They should be able to recognize that each sentence in the 'biography' begins with the same theme and that in the 'process' text, the rheme of one sentence often becomes the theme of the following sentence. Monitor their discussions. Students do not report to the whole class at this stage.

4   Create new pairs consisting of one student from Group A and one from Group B. The students talk to each other about their observations in Step 3.

5   Hand out the academic texts: one 'biography' and one 'process'. Ask: 'Do these texts follow the same patterns you observed in Step 3?' The pairs work together to highlight the themes of both texts and underline the rhemes. See Box 4.13c and Box 4.13d. Students then decide on their answer to your question.

6   Conduct a class discussion about the difference in the sentence patterns of the two genres and how these patterns have achieved cohesion and coherence in the texts.

Box 4.13a: Biography and process – simple texts

Biography: The authors of your textbook

… **and** … **are the authors** of our textbook. **They** have been writing these sorts of materials since … **Both these authors** are experienced and well-qualified language teachers. **Their work** covers areas including … and …

Pattern; Constant theme throughout

Process: Enrolling in a course

Some of you may want to <u>enrol in the … course</u> next term. **This course** is offered each semester, but you will need to <u>enrol now</u> to ensure your place. **The first step** is to download an <u>enrolment form</u> and fill it in. **The green form** is for international students. **Next,** select a date for your <u>entrance exam</u>.

Zigzag pattern: Theme → Rheme

Box 4.13b: Biography and process – academic texts

Biography

Stephen William Hawking is a British theoretical physicist. He is known for his contributions to the fields of cosmology and quantum gravity, especially in the context of black holes. Hawking was the Lucasian Professor of Mathematics at the University of Cambridge for thirty years, taking up the post in 1979 and retiring on 1 October 2009. He is author of a number of books, including *A Brief History of Time.* Hawking has ALS, a form of motor neurone disease: a condition that has progressed over the years and has left him almost completely paralysed.

© Doug Wheller/Flickr.

continued

Box 4.13b: (*cont.*)

Process: Steps of mine development

The process of mining, from discovery of an ore body through extraction of minerals and finally to returning the land to its natural state, consists of several distinct steps. The first is discovery of the ore body, which is carried out through prospecting or exploration to find and then define the extent, location and value of the ore body. This leads to a mathematical resource estimation to estimate the size and grade of the deposit. The estimation is used to conduct a pre-feasibility study to determine the theoretical economics of the ore deposit. This identifies, early on, whether further investment in estimation and engineering studies is warranted and also identifies key risks and areas for further work.

From *Communicative Activities for EAP*

Box 4.13c: Biography – analysed text

Theme	Rheme
Biography:	
Stephen William Hawking ——————▶	is a British theoretical physicist.
He ——————▶	is known for his contributions to the fields of cosmology and quantum gravity, especially in the context of black holes.
Hawking ——————▶	was the Lucasian Professor of Mathematics at the University of Cambridge for thirty years, taking up the post in 1979 and retiring on 1 October 2009.
He ——————▶	is author of a number of books including *A Brief History of Time*.
Hawking ——————▶	has ALS, a form of motor neurone disease: a condition that has progressed over the years and has left him almost completely paralysed.
Pattern: Constant theme throughout	

Box 4.13d: Process – analysed text

Theme	Rheme
Process:	
The process of mining, from discovery of an ore body through extraction of minerals and finally to returning the land to its natural state, ⟶	consists of several distinct steps.
The first ⟵	is discovery of the ore body, which is carried out through prospecting or exploration to find and then define the extent, location and value of the ore body.
This ⟵	leads to a mathematical resource estimation to estimate the size and grade of the ore deposit.
The estimation ⟵	is used to conduct a pre-feasibility study to determine the theoretical economics of the ore deposit.
This ⟵	identifies, early on, whether further investment in estimation and engineering studies is warranted and also identifies key risks and areas for further work.
Zigzag pattern: Theme → Rheme	

Follow-up

The pairs jointly construct a biography and a description of a process, following the patterns in Box 4.13c and Box 4.13d.

4.14 Matching graphs to descriptions

Skill	Describing data
Outline	Students describe data in a range of graphs and then match the descriptions to the graphics.
Level	**
Time	20–30 minutes
Preparation	Collect examples of a number of different types of charts and graphs – enough for one type for each group. Examples of graphs can be found at http://www.swiftchart.com/example.htm On the board, write the generic structure and sentence stems from Box 4.14b.

Procedure

1 Divide the class into groups according to their academic interests. Distribute a copy of one type of graph to each group. Alternatively, students could choose their own graph type for their group. See Box 4.14a.

2 The students refer to the sample graph to discuss the sort of information that they could record in a similar graph.

3 They draw the graph and insert 'invented' categories and numbers.

4 On a separate piece of paper, they jointly construct a short description of the data. They could use the generic structure and sentence stems on the board as a scaffold for this writing.

5 Collect the graphs and the descriptions and number them randomly.

6 Display the graphs and the descriptions around the room. The groups then survey the displays and match the number on each graph to the number on the descriptions.

7 When they have finished, ask each group to identify their original graph and its corresponding description. Check which groups made accurate matches.

Box 4.14a: Graphic representations

Academic discipline	Graph/chart
Business	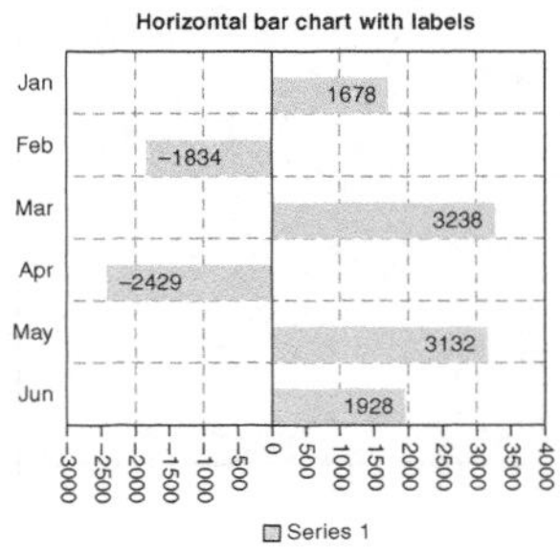
Financial markets	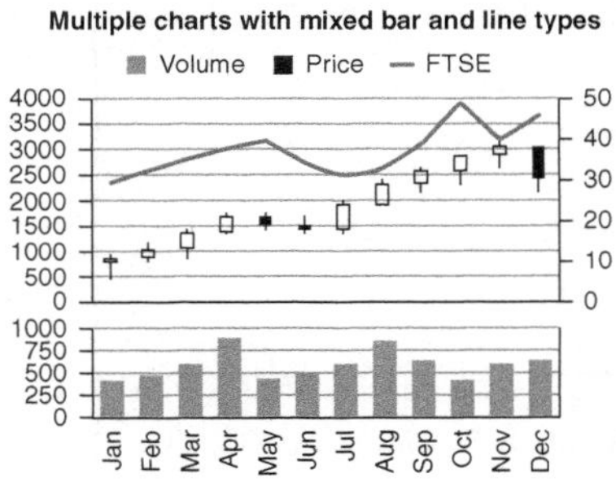
Economics	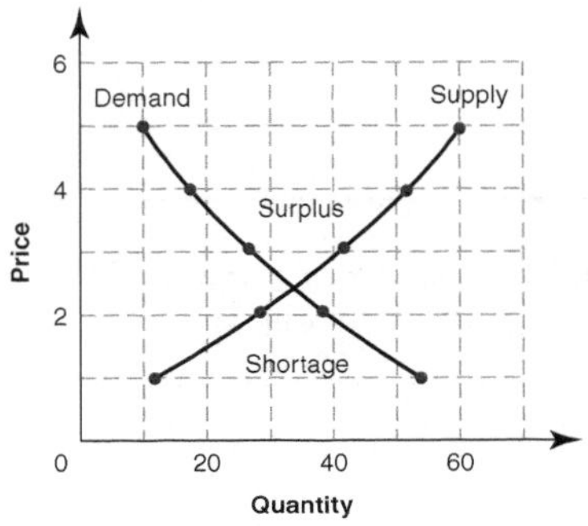

continued

Box 4.14a: (*cont.*)

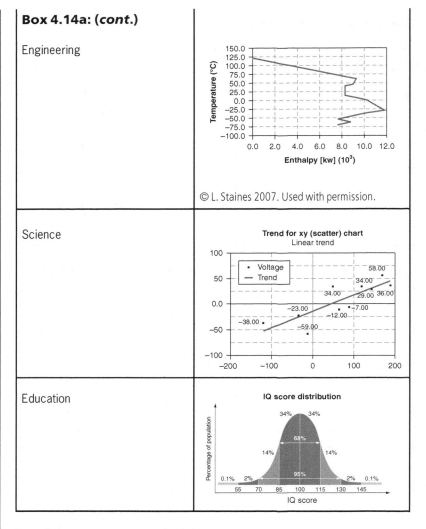

Engineering

© L. Staines 2007. Used with permission.

Science

Education

Box 4.14b: Describing graphs

Generic structure

Section 1

Begin by describing the graph and its features in general terms.

Section 2

Focus on details of the graph and explain why these are significant.

Language features

Section 1

Figure 1 illustrates/reflects the trend in/of …

The graph shows/depicts the relationship between …

Figure 2.5 represents/outlines …

Section 2

The results, depicted in Figure 1, reveal that … /… can be explained by …

As the graph indicates …

In comparison … is representative of …

According to the figures in …

The graph reveals a slight/significant reduction/increase in …

Figure 4.6 demonstrates that … is a result of …

Follow-up

Students create charts and graphs to represent the data that interests them.
They can access data from a range of categories at the following websites:

- http://www.abs.gov.au/
- http://www.statistics.gov.uk/hub/
- http://www.census.gov/

For other examples of the language features of graphs, see Activity 2.1
on p. 58.

TEXT USER

'Text users' apply their understanding of context, audience and purpose to create a range of staged texts with appropriate vocabulary and grammar choices. They also adapt the register of their texts to suit the context, audience and purpose of the writing.

4.15 Academic genres: round robin

Skill	Identifying purpose
Outline	Groups brainstorm a range of academic genres and describe the purpose of these texts.
Level	**
Time	20–30 minutes
Preparation	On the board, draw the table from Box 4.15. Write in the headings 'Genres' and 'Purpose', but leave the remainder blank.

Procedure

1 Divide the class into small groups and allocate a number to each group. Someone from each group copies the table from the board and records their group number at the top.
2 Demonstrate how to complete the table by using one example from Box 4.15.
3 Set a time limit (say, one or two minutes) for students to brainstorm the sorts of genres they are required to use in academic settings. They list these in the first column.
4 Rotate the pages to the next group. Students can either add to the list of genres or start describing the purpose of the genres.
5 Keep rotating the pages, allowing one or two minutes for each rotation. Students continue to add to the table or make corrections if necessary.
6 When the pages return to the original group, call for volunteers to read out their descriptions of the different academic genres. Add to their explanations and invite the class to provide examples from their own academic background.

Box 4.15: Academic genres

Genres	Purpose
Research proposal	To justify being accepted into postgraduate study
Report	To give an account of research, results and recommendations
Poster	To stimulate interest and present a summary of your research outcomes
Literature review	To demonstrate wide reading on a topic
Reflective writing	To link theories to personal, practical experience
Lab report	To describe the procedures and results of an experiment
Flow chart analysis	To explain a process
Examination: short answer	To briefly explain or describe something – usually within a paragraph
Academic essay	To respond to a set question in order to demonstrate understanding of key concepts
Critical essay	To interpret and evaluate the relevance of competing ideas, questions, theories, points of view, arguments or positions

© Garnet Education 2008

Follow-up

Students collect examples of academic genres, and following an analysis of the staging of these texts, groups identify the language features of each of the texts. Many examples of academic texts are available at http://unilearning.uow. edu.au/main.htm

4.16   Graphic organizers and essay planning

Skill	Planning and organizing information
Outline	From a fact sheet, students use a graphic organizer to select material and plan an essay.
Level	* *
Time	30–40 minutes
Preparation	Prepare a brief fact sheet on a current class topic by 'cutting and pasting' sections of a sample text in a random order. Write the topic to be discussed at the top of the fact sheet. See Box 4.16a. Copy the original text. See Box 4.16c. On the board, draw a number of graphic organizers. A range of graphic organizers is available at http://www.sdcoe.k12.ca.us/score/actbank/torganiz.htm See Activity 2.11 and Box 4.16b.

Procedure

1   Refer to the graphic organizers on the board and briefly explain how they can help to organize ideas for writing. See Activity 2.11 and Box 4.16b.

2   Divide the class into small groups. Hand out the fact sheet. The students read the topic at the top of the page and discuss the following questions: What type of question is this? What type of answer is required? (Cause/effect? Problem/solution? Listing of arguments/factors? Compare/contrast? For/against? A combination of one or more of these structures?)

3   Allow about five minutes for the students to read the material in the fact sheet. Assist with comprehension where required.

4   The groups select a graphic organizer from the categories on the board – one which matches the facts on the sheet.

5   They write the facts into the graphic organizer. See Box 4.16b.

6   Hand out the original text so that students can compare their plan with the organization of this text.

7   Invite the students to share their views on the way both the original text and their plans are structured. Ask 'Did you organize your response in a similar way? Why? / Why not? See Box 4.16c.

Box 4.16a: Hand hygiene facts

Topic: Challenges to measuring hand hygiene adherence (in hospitals): why it is not easy

1   There is no standard for measuring adherence to hand hygiene practices.

2   Few scientific studies have evaluated measurement techniques for adherence to hand hygiene practices.

3   The 'ideal' hand hygiene measurement method has been described as one in which 'for every health care worker opportunity for hand hygiene is observed by someone who is invisible, 24 hours a day, 7 days a week, 365 days a year'.

4   Reported compliance rates regarding hand washing vary considerably across studies.

5   Many standardized data collection tools and training materials are currently or will soon be widely available.

6   Methodology between studies varies a great deal, including how adherence or non-adherence is defined.

7   Sufficient details concerning the methods and criteria used to evaluate adherence to hand hygiene practices are often lacking.

8   Using validated methods saves time and resources by allowing organizations to avoid reinventing the wheel and also provides strategies to obtain better data.

9   Only 28% of research articles and guidelines related to hand hygiene measurement included any mention of reliability or validity.

10 Several countries or regions have invested considerable resources in developing and testing standardized data collection tools and training materials for hand hygiene.

From *Communicative Activities for EAP*

PHOTOCOPIABLE

Box 4.16b: Problem/solution – graphic organizer

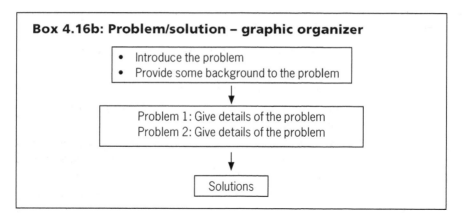

- Introduce the problem
- Provide some background to the problem

↓

Problem 1: Give details of the problem
Problem 2: Give details of the problem

↓

Solutions

Box 4.16c: Problem/solution essay – hand hygiene adherence

CHALLENGES TO MEASURING HAND HYGIENE ADHERENCE (IN HOSPITALS): WHY IT IS NOT EASY

Introduction: Establishes the problem of measuring adherence to hand hygiene. The position is that the writer agrees with the topic.

While most would agree that hand hygiene is of critical importance, many researchers have found that measuring adherence to hand hygiene guidelines is not a simple task. Haas and Larson recently concluded that there is no standard for measuring adherence to hand hygiene practices, and each method has advantages and disadvantages: 'Without a standard definition of hand hygiene compliance, and/or lack of standardized methods of training observers, or defining who should be observers, it is easy to see why reported compliance rates vary considerably across studies.'

continued

Box 4.16c: (*cont.*)

PROBLEM 1: Current research has not addressed reliability and validity issues

Few scientific studies have evaluated measurement techniques; a recent review of the reliability and validity of hand hygiene measures found that only 28% of research articles and guidelines related to hand hygiene measurement included any mention of reliability or validity.

PROBLEM 2: Methodology and definitions differ between studies

Methodology between studies varies a great deal, including how adherence or non-adherence is defined and how observations are carried out; in addition, sufficient details concerning the methods and criteria used are often lacking. Commenting on the inherent difficulties in measuring hand hygiene adherence, Marvin Bittner, MD, VA Medical Center, Omaha, Nebraska, described the 'ideal' hand hygiene measurement method as one in which 'for every health care worker opportunity for hand hygiene is observed by someone who is invisible, 24 hours a day, 7 days a week, 365 days a year'.

SOLUTION

It is noteworthy that several countries or regions have invested considerable resources in developing and testing standardized data collection tools and training materials for hand hygiene in order to assess the effectiveness of broadscale improvement initiatives. Many of these materials are currently or will soon be widely available for use around the world and should be considered for use by those searching for ways to improve their measurement strategies. Using validated methods saves time and resources by allowing organizations to avoid reinventing the wheel and provides strategies to obtain better data.

http://www.jointcommission.org/NR/rdonlyres/68B9CB2F-789F-49DB-9E3F-2FB387666BCC/0/hh_monograph.pdf

From *Communicative Activities for EAP*

Follow-up

Provide a number of essays and ask groups to devise a graphic organizer to match the essay. Models of essays can be found at the following websites:

> http://exampleessays.wordpress.com/essay-types/
> http://www.custom-essays.org/types_essays.html
> http://www.ukessays.com/essays/

4.17   Joint construction

Skill	Establishing thematic progression
Outline	Through a series of prompt questions, the teacher and the class construct a text together.
Level	*
Time	20–30 minutes
Preparation	This activity could follow a brainstorming activity in which ideas for writing have been explored and recorded on the board. Write the topic of the writing task on the board. See Box 4.17a.
Background	The 'teacher talk' in Box 4.17b demonstrates how teachers can assist student writers to achieve cohesion in their written texts.

Procedure

1   Read the topic question and ask the class to decide on the position they want to take.

2   Together, the teacher and class will construct a paragraph which represents this view. Drawing on the brainstorming notes on the board, invite students to suggest sentences which introduce the main idea of their paragraph. Write these on the board.

3   In collaboration with the class, choose one of these sentences to begin the jointly constructed paragraph.

4   Use prompt questions to elicit sentences to elaborate on the first topic sentence. See Box 4.17b.

5   Ask the class to enhance the answer by including reasons or effects.

6   Invite the students to make suggestions on how to link the ideas in the paragraph.

7   Finally, return to the topic question and jointly construct a concluding sentence. See Box 4.17c.

Box 4.17a: Comparing/contrasting social networks

Topic: Are virtual networks the new community?

Brainstorming notes

CONTRAST		COMPARE
Virtual networks	**Conventional networks**	
Are accessible at any time	Are accessible only when friends plan to meet	Both systems aim to maintain relationships with friends
Allow information to be shared with a range of friends and contacts simultaneously	Allow information to be shared with those physically present	Both allow friends to share information about themselves
Allow relationships to be maintained with friends who do not live locally	Allow relationships to be maintained with local friends only	Both offer opportunities to introduce friends to each other
Allow communication in pictures and written text	Allow communication in oral text. Non-verbal communication is also a factor	
Tend to entail delayed responses	All responses are instantaneous	
May allow strangers access to personal information	Usually prevent strangers from sharing in interactions	
Will most likely share factual, non-personal information	May share very personal details and information, e.g. personal problems	

Box 4.17b: Teacher talk

Topic: Are virtual networks the new community?

Teacher's comments and prompts	Comparative paragraph
How will this paragraph answer the topic question?	If we are comparing the two network systems, then we could argue that virtual networks are NOT exclusively the new community.
Let's start with a sentence which **makes the point** that these two forms of networking are related.	Virtual networks and conventional networks are complementary.
Now let's **pick up on the last part of this sentence**. We have said that the networks are complementary. How can we **elaborate** on this?	Both systems aim to maintain relationships with friends.
Could we use a phrase at the beginning to **signal** that we are going to elaborate?	That is to say, both systems aim to maintain relationships with friends.
We should add more examples to **extend** our answer. What words could we use to **signal** that we are adding extra examples?	In addition, both networks allow friends to share information about themselves.
We have said 'both' twice so far. How can we **write this in another way**?	In addition, these two networking systems allow friends to share information about themselves.
Could we use 'and' here, and **extend** the answer further?	In addition, these two networking systems allow friends to share information about themselves and to introduce their friends to each other.
We could **enhance** this answer by writing about the **effect** of these networks. What language **signals** 'effect'?	Because of this, friends today are not restricted by time or place.
Go back to our first sentence. We said that the networks were complementary. Let's return to this **theme**. Let's also look again at **the question**: are virtual networks the new community?	These similarities demonstrate that virtual networks are not necessarily 'the new community'. They simply add an additional means of creating community to the conventional method.

Box 4.17c: Jointly constructed paragraph

Virtual networks and conventional networks are complementary. That is to say, both systems aim to maintain relationships with friends. In addition, these two networking systems allow friends to share information about themselves and to introduce their friends to each other. Because of this, friends today are not restricted by time or place. These similarities demonstrate that virtual networks are not necessarily 'the new community'. They simply add an additional means of creating community to the conventional method.

Follow-up

Here are some other instances where joint construction of text can be used:

- Teacher plus class jointly construct topic sentences, and then each group collaborates to write one paragraph using the topic sentence from the board.
- Teacher plus class jointly construct the introduction to an essay, and then groups jointly construct an introduction to an essay on a different topic.
- Teacher plus class plan subheadings for a report. They jointly construct one paragraph. Then each group constructs one section of the report. The sections are gathered to create a class report.

4.18   Joint editing

Skill	Re-drafting, reviewing and self evaluation
Outline	Students plus teacher and/or student groups proofread texts.
Level	*
Time	20–30 minutes
Preparation	On the board, write a sample paragraph of student writing. This could be from an anonymous volunteer in the class or from a previous class. It is preferable that the writing is relevant to a current class theme and reflects the writing needs of the class. Students will also need a sample of their own writing.

Procedure

1   Divide the class into small groups and introduce the topic of the sample paragraph.

2   Allow a few minutes for the students to read the paragraph on the board.

3   The aim of this joint editing activity is to model to the students the thinking processes of an editor. Invite the students to make suggestions on how to improve the sentences. You could ask: 'Are there any grammar errors?' 'Could we join two of these sentences to make a complex sentence?' 'Can you think of a better word?' The example in Box 4.18 demonstrates both the students' suggestions and the thinking and dialogue which accompany the editing of the paragraph.

4   On the board, create a summary of the changes you made to the paragraph. For example:
   * word choice
   * grammar: use of gerunds
   * academic vocabulary
   * modifying language

5   Students now choose a partner. They read each other's writing and make some initial notes about how to improve the text. These notes could include some of the examples listed in Step 4.

6   The pairs then work together to edit their writing, one piece at a time. Encourage them to follow the example of joint editing 'talk' which you modelled in Step 3.

7   Students then re-draft their original texts.

Box 4.18: Joint editing

Original text plus editing

(Modify 'social networks' with adverb or phrase: Add 'Traditionally') social networks have formed naturally when friends meet ~~for a variety of purposes~~ (reword) in a range of different contexts. However, ~~as people began to meet online~~ (reword using academic register) with the emergence of online social networks (add an example: Facebook®) friends can maintain relationships by ~~create~~ (correct grammar error) creating virtual meeting spaces online (repetition of online. Choose another word.) on the internet. (Add a modifying phrase: 'On the surface'), these two methods of socializing appear to be vastly different.

Modified text

Traditionally, social networks have formed naturally when friends meet in a range of different contexts. However, with the emergence of online social networks like Facebook®, friends can maintain relationships by creating virtual meeting spaces on the internet. On the surface, these two methods of socializing appear to be vastly different.

Follow-up

You could set up a more formal arrangement of 'editing buddies' to
encourage learner autonomy. Partners work together to edit each other's
work, and then join with another pair to continue the editing process. Each
group of four identifies the areas of writing which need attention. The class
then makes suggestions for the focus of the next editing lesson.

4.19 Composing assessment questions

Language	Direction words in assessment questions
Outline	Students are grouped according to their academic backgrounds. They create assessment questions using direction words.
Level	*
Time	20–25 minutes
Preparation	On the board, write a number of assessment direction words. See Box 4.19.

Procedure

1 Ask the students to form small groups according to their academic
   background or interest.
2 Allocate one direction word to each group. They write this word at the
   top of a blank page. See Box 4.19.
3 Draw on the students' knowledge of university assessment to clarify the
   difference between these words.
4 The groups compose one assessment question using their direction word.
5 Rotate the papers, allowing time for each group to add to the questions.
   Each group's question will reflect their academic background. Some
   students may have difficulties distinguishing between the words, so assist
   where necessary. You could also provide scaffolding by drawing on the
   sentence stems from Box 4.19.
6 When the papers return to the original groups, they should contain
   questions from a range of academic disciplines. Display these in the
   classroom or ask volunteers to email copies of the questions to the others
   in the class.

Box 4.19: Assessment questions

Direction word	Sentence stems
list	List the three major components of ...
outline	Outline the contributing factors to ...
identify	Identify the underlying causes of ...
discuss	Discuss the role of ...
comment on	Comment on the relationship between ...
examine	Examine the major characteristics of ...
appraise	Appraise the contribution of ...
analyse	Analyse the current theories and justify ...
describe	Describe the essential elements of ...
review	Review the debate over ...

Follow-up

The students group direction words of similar meaning, e.g.:

- *list, outline, identify, state*
- *discuss, comment on, examine, appraise, analyse, justify, evaluate*
- *describe, define, characterize*
- *explain, clarify, interpret, elaborate, give reasons for*

TEXT AGENT

'Text agents' use written texts to influence others. They express values, judgements and attitudes within a social context. They also present alternative positions and points of view.

4.20 Fish bowl discussion: summarizing and paraphrasing

Skill	Summarizing and paraphrasing
Outline	Small groups discuss a topic and then summarize and paraphrase the content of the discussion.
Level	* * *
Time	30–40 minutes
Preparation	Drawing on a topic from a listening or reading class, create a question for discussion and write it on the board.

Procedure

1 Briefly explain the difference between summarizing and paraphrasing. You could use the models in Box 4.20 to illustrate. At this point you could also remind the class that summarizing and paraphrasing skills help them avoid plagiarism.

2 Divide the class into groups of six or eight. Half the students (Group A) sit in a tight circle (facing in), and the others (Group B) sit outside the circle looking into the 'fish bowl'.

3 Allow about ten minutes for Group A to discuss the question on the board. This question should be based on prior reading or listening classes so that everyone is familiar with the concepts. Encourage all the students in the 'fish bowl' to participate in the discussion.

4 The students in Group B take notes about the content of the discussion and indicate who said what.

5 Each member from Group B chooses a partner from Group A. Firstly, the pairs write a statement which summarizes the discussion. See Box 4.20.

6 Next the pairs write a paragraph to paraphrase what was said. Their writing should include references (i.e. the speakers) and 'invented' dates to simulate an academic paper.

7 Bring the original groups back together to compare their summaries and paraphrasing.

Box 4.20: Summarizing and paraphrasing

Question: What are the needs and gratifications of television audiences?

Summary statement	Paraphrasing
The group discussed the social and psychological origins of the needs and gratifications of television audiences. They concluded that the most common reasons for watching television are information, personal identity, integration and entertainment.	Jones (2008) suggests that entertainment is the primary focus of television audiences. Smith (2007) and Brown (2009) also endorse the view that deriving cultural and aesthetic enjoyment from television contributes to the motivation of viewers. Harvey (2000), however, contends that finding out about the world – both the immediate surroundings and the wider world – is of equal importance when viewers watch television.

http://www.aber.ac.uk/media/Documents/short/usegrat.html

Follow-up

Students start a collection of words to use when incorporating references, e.g.:

- *states*
- *acknowledges*
- *suggests*
- *points out*
- *confirms*
- *admits*
- *denies*
- *insists*
- *agrees*
- *rejects*

4.21   From subjectivity to objectivity

Language	Subjective and objective language features
Outline	Pairs read a letter to the editor, noting the subjective-sounding language. They rewrite the text in a more objective style.
Level	* * *
Time	30–40 minutes
Preparation	Photocopy a letter to the editor on an academic topic of interest. On the board, write the language features for both subjective and objective writing. See Box 4.21.
Reference	This activity is based on an idea presented in an unpublished paper by Suzanne Courtice (2009). Used with permission.

Procedure

1   Give an overview of the activity, pointing out that students will transform the subjective language of one text into more objective-sounding language.

2   Hand out the letter to the editor and allow a few minutes for the students, in pairs, to read the text and clarify the gist with each other and, if necessary, with you. See an example in Box 4.21.

3   Refer to the language features on the board and ask the pairs to highlight the personal and subjective language in the text.

4   Provide a context where more objective-sounding texts are published, e.g. a report for an academic journal. The pairs now rewrite the subjective-sounding text using impersonal and objective language. See Box 4.21. Clues to this sort of language are on the board.

5   The pairs now report to the class on the changes they have made and give reasons for these changes.

Box 4.21: Collecting ancient seeds

Note: The sample text is from a letter to the editor about the work of the International Centre for Agricultural Research in Dry Areas (ICARDA).

Task 1: Highlight subjective language from a letter to the editor.	Task 2: Write a report for a science journal about the work of the International Centre for Agricultural Research in Dry Areas.
Personal and subjective language	**Impersonal and objective language**
<ul><li>Personal pronouns: *I*</li><li>Personal circumstances: *rugged and often dangerous terrains*</li><li>Acronym: *ICARDA*</li><li>Verbs describing feelings: *encouraged, heartened*</li><li>Attitudinal language: *brave, dangerous, precious*</li><li>Exclamation: *Thank goodness!*</li><li>Modality: *hopefully*</li><li>Rhetorical question: *Isn't it about time?*</li></ul>	<ul><li>Generic terms for people, e.g. organizations: *The International Centre for Agricultural Research in Dry Areas*</li><li>No personal pronouns or circumstances</li><li>Nominalization: *sustainability, production*</li><li>Declarative mood: *ancient seed types provide the genetic material*</li><li>Limited use of modality: *may*</li></ul>
Sample text Thank goodness for ICARDA! I have been encouraged by the work of scientists who collect seeds which are on the brink of extinction. I'm heartened to know that seed collectors brave the rugged and often dangerous terrains of central Asia to collect ancient varieties of grains. Hopefully, many of these precious varieties will be resistant to pests and the effects of global warming. Isn't it about time our government got behind this potentially life-saving venture?	*Sample text* The International Centre for Agricultural Research in Dry Areas is addressing the issue of sustainability by collecting and storing rare seed varieties. While the effects of global warming pose considerable threats to future food production, ancient seed types from central Asia may provide the genetic material necessary for breeding disease-resistant and heat-resistant crop varieties in the future.

Follow-up
* Following a class debate, students transform the content into an objective-sounding essay or report.
* This activity also lends itself to an analysis of a text's tenor. In small groups, the students compare the two texts and describe the author of each text in terms of:

> social background
> academic background
> ideological stance
> status with the reader: equal/unequal
> attitude towards the reader: friendly/neutral

They could highlight the language which helped them form their conclusions.

4.22 Drawing on a range of sources

Skill	Incorporating citations
Outline	Students paraphrase ideas and then recreate the text including references.
Level	***
Time	20–30 minutes
Preparation	Photocopy a text which contains a number of citations. See Box 4.22a.

Procedure

1 Divide the class into groups. Explain that authors use a number of techniques to incorporate a reference into a text.

2 The groups read the text and note the language the author has used to incorporate references.

3 Volunteers from the groups record this language on the board. See Box 4.22b.

4 Still in the same groups, the students paraphrase the idea that each reference represents. You could say: 'What does Gee believe? What does Kuang believe?' Students record their findings in a table. See Box 4.22c.

5 Collect the photocopied texts. The groups now use the information from Steps 3 and 4 to reconstruct the paragraph.

6 Hand back the photocopies so that the students can compare their paragraphs with the original text.

Box 4.22a: Intercultural competence

Introduction

It is evident that culture and language can never be discussed separately (Gee, 1993; Kuang, 2007; Lankshear, 1994). On the one hand, Crozet and Liddicoat (1997) assert that culture reflects how text is produced by language, in either the oral or the written form; on the other hand, the language people use to interact with these texts also incorporates their culture. In other words, language is the carrier of culture and culture is the content of language (Kuang, 2007). In the context of the English Language classroom, when learners learn about language they learn about culture simultaneously (Byram, 1989). In fact, it has been suggested that, theoretically and practically, language teaching should involve the instruction of both linguistic knowledge and cultural competence (Tsou, 2005). Indeed, the importance of incorporating the intercultural dimension in the language class has been noted by both researchers and language instructors (Castro, Sercu and Garcia, 2004).

Kai Lian (Lillian) 2008. Unpublished paper. Used with permission.

From *Communicative Activities for EAP*
© Cambridge University Press 2011   PHOTOCOPIABLE

Box 4.22b: Incorporating references

1 **It is evident that** culture and language …
2 Make a statement: 'Language is the carrier of culture.'
3 Crozet and Liddicoat (1997) **assert** …
4 **It has been suggested that**, theoretically and practically, …
5 Indeed, the importance of incorporating … **has been noted by** …

Box 4.22c: Paraphrasing ideas

Gee	Culture and language cannot be discussed separately
Kuang	Culture and language cannot be discussed separately. Language is the carrier of culture / culture is the content of language
Lankshear	Culture and language cannot be discussed separately
Crozet and Liddicoat	Culture reflects language / Language incorporates culture
Byram	Language learners learn language and culture simultaneously
Tsou	Language teaching should involve linguistic and cultural instruction
Castro, Sercu and Garcia	Researchers and teachers note the importance of incorporating the intercultural dimension in the language classroom

Follow-up

Each group chooses a paragraph containing citations from their own writing. They create a table similar to Box 4.22c. They then challenge other groups to use their table to reproduce the paragraph. The students' writing should reflect the essence of the original paragraph.

4.23　Creating conference posters

Skill	Evaluating and selecting relevant information
Outline	Groups use information from a research paper to create an academic poster.
Level	***
Time	30–40 minutes
Preparation	Groups will need to pre-read a research paper – either one that they have written or a published text of interest. Supply stationery, e.g. coloured marker pens and cardboard, or provide access to computers. Photocopy the conference poster guide in Box 4.23.
Background	Examples of scientific posters that could help your students with their designs are available at http://www.flickr.com/groups/368476@ N21/pool/ PowerPoint® templates for conference posters are available at http://www.postersession.com/templates.php

Procedure

1　The class has already been divided into groups to select and read a suitable research paper for this activity.

2　Hand out copies of the guide to creating a conference poster and check that the students understand the key points. See Box 4.23.

3　The groups examine their research paper carefully and decide on the information to be included in their conference poster.

4　They make either a hard copy or an electronic poster. See Background for online PowerPoint templates and examples of scientific posters.

5　Posters are displayed in the classroom or emailed to the other groups.

> ## Box 4.23: Conference poster guide
>
> **Context:** A large, crowded conference room in which a range of posters is displayed.
>
> **Audience:** People attending the conference who are interested in this research.
>
> **Purpose:** To allow participants to interact personally with others who share a common research interest.
>
> **Tips:** Create a catchy title
>
> Establish a context: briefly explain the relevance of your research
>
> Use graphic representations to present your methods and results, e.g. tables, graphs, charts, photographs
>
> Outline future directions
>
> Include relevant references
>
> Have your email details for those who want to continue the dialogue with you
>
> Keep the whole poster within an 800-word limit
>
> Make sure the poster is colourful, engaging and easy to understand
>
> Sections should be clearly labelled
>
> The layout should be well balanced
>
> From *Communicative Activities for EAP*
> © Cambridge University Press 2011   PHOTOCOPIABLE

Follow-up

Conduct a mini conference where students display and talk to each other about their posters. If students have created posters about their own research, they may want to publish them free at http://www.eposters.net/ This site also provides opportunities for others to comment on the published posters. If students are preparing to present a poster at a conference, they could get feedback at this site before the presentation. Students could also comment on the other posters published here.

4.24　Contrary views exemplified

Language	Contrast and exemplification
Outline	Individuals plan key points in an argument and then pairs represent both views in a paragraph.
Level	**
Time	30–40 minutes
Preparation	On the board, write a number of controversial topics. See Box 4.24a. Also, display the language features from Box 4.24b.

Procedure

1　Divide the class into groups of four. You could supply a topic from a class theme, or students could decide on an academic topic of interest. See Box 4.24a.
2　Within the groups, students choose a partner. Each pair takes a different point of view in relation to the topic. Together with their partner, they write a general statement outlining their position.
3　The pairs then write a sentence justifying their position with an example. See Topic 2 in Box 4.24a. Examples could:
- positively illustrate (recovery in an economic downturn is more likely in countries with a regulated banking system);
- negatively illustrate (countries with a free market have suffered most from the global recession);
- present a specific case (China's economy continues to grow, in part because of policies which promote financial supervision and regulation).

4   The students swap partners. Following a brief discussion about both aspects of the topic, the pairs decide on the viewpoint they prefer.
5   Together, they use linking language to construct a paragraph in which both points of view are represented and which concludes with their preferred view. See Box 4.24b.
6   The pairs go back to their original group of four and compare the two paragraphs. They help each other to make any corrections necessary.
7   Invite a number of pairs to read their paragraphs to the class.

Box 4.24a: Controversial topics

Topic	Point of view (1)	Point of view (2)
1 Climate change	Human activity threatens the capacity of the landscape to sustain life on earth	Climate change is a naturally occurring event
2 Financial institutions	should be regulated by governments	should have minimal government involvement
3 Hospital systems	should be privatized	should be public and funded by the taxpayer
4 The role of the media	is to investigate and report	is to entertain
5 Architecture	The function of the structure is paramount	The form of the structure is paramount
6 The human condition	People are naturally social with altruistic potential	Individuals are flawed and need the rule of law
7 The internet	cultivates reading habits	leads to a decline in reading capacity
8 Oral language	Accent reveals most about a person	Communication content reveals most about a person
9 Business	Employees are a business's main asset	Effective management is a business's main asset
10 International aid	Poorer countries are best supported through trade	Poverty is best targeted through aid projects

---

Box 4.24b: Language to anticipate a contrary view

Some could argue that ... but we assert that ...

While ... contests the notion that ... we would assume that ...

In some respects, the claims of ... could be challenged when one takes into consideration ...

Previously, it has been suggested that ... but new research has revealed ...

These views could be seen as ... (outdated/irrelevant/unjustified) in the light of ...

Follow-up

Many ideas for debates and argumentative essays, including supporting details, are available at http://wiki.idebate.org/index.php

5 Vocabulary development

PHASE 1: NOTICING

Phase 1 provides consciousness-raising activities. New vocabulary input is either explicitly or implicitly highlighted in order to meet a communicative need.

5.1 Reflecting on strategies

Outline	Students brainstorm and then talk about the strategies that they use to store and retrieve new vocabulary.
Level	*
Time	30–40 minutes
Preparation	On the board, draw the vocabulary development table. See Box 5.1a.

Procedure

1 Organize the class into pairs. Draw their attention to the table on the board and explain the headings. See Box 5.1a.
2 Ask half of the pairs to record new vocabulary *input* from their previous classes – say over the last two or three lessons. Encourage them to think about whether they heard the new words or whether they read them.
3 The other pairs record their new vocabulary *output* from the previous week. Once more, ask them to reflect on whether they spoke the new words or wrote them. For both input and output there should be some overlap between the macro skills of speaking, listening, reading and writing
4 Now two sets of pairs make a group of four: one pair commenting on input and the other commenting on output. Ask them to compare their lists of words. Are they the same or different? Why?
5 The groups then discuss the methods they used to store and retrieve the new vocabulary. If you do not want to use the terms 'store' or 'retrieve' you could ask: 'How do you remember new vocabulary?'
6 List these strategies on the board. Invite the class to comment on why certain strategies were more successful for them, keeping in mind that all learners are different and what works for one may not work for another.

7 Check the strategies in Box 5.1b and, if necessary, add new strategies to the list generated by the class.

8 Display this list in the classroom to remind students of these language learning strategies.

Box 5.1a: Vocabulary development

INPUT		STORE AND RETRIEVE	OUTPUT	
Listening	Reading	Strategies	Speaking	Writing

Box 5.1b: Storing and retrieving vocabulary

1 Recording new vocabulary according to a topic.

2 Recording new vocabulary with other words of similar meaning or words of opposite meaning.

3 Recording words which go together (collocation), e.g. *effective, successful, clear overall strategy.*

4 Recording new words according to part of speech, e.g. noun, verb.

5 Recording the various forms of the word, e.g. *educate, education, educated, educational.*

6 Writing an example sentence using new words.

7 Regularly reviewing new vocabulary.

8 Taking risks. Trying to use new words in oral and written work.

9 Learning from mistakes. Noticing and self-correcting when you make an error.

10 Noticing the new words when listening and reading.

11 Using context clues to guess the meaning of new vocabulary.

12 Creating your own memory hooks – perhaps a new word reminds you of a word in your first language. You could also use pictures or diagrams as memory hooks.

continued

Box 5.1b: (*cont.*)

13 Choosing to learn words which help you in genuine communication.

14 Noticing when there's a gap in your vocabulary knowledge, i.e. you want to express an idea but you do not have particular words in your bank of vocabulary.

15 Asking the teacher or checking the dictionary for specific vocabulary you want to learn.

© Macmillan Education 1994

Follow-up

At the end of a project or unit of work, lead a class discussion about what new vocabulary students have learnt and the strategies they have used to store and retrieve this vocabulary. Encourage individuals to talk about any new strategies they have tried.

5.2 Let's get rich!

Outline	In a quiz game, students choose words which go together.
Level	* *
Time	20 minutes for preparation plus 20 minutes to play the game
Preparation	On the board, write five verbs: *do, make, have, take* and *give*. See Box 5.2a. Students will need access to a collocations dictionary. Collocations can be explored online at http://193.133.140.102/JustTheWord/index.html

Procedure

1 Refer to the five verbs on the board. The students will all be familiar with these words. Ask the class to suggest words within an academic register which may follow these verbs. Record their ideas on the board. See Box 5.2a.

2 Divide the class into five groups and allocate one verb to each group. Using a collocations dictionary (either paper or online version) the groups find examples of common collocations which come after their verb.

3 Create teams consisting of one member from each of the original groups. Based on their research, students then create quiz cards containing four possible answers. They write the four options on one small card. See Box 5.2b. Allow about 15 minutes for this research and then collect all the cards. Ideally, each team should create at least two cards.

4 Now the quiz game begins. One team nominates the first player. Choose one card and read out the four options. See Box 5.2b. If the player chooses the correct answer, he/she earns $100 for the team and continues to play. With each turn, the prize money doubles. If the player does not know the answer, he/she has three options:

- Ask a friend.
- Ask the team.
- Use a collocation dictionary.

During the game, the teams can use each of these options once only.

5 For some cards there may be two correct answers, e.g. *take effect* + *have an effect*. If the player guesses both correct answers, then the prize money doubles and the player continues.

6 When a player chooses incorrectly, the next team has a turn and the prize starts again at $100. The team which wins the most money wins the game.

Box 5.2a: Collocations

do	make	have	take	give
homework	an attempt	difficulty	action	the impression that
an exam	a decision	an interest in	notes	an opinion
research	a suggestion	an idea	effect	priority to (something)

Box 5.2b: Quiz card

A	make an effect	C	give an effect
B	take effect	D	have an effect

Follow-up

Students research adjectives which collocate with the nouns on their cards, e.g. *take appropriate/direct/drastic/further action*. They make additional quiz cards and play the game again.

5.3   Origins of words

Outline	Students use etymology resources to enhance vocabulary learning.
Level	*
Time	15–20 minutes for preparation plus 20 minutes for presentations
Preparation	On the board, write a number of concept words from a class theme. For example, words from a theme on 'globalization' could include: *culture, global, migrate, nation*. Students will need access to etymology resources, e.g. an online etymology dictionary. See, e.g. http://www.etymonline.com/index.php?search

Procedure

1   Explain to the class that when they understand where words come from and how words are formed, then they are more likely to remember and use the vocabulary.
2   Choose a number of concept words you would like your class to explore. Write the words on the board.
3   Divide the class into small groups and allocate one word to each group. Ask the students to discuss what they understand by the word.
4   The students use an etymology dictionary to research the history of the word. See Box 5.3.
5   They then find other words or phrases which contain the word.
6   Each group introduces their word in a small-class presentation.

Box 5.3: Investigating 'culture'

From *cultura* meaning 'to tend, guard, cultivate, till'
Original meaning: 'tilling the land'
Figurative meaning: 'cultivation through socialization'

Farming the land	Cultivation through socialization
cultivate	acculturation
viticulture	counter-culture
horticulture	subculture
agriculture	monoculture
	culture shock

http://www.etymonline.com/index.php?search

Follow-up

Using a good learners' dictionary, or an online concordance website, groups research words and phrases which collocate with their word. For example:

- *dominant, indigenous, mainstream, youth **culture***
- *assimilate into the **culture**; adopt the **culture** of …; adapt to the **culture***

For an online concordance resource, see http://www.xiaolai.net/ocd/

5.4 Search for suffixes

Outline	Students create and display suffix posters.
Level	*
Time	25–30 minutes
Preparation	On the board, write the common suffix endings from Box 5.4a. Provide each group with a blank poster and large marker pens. Students will need a range of academic texts for this activity.

Procedure

1 Divide the class into groups and allocate one suffix to each group. See Box 5.4a.
2 Ask students to scan through their textbooks and texts from their reading class and locate five words with the suffix ending.
3 The groups use their dictionaries to find the part of speech and the meaning of each word in their list.
4 They then create a poster about their suffix. See Box 5.4b. The posters contain:
   - the suffix at the top
   - words grouped according to their part of speech
   - the definition of each word
   - a sample sentence for each word
5 Display the posters in the room and allow time for the groups to look at them carefully.
6 Ask the class to identify which suffixes create particular parts of speech.

Box 5.4a: Common suffixes

-ment, -ity, -tion/sion, -ence/ance, -ent/ant, -ate, -ify, -ic, -al

---

Box 5.4b: Suffix poster

-ate	
Nouns	**Verbs**
Aggregate: the sum, the mass, the total amount	**Innovate:** to make changes, to make something new
Rather than comparing the votes for each state, this table represents the aggregate of the votes for the entire country.	*To remain viable, the company needs to innovate and reform some of its business practices.*
	Investigate: to examine or study
	The scientists investigated a number of possible causes for the spread of the virus.
	Integrate: to bring together
	This medical practice has integrated alternative medicine and Western medical traditions.
	Fluctuate: to change continually
	The value of the currency fluctuates in relation to the value of gold.

Follow-up
- Students research the meaning of suffixes using a good student dictionary. Meanings are also available at http://grammar.about.com/
- Students create posters with prefixes. For common English suffixes and prefixes, see http://grammar.about.com/
- Students scan academic word lists and add to their posters. Lists of the most frequently used words in the academic corpus are available at http://www.academicvocabularyexercises.com/

5.5   Work out the code

Outline	The aim of the activity is to familiarize students with the phonemic transcriptions in dictionary entries. Pairs write new vocabulary items in phonemic script and challenge others to read and spell the words.
Level	*
Time	20–30 minutes
Preparation	Photocopy two recent reading texts. Students will need either paper or online dictionaries which include phonemic scripts with the entries. For those who are unfamiliar with this script, the phonemic chart, including an audio function, is introduced (online) at http://www.britishcouncil.org/parents-help-pronunciation.htm PDF versions of the phonemic chart can be printed from http://www.antimoon.com/how/pronunc-soundsipa.htm If you or your students want to word-process using phonemic script, a very accessible online typewriter is available at http://ipa.typeit.org/

Procedure

1   Explain the aim of the activity. See Outline. Then choose one item of new vocabulary taken from a recent reading text. Write the word on the board using phonemic script. Demonstrate how the script can guide pronunciation.
2   Divide the class into pairs and provide a copy of the phonemic chart if students are unfamiliar with it. See Preparation. Distribute the two reading texts evenly throughout the class.
3   Each pair chooses ten new words from their reading text. Using entries from either a paper or an online dictionary, the students transcribe the vocabulary items using the phonemic script. Some classes may want to use the online typewriter to word-process these words. See Preparation.
4   The pairs swap papers with another pair who has worked with a different text. They use the phonemic chart to write the orthographic version of the words, i.e. write the words with conventional spelling.
5   In groups of four, the pairs check each other's work.

Follow-up

The group of four scans both reading texts and locates all the words they have used in the activity. They note how the word is used in the context of the passage.

5.6   Noughts and crosses

Outline	Students create a noughts and crosses puzzle.
Level	*
Time	20–30 minutes
Preparation	Each group will need a different academic text which relates to the class theme. Students could use texts from previous reading classes, listening transcripts or sections of their textbook. Alternatively, they could conduct online searches to identify a suitable text on the set theme.

Procedure

1   Divide the class into small groups and assign a different text to each group. The students scan their text and choose unfamiliar or new items of vocabulary. All the words should be topically related. These will be recorded in the puzzle.

2   Groups write their topic words in a grid and number each square. They decide on a key concept word to display in Square 5. This word will reflect the theme of the text used in Step 1. See Box 5.6a.

3   The groups then compose eight clues to accompany the words in the grid. These clues are in the form of a gap-fill exercise. See Box 5.6b.

4   The groups take turns to draw their grid on the board. The only word displayed should be the concept word in the middle square (Square 5).

5   The other groups take turns to nominate a number. The clue is given by the authors, and the competitor tries to guess the word. If they are correct, the creators of the puzzle write it into the grid. If the class cannot guess the word, then they should be given the first letter of the word as an additional clue.

6   The team who can make a line (either horizontal, vertical or diagonal) is the winner.

7   Continue with the other puzzles until each team has had a turn.

Box 5.6a: Conservation grid

1 species	2 emissions	3 renewable
4 erosion	**5 conservation**	6 environment
7 toxic	8 threatening	9 extinction

Box 5.6b: Clues

1 Global warming is threatening endangered .... (species)

2 Governments worldwide are being encouraged to control carbon .... (emissions)

3 Fossil fuels could be replaced by .... energy. (renewable)

4 Farmers revegetate banks of creeks and rivers to prevent soil .... (erosion)

6 To protect the .... we are advised to reduce household waste. (environment)

7 Mines need to find ways of storing or disposing of .... waste. (toxic)

8 Increases in sea temperatures are .... coral reefs. (threatening)

9 Animals in Africa are in danger of .... due to poaching. (extinction)

Follow-up

Over time, collect copies of the students' cards. These then become a resource for pairs to revise vocabulary items as they play the noughts and crosses game.

5.7 Card games

Outline	Students create card games using matching words.
Level	*
Time	20 minutes for preparation plus 15 minutes for each game
Preparation	Cut cardboard into packs of about 20 blank cards. The cards should resemble a pack of playing cards. Each group will need one pack of 20 cards. They will also need texts from previous reading or listening classes.

Procedure

1   Divide the class into small groups. Provide each group with a pack of 20 blank cards.
2   Students decide on ten new vocabulary items taken from recent reading or listening classes. The words should be either nouns or verbs. For each word chosen, they find a matching word. If the word is a verb, for instance, the matching word would be the object of the verb, e.g. *reduce waste*. If the word is a noun, the matching word would be an adjective, e.g. *toxic waste*.
3   Go from group to group and check the matching pairs of words.
4   Introduce the game of Snap. See Box 5.7. Allow about five minutes for the group to play the game, using their own set of cards.
5   The groups pass their cards to the next group, who play another game of Snap. During the game, encourage students to justify to each other why they believe they have recognized a pair of words. The winner of all the cards scores one point.
6   Keep rotating the cards for as long as the students are engaged in the game.
7   At the end, find the most successful player from each group. You could have a Snap championship where each group's winner competes for the grand champion Snap player of the class.

Box 5.7: Card games

Snap

Divide the cards among the players. Players do not look at their cards. Each player takes a turn to place one card (face up) on the table. When the next card is revealed, players decide if there is a pair. The first player to slap a hand over the cards and call out 'snap' gets to keep all the cards on the table. Keep playing until all the cards have been won. This player scores a point.

Concentration

Place all the cards face down on the table. Players take turns to turn over two cards. If they have a pair, they keep the cards. If the cards don't match, they replace the cards in the same spot. Keep playing until all the pairs have been claimed. This player scores a point.

Follow-up

Using the same sets of cards, students play a game of Concentration. See Box 5.7.

5.8 Bingo

Outline	Students create Bingo cards and clues based on word definitions.
Level	*
Time	30–40 minutes
Preparation	Create blank Bingo cards consisting of 3 × 3, 4 × 4 or 5 × 5 squares, depending on the number of vocabulary items you wish to revise. Copy one blank card per group. See Box 5.8. Students will also need a number of small objects to use as markers – one for each square on the Bingo card. Students should have access to dictionaries. Medical, financial and legal dictionaries are available at http://www.thefreedictionary.com/

Procedure

1 Divide the class into small groups and provide each group with a blank Bingo card.
2 Students choose vocabulary items using texts from a current class theme.
3 In each square they write one vocabulary item. Using their dictionaries, they write a definition for each word on separate pieces of paper. These will be the clues in the game.

4   Collect all the clues and place them in a container and then redistribute the Bingo cards to new groups.
5   Draw out definition clues and then students who have the word which 'goes with' the clue place a marker over the word.
6   Winners are the first to call out 'Bingo'. These could be either groups who cover every square, or those who end up with one complete row of covered squares.

Box 5.8: Bingo card – legal language

mediation	limited liability	negligence
plaintiff	defamation	malpractice
bankruptcy	equity	plea

Bingo clues

Mediation: When an independent person brings about a settlement between two opposing parties.

Limited liability: This is the maximum amount of money that can be claimed by creditors.

Negligence: Behaviour which, according to the law, places a person at risk of harm.

Plaintiff: The party who initiates proceedings in a court of law.

Defamation: Any written or spoken attack on a person's good reputation.

Malpractice: An infringement of a professional standard.

Bankruptcy: When a party is unable to repay debts.

Equity: The net worth of an asset.

Plea: A defendant's response (in court) to a criminal charge.

Follow-up

Rather than writing definitions, students could compile a list of clues, e.g. for *mediation*:

- This word is a noun.
- It starts with 'm'.
- It has four syllables.
- It describes a process.
- It involves at least three people.

5.9   Creating vocabulary cards

Outline	Students record information about words on a vocabulary card.
Level	*
Time	30–40 minutes
Preparation	Make one card for each student. The ideal size would be four cards from one A4 sheet. Each student will need a dictionary.
Reference	The framework for this activity is based on the work of T. Hedge (2000) *Teaching and Learning in the Language Classroom*. Oxford: Oxford University Press. Online support: http://www.thefreediction ary.com/

Procedure

1   Lead a brief sharing time about how to learn and record new vocabulary. If some students keep a vocabulary notebook, ask them to tell the class the sort of information they write next to each new vocabulary item.

2   On the board, draw a table with six squares. Each square will represent information to support vocabulary learning. Start by filling in one square, and then ask the students to suggest other items for the remaining squares. See Box 5.9 for suggestions.

3   Each student chooses one new vocabulary item from a current theme or project. Using their dictionaries, they create a vocabulary card for this word. See Box 5.9.

4   In pairs, students engage in a peer-tutoring activity and introduce their new word to their partner.

5   If you do this activity a number of times, pairs can use their cards to test each other. For example, one person could provide a phonemic transcription or a definition and ask for the word. Or they could provide the word and ask for a sample sentence which incorporates the word.

Box 5.9: Vocabulary card (consider)	
Word in learner's first language (e.g. French) *réfléchir à*	**Phonemic transcription of word in English** (kən'sɪdəʳ)
Orthographic version of the word in English + part of speech *consider* (verb)	**Example phrase or sentence** *Consider the implications of this research before proceeding further.*
Definition To think carefully about / to judge	**Other forms of the word** *consideration* (noun) *considerable* (adjective) *considerably* (adverb)

Follow-up
Additional categories for vocabulary cards could include:
- an illustration
- collocations
- synonyms
- antonyms
- semantic map, i.e. logical connections to other words

PHASE 2: EXPERIMENTING	

In Phase 2, students reason, hypothesize, experiment and organize vocabulary as they move towards language acquisition.

5.10   What's the difference?

Outline	Groups determine the difference between commonly confused words.
Level	* *
Time	20–25 minutes
Preparation	Create a number of small cards which contain two words that are commonly confused. See Box 5.10. Place the cards in a container. You could use a ball to toss to the team in the 'hot seat'. Students will need dictionaries for this activity.

Procedure

1   On the board, write two words which are often confused, e.g. *affect* and *effect*.

2   Ask the students to explain the difference between these two words using sentences to illustrate. Point out that this will be the task for the 'hot seat' game to follow.

3   Divide the class into teams consisting of four or five members. Each team will take a turn to be in the 'hot seat'.

4   Toss the ball to the first team and draw out the first pair of words. The team has a time limit, e.g. two to three minutes, to come up with an explanation of the difference. This could include either a definition or a sample sentence. Members can refer to their dictionaries if required. The other teams should also be discussing their response in case the first team is unsuccessful and the ball is tossed again.

5   Decide whether the response merits a point. If necessary, throw the question to the other teams until you receive a satisfactory explanation. The team that answers correctly scores a point.

6   Toss the ball to the next team and draw out another card. Continue until all the teams have had a turn.

7   Tally the points and award a small prize to the winning team.

Box 5.10: Commonly confused words

imply	*infer*
accept	*except*
elicit	*illicit*
eminent	*imminent*
precede	*proceed*
adapt	*adopt*
cite	*site*
continual	*continuous*
definite	*definitive*
impractical	*unpractical*

Follow-up

From the students' writing, collect words which have been confused and used incorrectly. Add these to your cards when you play the game again.

5.11 Words in context

Outline	Students use dictionaries to create a gap-fill activity.
Level	*
Time	20–30 minutes
Preparation	On the board, write or project a short academic text. Remove one unfamiliar vocabulary item to create a gap-fill exercise. See Box 5.11. Students will need a dictionary and a short academic text from a class theme.

Procedure

1   Refer to the text on the board and allow a few minutes for the students to read it.
2   Ask the class to use the context to guess the meaning of the missing word. Write their suggestions on the board. Then reveal the missing word. See Box 5.11.
3   Divide the class into pairs and check that the class has selected a variety of academic texts. They read the text and select one new vocabulary item that they would like to learn. Firstly, they check the meaning of the word

in their dictionaries, and then they write the text on a strip of paper and omit the vocabulary item. They write the missing word on a separate card and a definition from their dictionaries on the back of the card.

4   Collect the cards. The pairs then display their sentence strips around the classroom.

5   Redistribute the cards randomly – one for each pair. The students then move about the class, searching for a text to match their word. An extra clue is available in the form of the definition on the back of the card. They attach the word under the text.

6   The activity concludes when all words have been successfully matched to their texts.

Box 5.11: Sample gap-fill

Text on the board:

'Fisheries science is driven by the need to regulate fishing to achieve .... yields.'

Student suggestions:

continuing, ongoing, greater, improved

Missing word:

sustainable

Word card: Side 1	Word card: Side 2
SUSTAINABLE	capable of being continued with long-term effect on the environment (http://dictionary.reference.com/)

Follow-up
Pairs use sets of cards to test each other on new vocabulary items.

5.12   A matter of choice

Outline	Students use dictionaries and thesauruses to create a multiple-choice activity.
Level	* *
Time	30–40 minutes
Preparation	On the board, write or project a short academic text with one unfamiliar word omitted. See Box 5.12a. Students will need a dictionary and/or a thesaurus. A helpful online resource is available at http://dictionary.reference.com/ Each group will need a different short academic text from a class theme.
Background	When students create 'incorrect' options for this multiple-choice activity, they could draw on their knowledge of errors in their own or their colleagues' work. Some 'incorrect' options could include: wrong part of speech, commonly confused words, not taking account of a referent, or inappropriate connotation.

Procedure

1   Introduce the topic of the sample text. On the board, write four words which could fill the gap in the text. See Box 5.12b. The students use their dictionaries and thesauruses to decide which word fills the gap.

2   Invite volunteers to nominate the correct word and explain why the other words are not suitable. These explanations will help the groups create their own multiple-choice options in the next step. See Background and Box 5.12b.

3   Divide the class into groups. Students create a similar gap-fill activity from the short academic text they have brought to class. They use their dictionaries and thesauruses to create four multiple-choice options for one gap in the text. Go from group to group monitoring their discussions.

4   Set a time limit for each rotation in this stage. The gap-fill exercises and multiple-choice answers are rotated around the class until they return to the original group. With each rotation, students record the word they have chosen to fill the gap.

5   Each group reads out the answer for their gap-fill activity. They should be prepared to explain why their answer is the correct one and why the other options are incorrect.

Box 5.12a: Defining power

Although we use the term 'power' frequently in our everyday lives and seem to have little trouble understanding what is meant by it, the concept has sparked widespread and seemingly intractable disagreements amongst those philosophers and social and political theorists who have devoted their careers to analyzing and … it.

http://stanford.library.usyd.edu.au/archives/fall2008/entries/feminist-power/

Box 5.12b: Multiple-choice

Clues	Answers + rationale
A conceptualizing	**Correct word:** *conceptualizing* is the correct word. It means 'thinking about its meaning'.
B debate	**Incorrect word:** *debate* does not follow the parallel structure created by 'analyzing'.
C quarrelling	**Incorrect word:** You 'quarrel <u>about</u>' something. Also *quarrelling* has the wrong connotation. In formal writing we would say that social and political theorists debate and contest rather than 'quarrel'.
D wielding	**Incorrect word:** *wielding* is incorrect. Knowing that 'it' refers to 'power' is essential here. The paragraph makes clear that the philosophers and social and political theorists are interested in exploring the concepts of power: they do not seek power for themselves.

Follow-up

In this example, understanding the role of the referent 'it' is essential for comprehension. Ask the students to find referents in their texts and identify the word/words that are being referred to. Invite volunteers to share their examples with the class.

5.13 Analysing academic vocabulary

Outline	In this jigsaw activity, students divide vocabulary into three categories: technical, semi-technical and general academic vocabulary.
Level	* * *
Time	30–40 minutes
Preparation	Provide copies of a short, familiar academic text which contains technical, semi-technical and general academic vocabulary. A text from a reading class or a textbook would be suitable. On the board, write the vocabulary categories and their explanations. See Box 5.13.
Background	The aim of this activity is to emphasize that general academic vocabulary is the most common category and that learning this vocabulary will benefit the student in both their writing and their reading comprehension skills.

Procedure

1   Introduce the idea that academic vocabulary can be analysed according to three different criteria: technical, semi-technical and general academic. Refer to the table on the board, and allow students a little time to read the explanations of these terms. Then invite them to suggest vocabulary from their own academic discipline to illustrate.

2   Divide the class into three groups and hand out the text to be analysed.

3   Assign one vocabulary type to each group, e.g. Group A: technical, Group B: semi-technical, Group C: general academic. The students scan for examples from the article. If they cannot decide on the category, they should refer to the explanations on the board.

4   Form groups of three, and include one person from Group A, one from Group B and one from Group C. Ask the students to share their findings from their previous group. Be on hand to help groups come to a consensus. Use prompt questions, e.g. 'Is this word used solely in one academic field, or could it be used across a range of fields?'

5   Finally, point out that most words fall into the general academic vocabulary category. Emphasize the importance of gaining control of general academic vocabulary, because these words occur across a range of academic disciplines.

Box 5.13: Vocabulary categories

Vocabulary categories	Explanation	Examples from an academic text (field: language education)
Technical	Terms specific to an academic field	*rhetorical skill, language proficiency, EAP*
Semi-technical	Words from an academic discipline that non-academics may have heard of	*course, curriculum, grammar*
General academic vocabulary	Vocabulary that could be present in a range of academic fields	*participants, required, rank, scale, adequately, indicate, specifically, performance, perception*

© Garnet Education 2008. Adapted with permission.

Follow-up
Students could sort the general academic vocabulary into parts of speech, e.g. noun, verb, etc., and then note other forms of the words: e.g. *perceive* is a verb; *perception* is the noun form of *perceive*; *perceptive* is the adjective form. They should be encouraged to use this vocabulary in their own writing.

5.14   Concept clusters

Outline	Students group words into concept clusters.
Level	*
Time	10–15 minutes
Preparation	Decide on the topic to be explored, e.g. information technology. Provide two blank pieces of paper per group.

Procedure

1   Divide the class into small groups. Provide each group with a blank piece of paper and introduce the concept to be explored, e.g. *information technology (IT)*.

2 Tell the students that they have five minutes to write all the vocabulary they know in this field.

3 On another blank page the students draw three concentric circles. The circles should be large enough for the students to record their vocabulary within each circle. Ask them to write the concept word in the middle circle. See Box 5.14.

4 Using their brainstorming page, the students choose words to write in the next circle. They need to decide on a category of words that represents a concept in the field, e.g. *IT hardware*.

5 Students then decide on the vocabulary for the outer circle. In Box 5.14 the words reflect some of the functions or applications of technology.

6 Ask the groups to talk to the class about their circles and how they made decisions about where to place the vocabulary.

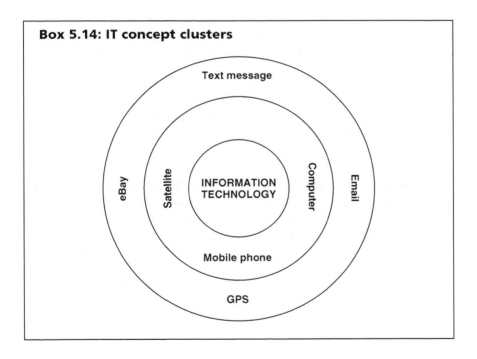

Box 5.14: IT concept clusters

Text message

eBay

Satellite

INFORMATION TECHNOLOGY

Computer

Email

Mobile phone

GPS

Follow-up

This model uses circles to represent concepts. Some students may want to use circles when brainstorming for an oral or a written task. Others may prefer alternative diagrams, e.g. flow charts. Encourage the students to explore ways of brainstorming and planning which suit their learning style.

5.15 Concept map

Outline	Students use word networks to build a concept map.
Level	*
Time	10–15 minutes
Preparation	Provide blank pages and marker pens. Students will need their dictionaries for this activity.

Procedure

1 This activity is a task for the whole class. You want them to create a concept map on the wall. Start with a large heading drawn from a current class theme. See Box 5.15.

2 Divide the class into small groups. The students brainstorm broad categories of words which fall under the heading. Assign one of these categories to each group, e.g. names of body systems.

3 Together, decide on a vertical thread, e.g. body part → disease → specialist doctor.

4 Using their dictionaries, the groups research their category and choose vocabulary for the concept map. They write their words on pieces of A4 paper and use dark, thick marker pens so that the information is clearly visible in the classroom. Word cards are then attached to the wall.

5 When the concept map has been created, ask the class to look for any gaps. For instance, have they missed any illnesses or injuries for each of the body systems? The groups continue their research in order to elaborate on the ideas presented in the concept map. This then becomes a resource for speaking and writing activities.

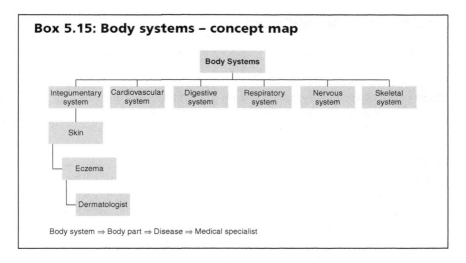

Box 5.15: Body systems – concept map

Body system ⇒ Body part ⇒ Disease ⇒ Medical specialist

Follow-up

Other topics to explore:

- University studies → Name the faculties → List the subjects → Identify career options.
- Engineers → Type of engineer (electrical, mechanical, chemical, civil, geotechnical) → Specialization (geotechnical: gas, oil, petroleum) → Tasks (exploration, recovery, processing).
- Legal system → Participants (judge, lawyer, solicitor, attorney, barrister, jury, litigant, defendant, witness, police) → Tasks (prosecute, defend, research, investigate, argue, interview, advise, deliberate) → Outcomes (suspend, reserve, convict, dismiss, charge, render, acquit).

5.16   Spot the 'odd' word

Outline	Students create lists of words which include one 'odd' word.
Level	*
Time	20–30 minutes
Preparation	Decide on the words you want to reinforce, e.g. content words from a class theme, direction words in exam questions, words to introduce a citation in an academic paper. See Box 5.16.

Procedure

1   On the board, provide a few examples of the words which will be the focus of the activity. See Preparation.

2   Divide the class into groups of three and ask the students to brainstorm other words in this category. Offer assistance to groups where needed.

3   The groups use their brainstorming to create a list of five words in which one word is the 'odd word out'. See Box 5.16. Check that there is a variety of lists across all the groups.

4   The students write their word list on a blank page. Allocate a number to each group and ask them to record it at the top of their page.

5   The word lists are rotated from group to group within a time limit, e.g. one minute. The groups record the number of the page and the word which is the 'odd word out'.

6   When the lists return to their original group, a member of each group justifies the answer for the class. Tally the points and announce the winning group.

Box 5.16: Odd word out

	Words from a class theme (finance)	Direction words in an exam question	Words to introduce a citation in an academic paper
	stocks, **mortgage**, commodities, futures, broker	evaluate, justify, examine, **define**, discuss	**contend**, mention, show, express, state
Justification	'Mortgage' refers to houses whereas the other words refer to shares.	'Define' does not entail a detailed explanation. The other words require critical appraisal.	'Contend' suggests an issue is being debated, whereas the other words imply a statement of fact.

Follow-up
Students create lists of synonyms and include one antonym as the 'odd word out'.

5.17 Visual thesaurus

Outline	Students use paper or online dictionaries and thesauruses to create a 'visual thesaurus'.
Level	*
Time	20–30 minutes
Preparation	Using an academic word list, choose one word for each group. Academic word lists can be found at http://www.academicvocabularyexercises.com/

Procedure
1 Select one word from an academic word list. On the board, demonstrate how to draw a 'visual thesaurus'. Alternatively you could use an online resource to demonstrate. See Box 5.17.
2 Students choose a partner. Assign one word from an academic word list to each pair.
3 The students use either paper or online dictionaries and thesauruses to create a visual thesaurus for their word. They also write short example sentences demonstrating the different uses of the word.

4 Create groups consisting of four pairs. The partners take turns to show their visual thesaurus and introduce their word to the group. They explain how the word is used by providing examples in a context.

5 Display the students' work in the classroom.

Box 5.17: Exploring 'endorse'

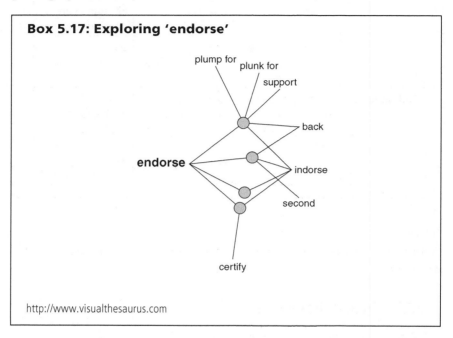

http://www.visualthesaurus.com

Follow-up

Students add collocations to their display, e.g. 'endorse' – *explicitly, officially, publicly endorse*; *fail to / refuse to endorse*. An online collocations resource is available at http://www.xiaolai.net/ocd/ See also *Oxford Collocations Dictionary for Students of English* (2008). Oxford: Oxford University Press.

5.18 Matching words to categories

Outline	Students listen to words and then match them to a general category.
Level	*
Time	5–10 minutes
Preparation	Create a bank of words which belong to different categories. See Box 5.18. Write the categories on the board.

Procedure

1 Refer to the general categories on the board and invite the students to suggest one example for each category. See Box 5.18.
2 Divide the class into small groups. They write the categories as headings, one under the other, leaving space for examples.
3 Read out random examples. See Box 5.18. Students have a short period of time to discuss and then decide on the category. They write the word next to the heading.
4 Call on the groups to read out their answers. In instances where groups disagree on the category, debate the possibilities until they arrive at a consensus.

Box 5.18: Generalized participants

General category	Bank of words
Academic reading material	*textbook, journal, conference paper, website, reference book, manual, report*
Experts	*scholars, researchers, scientists, authorities, professors, authors*
Institutions	*government, political party, parliament, government department, church, bureaucracy, school, university*
Ideology/philosophy	*religious, political, feminist, conservative, liberal*
Research results	*data, statistics, outcomes, opinions, reports, findings, reforms, evidence*
Focus of academic study	*theories, hypotheses, programmes, systems, strategies, evidence*

Follow-up

Students write sentences expressing exemplification. For example:

> *Educational institutions including kindergartens, schools and universities engage in values-clarification exercises when reviewing their mission statements.*

Students write sentences using a referent. For example:

> *Kindergartens, schools and universities are usually required to review their mission statements regularly. All these institutions engage in values-clarification exercises to guide this process.*

PHASE 3: PRODUCING

The focus in Phase 3 is access and output. Students produce vocabulary in a meaningful social context.

5.19 Conversations

Outline	Pairs conduct a conversation based on their analysis of a vocabulary item and its context.
Level	✴ ✴ ✴
Time	30–40 minutes
Preparation	From a class theme, choose a number of topic-related words from previous reading or listening classes. Write these on the board. Students will need to access a corpus such as the British National Corpus (http://www.natcorp.ox.ac.uk/) or the Corpus of Contemporary American English (http://www.americancorpus.org/).

Procedure

1 Refer to the topic-related words on the board. Explain that, in pairs, students will find words or phrases which 'go with' these vocabulary items.

2 Divide the class into pairs and ask the students to choose one word from the board. Cross words off as each pair makes a choice.

3 Using an online corpus or a good corpus-based learner's dictionary, individual students research collocations for their topic-related word and create a list. They should choose examples from academic texts. See Box 5.19a.

4   The pairs then decide on a context in which people would use the word
    they have researched. In the example in Box 5.19b, the conversation could
    be between two law students who are reflecting on a newspaper article.
    Move around the class, and assist where necessary.

5   The pairs adopt a role and have a conversation about their topic. They
    try to incorporate the words from their list and mark off each item as they
    use it in the conversation.

6   The pairs then swap lists and repeat the activity.

Box 5.19a: Exploring 'malpractice'

Word analysis: *malpractice*

some malpractice is occurring in connection with …

… is facing indictment for malpractice

medical malpractice lawsuits

breach of contract and accounting malpractice

extreme examples of boardroom malpractice

there was no hard evidence of any malpractice

unaware of any allegations of malpractice

… springs from malpractice

suspicion of malpractice

uncover malpractice

http://www.natcorp.ox.ac.uk

241

Box 5.19b: Boardroom malpractice – dialogue

Speaker 1: Have you heard that the board of Smith and Co. are facing indictment for malpractice?

Speaker 2: No. I was unaware of any allegations of malpractice against the company or its board.

Speaker 1: I heard that there had been some suspicion of malpractice but that there was no hard evidence of any.

Speaker 2: I must say I'm surprised. I am familiar with medical malpractice lawsuits and breach of contract and accounting malpractice, but such extreme examples of boardroom malpractice are virtually unheard of in this country.

Speaker 1: It's a new phenomenon, for sure, that some malpractice is now occurring in connection with company boards. However, in the light of recent events, I'm not surprised.

Follow-up
- The pairs share their word analysis with the class, either electronically or in the form of a class poster.
- Following a short practice, they could also take turns to 'perform' their conversation for the class.

5.20 Avoiding plagiarism

Outline	Students rewrite a paragraph in their own words.
Level	* * *
Time	30–40 minutes
Preparation	Photocopy a paragraph for students to rewrite in their own words. See Box 5.20a. Groups will need a thesaurus and a dictionary. Both of these resources are available at http://dictionary.reference.com/

Procedure
1 Divide the class into groups of three and hand out the paragraph. Allow a few minutes for the students to read and discuss the content of the text to the best of their ability. Initially students will not use dictionaries, so suggest that for unfamiliar vocabulary they guess the meaning from the context.
2 The groups write short statements based on the text. See Box 5.20a. Collect the original paragraph.

3 Ask the students to highlight the technical and semi-technical vocabulary. See Box 5.20a. This will not change when they rewrite the paragraph. For more information about academic vocabulary categories, see Activity 5.13 on p. 231.

4 Now the students underline the general academic vocabulary. These are the words they will research in the activity. See Box 5.20a.

5 Each group member selects a number of underlined words from Step 4. Firstly, they use a thesaurus to discover a range of meanings. Here it is important to emphasize that not all words listed in the thesaurus can be substituted into the original paragraph. Students should check the context and select a word that will make sense in the text. If they are uncertain, they can double-check the meaning in a dictionary. See Box 5.20b.

6 The group uses their vocabulary research and their statements from Step 4 to write the paragraph in their own words.

7 Display the paragraphs so that the groups can compare their work.

Box 5.20a: Computer security

Modern-day computer networks must employ mechanisms for securing the components of the network. Malicious user activities will continue to increase and their tools and procedures will become ever more sophisticated as more and more devices are connected to the network. Because of this, novel techniques for detecting malicious activities and network anomalies will need to be employed.

Statements:

- Modern **computer networks** must employ mechanisms for securing **components** of the network.
- Malicious user activities are increasing.
- Malicious **tools** and **procedures** are becoming more sophisticated.
- More **devices** are being connected to the **network**.
- Novel techniques are needed to detect malicious activities and network anomalies.

Note: The words in bold represent semi-technical vocabulary, i.e. words or phrases in general use which also have a restricted or special meaning in a particular discipline. General academic vocabulary has been underlined.

http://portal.acm.org/citation.cfm?id=1185513

Box 5.20b: Vocabulary research

Vocabulary	Acceptable meanings	Inappropriate meanings or usage
employ	use	give a job to someone
mechanism	method, procedure and/or device	
securing	protecting, defending, guarding	fastening, tightening
malicious	damaging, destructive	sinful, spiteful
sophisticated	complex, advanced	polished
novel	new, original	book
detect	discover	
anomalies	things that differ from standard expectations	

Rewritten paragraph:

Modern computer networks must use procedures for defending the components of the network from destructive attacks. As more devices are being connected to the network, damaging user-activities will continue to increase and their tools and procedures will need to become more complex. New and original techniques are needed to discover activity which differs from standard expectations.

Follow-up

Paraphrasing involves more than simply replacing words with synonyms. Following this lesson, review techniques for creating cohesion in a text. See Activities 4.8, 4.9, 4.10 on pp. 66–73. Then ask the students to write a second draft of their text from this activity.

5.21 Writing definitions

Outline	Students research the origins of words and write definitions.
Level	**
Time	30–40 minutes
Preparation	Students will need access to a dictionary and a thesaurus, as well as a resource containing Greek and Latin roots. See the Websites section, pp. 309–10, for useful links. Select words from a class theme for students to define.

Procedure

1 Explain to the class that learning vocabulary by researching the origins of words enables them to transfer this knowledge to other contexts. See Box 5.21a.

2 Choose one word from a class theme. With the class, jointly construct a definition of the word. Highlight scaffolding that will enable students to write their own definitions. See Box 5.21b.

3 Using the same word, point out how knowledge of the derivation of the word assists with comprehension. See Box 5.21b.

4 Divide the class into pairs and give each pair one word to research. Student A writes a definition, using the scaffolding from Step 2. Student B researches the derivation of the word, i.e. the Greek or Latin root, prefixes and suffixes. Student B also finds other words which are based on the same root.

5 When they have finished, the partners share their findings with each other. They create a resource (a chart, a PowerPoint® slide) for communicating their knowledge to others in the class.

Box 5.21a: Word knowledge

A student may encounter the word *osteopath* and discover that this doctor specializes in 'bones'. In another context, the student may come across the following illnesses: *osteoporosis* or *osteoarthritis*. They immediately understand that the conditions are related to 'bones'.

Box 5.21b: Definition display

Student A: A definition of the work of a dentist

Dentists are doctors who specialize in the teeth. **Their work is generally focused on** patients with cavities or damaged teeth. **They also treat problems with** the gums and the tissue of the mouth. **Most modern dentists** inform their patients about preventative measures like effective brushing and flossing.

Student B: Derivation of 'dentist' + related vocabulary

dent-/dont-: teeth

-ist: a person who …

Other words: *dental, denture, dentistry, dentate, dentine, dentition*

Follow-up
Here is a selection of other medical professions to define:

psychiatrist	neurologist
podiatrist	cardiologist
paediatrician	surgeon
obstetrician	anaesthetist
nutritionist	optometrist
orthodontist	oncologist
psychologist	geriatric specialist

5.22 Reporting to the class

Outline	Students use topic-related vocabulary to report on an oral text.
Level	* *
Time	30–40 minutes
Preparation	This activity could follow a lecture or broadcast.

Procedure

1 Following a lecture or broadcast, ask the class to suggest sub-topics within the overall content. Write these on the board.
2 Divide the class into small groups and allocate one sub-topic to each group. Then hand out marker pens for students to record vocabulary from the lecture or broadcast on the board. Simultaneously, students from each group write vocabulary from the lecture under their sub-topic. After they have written a word, they pass the pen to a colleague to continue recalling vocabulary. If they have missed important content words at the end of this brainstorming task, add these to the lists of words.
3 Groups use the vocabulary from the board to jointly construct a written summary of their section of the lecture.
4 Each group presents their summary to the class. Choose students from the other groups to stand at the board and tick the vocabulary items as they hear them.
5 Did the class use most of the words on the board? Were the vocabulary items used correctly? Congratulate the students for their efforts and, if necessary, correct any errors.

Follow-up
Collect the students' work and publish a class summary of the oral text.

5.23 Creating academic register

Outline	Students create a text which reflects academic register.
Level	* * *
Time	30–40 minutes
Preparation	Each group will need a transcript from the popular media, e.g. a radio or television programme. Choose a topic related to an area of academic interest. See Box 5.23. Transcripts on a range of topics are available at http://www.abc.net.au/
Reference	The language analysis for this activity is based on work by Suzanne Courtice (2009). Unpublished paper.

Procedure

1 Divide the class into small groups and hand out the transcript. Allow time for the students to read the text. Clarify their comprehension questions.

2 Working with the whole class, scan the first section of the transcript. See Box 5.23, where the following language features have been highlighted. Point out examples of the following:
- subjective-sounding language
- personal language
- informal language
- everyday language

3 The groups then use coloured pens to highlight other examples of this kind of language in the remainder of the transcript.

4 Going back to the first section, ask the class to suggest alternative language using the following:
- objective-sounding language
- impersonal language
- formal language
- technical language

5 Finally, the groups rewrite the transcript so that it reflects academic register.

Box 5.23: Economic stimulus

Original text	Text rewritten to reflect academic register
SUE LANNIN: Fewer people are **looking for work** and employers are **cutting** hours. **That's Australia's economic reality** as the country **copes** with the **fallout** from the global financial crisis. The unemployment rate **remained steady** in August at 5.8 per cent but 27,000 jobs were lost over the month. Citigroup senior economist Joshua Williamson expects unemployment to peak at up to 7%, better than the government's estimates.	In a recent Australian report, it was revealed that fewer people were seeking employment and employers were reducing workers' hours. The unemployment rate stabilised at 5.8% in August when 27,000 jobs were lost. In response to these statistics, a senior economist at Citigroup, Joshua Williamson, forecast that these figures would not exceed 7%. In contrast to the estimates of the government, Mr Williamson predicted that unemployment figures would improve within the next six months.
But looking ahead probably another six months along the horizon, the leading indicators for employment are **actually very, very good**.	

http://www.abc.net.au/worldtoday/content/2009/s2683047.htm

From *Communicative Activities for EAP*

© Cambridge University Press 2011   PHOTOCOPIABLE

Follow-up

Note that the original transcript is an oral text. The rewritten text relies on reported speech and internal cohesion in addition to the changes in vocabulary. This illustrates that both grammar and vocabulary influence academic register. Follow-up activities could explore the grammar of reported speech and techniques for creating a cohesive text. See Activities 4.8–4.12 on pp. 166–77 and Activity 6.17 on p. 287.

6 Grammar

Phase 1 provides consciousness-raising activities. New grammar input is either explicitly or implicitly highlighted in order to meet a communicative need.

6.1 Colour-coded errors

Skill	Error analysis
Outline	Students use colours to highlight errors in written work.
Level	*
Time	30–40 minutes
Preparation	As you read students' written work, identify three or four common errors. Record these examples of student writing. Write two sentences on the board, making sure that the common class errors are represented in these sentences. Prepare and photocopy a handout consisting of other examples of student errors, making sure that the authors remain anonymous. Students will need coloured highlighter pens, one colour for each category of error.
Background	Learners become more autonomous as they monitor their errors. Before deciding what grammar to introduce, teachers also usually analyse the errors that occur in their students' written work.

Procedure

1 Refer to the sentences on the board. Tell the students that these have come from their writing, but do not identify the authors of the sentences. Make the point that each sentence contains a number of errors, and that these sorts of errors have been quite common across the whole class.

2 Use different coloured markers to highlight each of the errors in the first sentence. Each colour represents a different problem.

3   Point to each highlighted text and invite the class to answer the following
    questions:
    • What is the problem?
    • Why is it a problem?
    • How would you fix it?
4   Write the corrected sentence underneath. Then repeat Steps 2 and 3 with
    the second sentence.
5   Divide the class into small groups and hand out the other examples of
    student work. Together, students use different coloured highlighter pens
    and your colour code from Step 2 to identify the errors in each sentence.
6   The groups then write the corrected sentences. Monitor their work and
    answer their questions as you move about the class.
7   There is no need for whole-class feedback unless you observe a common
    area of difficulty that you need to address with all the students.

Follow-up

As you mark students' written work over the next few weeks, use the
highlighter pens to identify the errors from the activity. Students create an
individual error log and record the number of times each error is highlighted.
They can trace their progress by recording the number of errors they make
over a period of time. See Box 6.1. The error log can be expanded as new
errors become obvious in students' written work.

Box 6.1: Error log

Error	Colour	Week 1	Week 2	Week 3
Articles: *the, a,* zero article	Blue	4	1	0
Singular/ plural nouns	Yellow			
Verb–subject agreement	Green			
Word order	Pink			

© Garnet Education 2008. Adapted with permission.

6.2 Interrogating the definite article

Language	Definite articles in definitions
Outline	Students identify anaphoric and cataphoric reference.
Level	* *
Time	15–20 minutes
Preparation	Copy a short academic text which contains a number of definite articles. The example uses a definition. On the board, draw the grid from Box 6.2.
Background	An understanding of how *the* works in a text helps writers create cohesive texts and assists with reading comprehension. In this activity, an understanding of anaphoric and cataphoric reference is essential. It is not necessary for students to use these terms; the explanations in Box 6.2 are probably more appropriate. Note also that the analysis in this activity explains only some of the many rules governing the use of the definite article.

Procedure

1 If the students are not already familiar with the role of *the* as a referent, then briefly introduce the concepts of anaphoric and cataphoric reference. See Background and Box 6.2.

2 Divide the class into small groups and hand out the text. Allow students a few minutes to read it, and then address any of their comprehension questions.

3 Ask the groups to locate all the definite articles in the text and write the article plus the following noun in their notebooks, e.g. 'the definition'.

4 The students draw the grid from the board, then ask: 'What?' about the noun, e.g. 'What definition?' See Box 6.2. As they answer this question, they should complete the grid by noting whether they looked forward or backward in the text. Examples that are not covered by this questioning should be recorded in the 'Other' column.

5 The students then draw arrows on the text to demonstrate what they have discovered in Step 4.

6 Lead a class discussion on rules governing the use of the definite article that have been discovered in the activity. For now, focus on anaphoric and cataphoric reference only. The students provide examples from the text as they contribute to the conversation.

Box 6.2: Reference categories

Anaphoric reference (looking backward in the text)	Cataphoric reference (looking forward in the text)	Other
4 What term? *bel canto*	1 What definition? – that of *bel canto* 2 What Italian vocal style? – that of the eighteenth and early nineteenth centuries 5 What time? – that of Rossini, etc.	3 the eighteenth and early nineteenth centuries

There is some debate amongst music theorists about (1) the actual definition of *bel canto*. In its broadest application, *bel canto* refers to (2) the Italian vocal style of (3) the eighteenth and early nineteenth centuries; more narrowly, (4) the term is applied exclusively to Italian opera at (5) the time of Rossini, Bellini and Donizetti (Jander and Harris).

© K. Rutledge 2009. Used with permission.

Follow-up

- Students use their grammar books to research the uses of *the* in the 'Other' column. See Box 6.2. 'the eighteenth and early nineteenth centuries' is a phrase of time with *the*. Other examples include: *the first of January, the summer of 2009, the day before yesterday*.
- The students repeat the activity using a sample of their own writing. This may provide opportunities for error correction and individual assistance as you monitor their work.
- For other examples of the use of articles, see Activity 6.12 on p. 275.

6.3 Creating parallel structures

Language	Noun groups, verbs and adjectives in parallel structures
Outline	Students listen for parallel structures and then complete a gap-fill activity.
Level	*
Time	25–30 minutes
Preparation	From listening transcripts or texts from a reading class, select about five sentences which contain parallel structures. See Box 6.3a. Create a gap-fill activity for each sentence, omitting one of the elements in the list. See Box 6.3b.
Background	Noticing parallel structures will assist with reading comprehension. When students write parallel structures, they should also check that the parallel elements are consistent.

Procedure

1   Divide the class into pairs. Tell the students that you are going to read out a sentence and that when you come to the parallel structure, you will omit one of the items in the list. At this point you could give an example: *An architect is trained to plan, design and … the construction of a building.* They should listen for and note the things which are listed in the sentence, i.e. 'plan and design'. See Box 6.3a.

2   The pairs discuss what was listed and how many things appeared in the list, including the item you omitted. In the example above, the author listed three things.

3   Before you read the sentence again, tell the students that they should decide if the lists are noun groups, verbs or adjectives. After you read the incomplete sentence for the second time, the pairs confirm or adjust their conclusions from Step 2 and then decide on the part of speech in the list. Do not ask students to share their answers with the class at this stage.

4   Write or project this same incomplete sentence on the board, and leave a space for the missing word. The pairs write the sentence and decide on a word to fill the gap. This word should be the same part of speech as the other words or groups of words in the list.

5   Invite volunteers to share their ideas. The class could then decide whether to accept these answers. They should give reasons for their opinions.

6 Compare the original text with the student answers. Accept their suggestions if they make sense and are grammatically consistent with the list.

7 Repeat the activity with the other sentences.

Box 6.3a: Examples of parallel structures

Environmental science	High temperatures, record drought, increased flooding and rising sea levels can all be attributed to global warming.
Architecture	An architect is trained to plan, design and supervise the construction of a building.
Business	In these economic times, it is essential to employers that prospective employees be flexible, skilled and experienced.
Music	Long after he had stopped composing operas, Rossini gave his three requirements for the correct approach to *bel canto* singing: a naturally beautiful voice; careful training to encourage effortless delivery of florid music; and mastery of Italian style (Buchau).
Economics	Economics analyses movements in the overall economy – trends in prices, output and unemployment.

> ## Box 6.3b: Gap-fill activity
>
> 1 High temperatures, record drought, increased flooding and
> .... can all be attributed to global warming.
>
> 2 An architect is trained to ...., design and supervise the
> construction of a building.
>
> 3 In these economic times, it is essential to employers that prospective
> employees be flexible, ... and experienced.
>
> 4 Long after he had stopped composing operas, Rossini gave his
> three requirements for the correct approach to *bel canto* singing:
> ....; careful training to encourage
> effortless delivery of florid music; and mastery of Italian style (Buchau).
>
> 5 Economics analyses movements in the overall economy – trends in prices,
> output and ....
>
> From *Communicative Activities for EAP*
> © Cambridge University Press 2011   PHOTOCOPIABLE

Follow-up
Divide the class into pairs. Each pair chooses a profession. Check that a
range of professions is represented. Then the pairs devise lists of nouns, verbs
and adjectives to match professions. For example, for *architect*:
- *houses, stadiums, public buildings* (nouns)
- *plan, design, supervise* (verbs)
- *precise, creative, thorough* (adjectives)

Using the models from the activity, the students create sentences which
include parallel structures.

6.4 Noun:verb ratios

Language	Nouns and verbs
Outline	Students record the noun:verb ratio in their own writing and compare this with a published academic text.
Level	*
Time	10–15 minutes
Preparation	Students will need a sample of their own writing based on a class theme. Write your own short formal text on the same topic, making sure that academic register is created through extensive use of noun phrases. Photocopy this text. See Box 6.4.
Background	Formal academic texts are more dense and concise than informal texts. This is achieved through the use of noun phrases.
Reference	This activity is based on an idea in S. Thornbury (1997) *About Language: Tasks for Teachers of English*. Cambridge: Cambridge University Press, p. 102.

Procedure

1   In small groups, the students underline the noun phrases in their writing sample. They record the number of nouns at the bottom of the page.
2   After the students compare the number of nouns they each have in their writing, they circle the verbs, count them and record the number at the bottom of the page. (Verb phrases count as one verb.)
3   Under these numbers, each student writes the ratio of nouns to verbs in their text. They compare ratios within the group.
4   Hand out your short academic text and ask the groups to repeat the exercise.
5   The groups now compare their ratios with those of the academic text.
6   Conclude by asking the class to decide which texts most reflect academic register. In general, these texts will have a higher proportion of nouns to verbs.

Box 6.4: Informal and formal writing

Note: Noun groups are underlined and verb groups are in bold.

Informal reflection: an observation of an English class	Formal conclusions based on classroom observations
It **may be** better if the teacher **help** in a more subtle way. I **mean**, the teacher **can meet** the student after class. This **is** better because the student **won't feel** embarrassed. **Imagine** if you **are being called out** during the lesson because of lower English proficiency, you **will feel** bad.	Effective support of English language learners **requires** due consideration of the social and emotional needs of the learner. Some professionals **argue** that the singling out of less able students in front of the class **may have** consequences for the learner's self-esteem.
N:V ratio = 8:9 (51 words) [The author, a trainee teacher, is from a non-English-speaking background.]	N:V ratio = 11:3 (42 words)

Follow-up

Students rewrite their text and transform some of the verbs into nouns. This can be done in a number of ways:

- A noun is formed from the verb, e.g. *Students **correct** their errors* becomes *The **correction** of student errors* (noun + verb → new noun).
- A gerund is used, e.g. *The teacher can **meet** the student after class* becomes ***Meeting** a student after class could help to alleviate student embarrassment* (verb + -ing).
- The noun is formed metaphorically, e.g. *It may be better if the teacher **help** in a more subtle way* becomes ***Effective support** of English language learners ...*

Students identify other elements of informal register, e.g. contractions and personal pronouns. They scan the academic text for these features and compare this with the informal text.

6.5   Running dictation

Language	Use of Present Perfect Simple and plural nouns
Outline	Groups dictate to each other from a short academic text.
Level	∗
Time	25–30 minutes
Preparation	Make a number of copies of a short text which contains plural nouns and examples of the Present Perfect. See Box 6.5.
Background	While any point of grammar could be used in this activity, I have drawn attention to the pronunciation of word endings when forming plural nouns and the Present Perfect verbs because learners may omit these endings in their oral language, e.g. -*n* in *been*; -*ed* in *provided*, -*s* in *companies*. These omissions can then result in grammar errors when they write.

Procedure

1   Divide the class into small groups and explain how the running dictation works. See Steps 2 to 4.

2   Around the room, attach copies of the text you have copied. There should be one copy for each group. Place each text as far away as possible from the group who will be reading it.

3   The students decide on the order that they will 'run' to the text on the wall. The first student runs to the text, reads and memorizes a section, then runs back to the group to dictate the text. If the students have questions, or if the 'runner' forgets part of the text, they can return as many times as they like.

4   The next 'runner' has a turn. This continues until the complete text has been dictated.

5   Take the texts from the wall and distribute them to the groups. The students then highlight the Present Perfect verbs and plural nouns and check these against their work.

6   Lead a feedback session and explore these questions: Which groups have accurately dictated the text? What were the errors in the other transcriptions? Were these errors a result of inaccurate pronunciation? What other reasons explain the errors?

Box 6.5: Recapping

Our fundamental aim in this report has been to aid managers in terms of the performance of their companies. We have drawn upon data gathered from an intensive ongoing ten-year study. These data have provided a clear picture of the links between managerial practices and company performance.

© Institute of Personnel and Development 1997

Follow-up

Ask students to discuss and then recap on the aims and outcomes of nominated lessons. They should use the Present Perfect tense in their responses. For example:

> *The fundamental aim of this lesson has been to draw our attention to word endings when we speak and write plural nouns and the Present Perfect tense.*

6.6 Comparing texts

Language	Sentence types: simple, compound and complex.
Outline	Students compare two texts in terms of sentence types.
Level	*
Time	25–30 minutes
Preparation	Use a sample of informal text. It could be taken from students' written or oral work. Rewrite the sample so that it reflects a formal academic register. Make copies of both texts. See Box 6.6.
Background	This activity assumes that students know the difference between simple, compound and complex sentences. If necessary, you may want to revisit these sentence types before you start the activity.

Procedure

1   Divide the class into pairs. Give Student A the informal text and Student B the formal text. Allow a few minutes for the students to read the handout.
2   This step establishes that the two texts, while reflecting formal and informal register, contain the same basic information. The pairs take

turns to tell each other facts contained in their texts, one fact at a time. The conversation could go something like this:

> Student A: *My text says that Chinese people cook only Chinese food at home. Does your text say that too?*
>
> Student B: *Yes, it does. My text also says that Australians draw on a range of cuisines when they cook at home. Does your text say that too?*

3 When all the facts have been revealed, the students work individually to count the number of simple, compound and complex sentences in their handouts. They record the numbers at the bottom of the page.

4 Students label the sentences in the margin of the page.

5 The pairs then swap handouts. After they have read the text, ask the pairs, and then the class, to discuss how choice of sentence type influences the register of a text.

Box 6.6: Comparing cuisines

Student A: Informal comparison (sample of a student's writing)	Student B: Formal comparison (text rewritten by the teacher)
(1) From my observations I think about our diet and eating habits in China. (2) In the home, we cook only Chinese food. (3) When we want to eat cuisine from other countries, we always go to a restaurant. (4) This is a result of migration policy. (5) Australia is a multicultural country and many immigrants have changed the eating habits here but China has only a few immigrants. (6) Therefore China has not been influenced by other cuisines.	(1) A comparison between the cuisine preferences of Australians and the Chinese reveals that the former prepare meals in the home drawing on a range of cuisines, while the latter cook only Chinese food at home. (2) The habits of Australian home-cooks have been influenced by this country's multicultural and immigration policies, whereas minimal migration to China means that such policies have not influenced the home-cook.
Simple sentences: 4	Simple sentences: 0
Compound sentences: 1	Compound sentences: 0
Complex sentences: 1	Complex sentences: 2
Total: 6 sentences	Total: 2 sentences

Follow-up
Students scan through their textbook or material from their reading class to test the theory that fewer sentences and the use of complex sentences help to create formal academic register.

PHASE 2: EXPERIMENTING

In Phase 2, students reason, hypothesize, experiment and organize words, sentences and extended texts as they move towards language acquisition.

6.7   Rotating questions

Language	Reported questions
Outline	Students write questions and then convert them into statements.
Level	* *
Time	30–40 minutes
Preparation	Provide a blank piece of paper for each group. On the board, display the scaffolding from Box 6.7b.
Background	In responding to an assessment question, it may be helpful for students to begin by converting the question into a statement.

Procedure

1   Divide the class into groups, according to the number of question types you want to explore. The example has five question types. Allocate one question type to each group. See Box 6.7a.

2   Model the construction of the questions. In the example, you would model the word order of yes/no questions and Wh- questions ('How' is included among the Wh- questions).

3   Drawing on a class theme, each group constructs one question. The questions could be titles of essays or debates that the students have encountered recently, or the groups could draw on the content of class reading and listening texts and predict questions that may appear in an exam or a language test. They write the question at the top of a blank page. See Box 6.7a. While the students are engaged in the activity, go from group to group, monitoring their work and collecting their questions. Write these on the board, leaving space for students to write statements under the questions later on.

4 On the board, model how to convert questions into statements, using your questions from Step 2. See Box 6.7a.
5 The students pass their page to the neighbouring group. They jointly construct a statement based on the question and write this under the question. For additional support, refer students to the scaffolding on the board. See Box 6.7b.
6 Keep rotating the pages. Each time, the students read the work of the previous groups. They correct any errors and then add a statement of their own. As you go from group to group, check the subject–verb–object word order in the subordinate clauses.
7 When the pages return to their original groups, invite the students to write one of their sentences under the question on the board. Briefly recap on the differences between the question and statement forms.

Box 6.7a: Converting questions to statements

	Yes/no question	'Why' question	'How' question	'Where' question	'What' question
Assignment questions	Is climate change the result of human activity?	Why are sea levels rising?	How have Pacific islands been affected by global warming?	Where have the economic repercussions of global warming been experienced?	What can governments do to combat the effects of climate change?
Statement	This paper investigates if/whether climate change is the result of human activity.	This essay explains why sea levels are rising.	This report describes how Pacific islands have been affected by global warming.	This table outlines where the economic repercussions of global warming have been experienced.	This website details what governments can do to combat the effects of climate change.

Box 6.7b: Scaffolding

This: essay/table/ paper/report/website/ article/diagram/author/ researcher	*investigates, discusses, examines, explores*	*if, whether*
	explains, notes, observes, justifies	*why*
	describes, outlines, points out, details	*how, where, when, what*

Follow-up

Provide a number of questions taken from exam papers. Groups draft the first sentence in their response by rewriting the question as a statement.

6.8   Sentence auction

Skill	Error analysis
Outline	Students bid for sentences in an auction.
Level	*
Time	20–30 minutes
Preparation	Collect examples of incorrect sentences from the students' writing. Choose examples which occur frequently rather than 'one off' errors. On the board, write or project accurate and inaccurate sentences in a random order. Do not write pairs of sentences, i.e. the correct and the incorrect version of the same sentence, and avoid sentences with very obvious errors. See Box 6.8.
Reference	This activity is based on a game from M. Rinvolucri (1984) *Grammar Games*. Cambridge: Cambridge University Press, p. 18.

Procedure

1   Refer the class to the sentences on the board and allow a little time for the students to read them. Do not tell the students how many sentences are correct or incorrect.

2   Divide the class into small groups and allocate a budget to each group, e.g. $1,000. The groups should also have a name or a number to identify them.

3   The groups have a few minutes to decide which sentences are correct and which ones contain errors. The amount they bid for a sentence will depend on how confident they are that this is an accurate sentence.

4   Adopt the role of an auctioneer and start the bidding at about $50 for the
     first sentence. Whoever is the highest bidder at the fall of the hammer can
     claim the sentence. You could use a student volunteer to keep a record
     on the board of the group who successfully bids for each sentence. This
     student could also record what was spent and how much is left in the
     budget of each group so that they do not overspend.

5   Continue until all sentences have been claimed or it becomes obvious
     that no groups want a sentence. Note that you do not have to auction the
     sentences in the order they appear on the board. This keeps the students
     guessing what might come next, and therefore engaged in the activity.

6   The group with the highest number of accurate sentences wins. Next,
     identify the incorrect sentences and ask the groups to discuss why these
     sentences are incorrect. They could use their grammar books here.

7   Call on volunteers to explain the rules or conventions for the inaccurate
     sentences.

Box 6.8: Accurate and inaccurate sentences

Inaccurate sentences	Accurate sentences	Reason
The advertising campaign for these publicly listed companies are similar in many ways.	The advertising campaign for these publicly listed companies is similar in many ways.	The controlling noun is *campaign*. The singular noun requires a singular verb – *is*.
Meteorologists outlined what would they forecast for the next season.	Meteorologists outlined what they would forecast for the next season.	Following a Wh- clause, use the subject–verb–object word order.
The identity of ethnic minorities has been threatened by the globalization.	The identity of ethnic minorities has been threatened by globalization.	*globalization* is a non-count noun with indefinite reference, so it takes zero article.
In spite of the tax was increased, consumption remained steady.	In spite of the tax increase, consumption remained steady.	*in spite of / despite* are prepositions, not conjunctions, so they cannot introduce a finite clause.

continued

Box 6.8: (*cont.*)

In the future, town planners can reduce our dependency on cars by constructing walkways, bike paths and designated public transport links.	In the future, town planners will be able to reduce our dependency on cars by constructing walkways, bike paths and designated public transport links.	*can* refers to a present ability, whereas *will be able to* reflects a future ability.
Because of feral cats have had to adapt to harsher environments they have become much larger than domestic cats.	Because feral cats have had to adapt to harsher environments, they have become much larger than domestic cats.	*Because of* is followed by a noun phrase; *because* is a conjunction and is followed by a clause.
Alternating current is easily made in generators, and this is the reason because countries choose alternating current rather than direct current.	Alternating current is easily made in generators, and this is (the reason) why countries choose alternating current rather than direct current.	Follow *reason* with 'why' or 'how', not 'because'.
This diagram describes how does a parallel circuit work.	This diagram describes how a parallel circuit works.	Following a 'How' clause, use the subject–verb–object word order.
The earth's crust is consists of seven large tectonic plates and approximately twenty smaller plates which are separated by fault lines.	The earth's crust consists of seven large tectonic plates and approximately twenty smaller plates which are separated by fault lines.	A Present Simple verb *consists* is required.
Employees will receive a 3% wage increase over the next two years. Besides, they are entitled to an additional taxable transfer allowance of £300 paid in three instalments over 16 months.	Employees will receive a 3% wage increase over the next two years. Besides this, they are entitled to an additional taxable transfer allowance of £300 paid in three instalments over 16 months.	*Besides this* means 'in addition to this', while *besides* means 'however/anyway' and is used in informal oral language.

Follow-up

Students create a similar auction using samples of writing from their group.
Check that they have successfully corrected the sentences and that they
understand the rules that apply to the incorrect sentences. Then call on the
groups to conduct the auction.

6.9 Spotting adverbial clauses

Language	Subordinate adverbial clauses
Outline	Students identify adverbial clauses in their writing.
Level	* *
Time	30–40 minutes
Preparation	On the board, write categories of adverbial clauses and their corresponding conjunctions. Display a text which contains adverbial clauses. See Box 6.9.
Background	The conjunctions I have chosen for this activity can all be followed by a subject–verb–object word order.

Procedure

1   Display a text containing examples of adverbial clauses. See the sample
    text in Box 6.9. Highlight each conjunction.
2   Ask the students to match the conjunctions to the categories on the
    board. Invite volunteers to share and justify their answers.
3   Draw attention to the word order in each of the clauses. See Background
    above.

4   Divide the class into small groups. Individually, each student scans a sample of their writing and identifies the adverbial clauses. They note the category of each conjunction.
5   The students share their findings in their groups. Are there categories that they do not use? Are there opportunities in their writing when they could include a different type of adverbial clause? Are the adverbial clauses used accurately?
6   Pairs of students help each other to edit their work. Monitor this process and assist where needed.

Box 6.9: Adverbial clauses

	Time	Condition	Contrast	Reason	Purpose
	since, until	*provided that, as long as*	*even though, whereas*	*as, because*	*so that, so*
Example sentence	Information has become more accessible since the invention of the internet.	The internet is reasonably secure provided that users have security systems in place.	Some users prefer conventional banking practices, even though internet banking is convenient.	The authorities have warned internet users to take security measures as crimes of identity fraud have increased.	Most businesses advertise online so that they can reach a wider audience.

Sample text: Business – e-commerce

The internet has revolutionized the way we work and communicate. Information has become more accessible **since** the invention of the internet. In addition, most businesses advertise online **so that** they can reach a wider audience. However, the authorities have warned internet users to take security measures **as** crimes of identity fraud have increased. **Because of** such security concerns, some users prefer conventional banking practices, **even though** internet banking is convenient. Most internet users, however, consider that the internet is reasonably secure **provided that** they have security systems in place.

Follow-up
Students display examples from their own writing which include adverbial clauses.

6.10 Cause/effect reconnaissance mission

Language	Cause and effect
Outline	Groups use a corpus to discover cause/effect language patterns.
Level	**
Time	30–40 minutes
Preparation	Groups will need access to the internet and a corpus, e.g. the British National Corpus (http://corpus.byu.edu/bnc/x.asp) or the Corpus of Contemporary American English (http://www.americancorpus.org/). They will also use dictionaries in this activity.

Procedure

1 Invite the class to embark on a reconnaissance mission to discover patterns in cause/effect constructions. In explaining cause and effect relationships, it may be helpful to think about the *cause* as the thing that happened first, and the *effect* as the thing that happened next. You could give an example from everyday life to illustrate. For example: *An accident on the highway causes traffic chaos.*

2 Give each group one cause/effect language exponent. See Box 6.10a. Using an online corpus, the groups find examples of texts which contain their language signal. Students should choose material from academic texts and take note of the field, e.g. commerce, law, etc.

3 Allow a few minutes for groups to check unfamiliar vocabulary in their dictionaries.

4 Before they write the examples, students should check that the sentences represent a cause/effect relationship. (For example, *causes* could be a plural of *cause*, but they are looking for the Present Simple, third-person verb form.)

5 Create new groups consisting of one student from each of the original groups. Draw the table from Box 6.10b on the board and write in the headings. The students copy the table and fill in each column using their research from Steps 2 to 4. They look for similarities in the sentence patterns.

6 Following a brief feedback session, ask the groups to examine each example and discuss if the cause/effect language exponents have a

positive, negative or neutral association. Is this always the case? In what contexts do the exponents have these associations? See Box 6.10a.

Box 6.10a: Cause/effect language exponents

Cause/effect language exponents	Example sentence from the British National Corpus (Positive (+), Negative (−) and Neutral (θ) associations)
produces	Agriculture: Aquaculture innovation **produces** a higher capital return to the farmer than traditional farming practices do, and such innovation can also be a natural way of managing aquaculture production to become more sustainable. (+)
causes	Engineering: The left-hand arm is positioned by a jack and a right-hand arm is set by the coupling linkage. The arrangement **causes** the two arms to open and close together. (θ)
results in	Law: It should be noted that positive discrimination would also be unlawful under the Act, since it inevitably **results in** one racial or ethnic group being treated less favourably than another on the grounds of their race, and so on. (−)
leads to	Commerce: Thus, in the Keynesian model, a fall in aggregate demand **leads to** a fall in real income and reduces employment. (−)
brings about	Education: The librarian has also found that close examination of data required in producing databases **brings about** an awareness of bias and the development of objective criticism. (+)
gives rise to	Veterinary science: The gene that causes the taillessness also distorts the rest of the spine, giving the cat a backbone with fewer and shorter vertebrae. In severe cases, it **gives rise to** the condition known as spina bifida. (−)

http://corpus.byu.edu/bnc

Box 6.10b: Cause/effect sentence pattern

The thing that happened first: noun phrase	Cause/effect language: verb phrase	The thing that happened next: noun phrase
aquaculture innovation	*produces*	a higher capital return to the farmer
the arrangement	*causes*	the two arms to open and close together
it (positive discrimination)	*results in*	one racial or ethnic group being treated less favourably than another
a fall in aggregate demand	*leads to*	a fall in real income
close examination of data	*brings about*	an awareness of bias and the development of objective criticism
it (the gene)	*gives rise to*	the condition known as spina bifida

Follow-up

Students use a corpus to research examples of language signals which create different patterns. For example:

Pattern 1

Cause/effect language	The thing that happened first: noun phrase	The thing that happened next: noun phrase
Owing to *Because of* *Due to* *As a result of*	a fall in demand	world copper prices have fallen.

Pattern 2

(With this pattern, ask: 'What happened first? What happened next?')

The thing that happened next: noun phrase	Cause/effect language	The thing that happened first: noun phrase
World copper prices have fallen	*owing to* *because of* *due to* *as a result of*	a fall in demand.

6.11   From informal to formal

Language	Phrasal verbs and their Latinate equivalents
Outline	Pairs rewrite a newspaper article replacing phrasal verbs with Latinate verbs.
Level	* *
Time	25–30 minutes
Preparation	Photocopy a short newspaper article on a topic of academic interest. If necessary, adapt the article so that it contains phrasal verbs. See Box 6.11a. Students will need a dictionary and a thesaurus during this activity. The thesaurus contained in word-processing software is ideal.
Background	Phrasal verbs generate an informal register, while their Latinate equivalents help to create a more formal register. See Box 6.11b.
Reference	Thanks to Marion Whittaker (QUT's International Short Course Coordinator: TESOL) for the inspiration for this activity.

Procedure

1   Divide the class into pairs and hand out copies of the newspaper article. See Box 6.11a.
2   Write a few phrasal verbs on the board to illustrate. In pairs, the students then underline the phrasal verbs in the article.
3   Choose one of these verbs and demonstrate its Latinate equivalent/s. Make the point that Latinate verbs help to create a formal register. See Box 6.11b.
4   Using a thesaurus (either paper or electronic), the pairs research the Latinate version of the phrasal verbs they have identified. They use dictionaries to check that their choice of word has the same meaning in the text as the phrasal verb. See Box 6.11b.

5 The pairs then rewrite the text and substitute Latinate verbs for phrasal verbs. See Box 6.11a.

6 Make groups of four. The pairs compare paragraphs and check that the replacement verbs make sense in the texts.

Box 6.11a: Two paragraphs – informal and formal

News report: informal register	Paragraph using Latinate verbs: formal register
As more people are put off by increasing health insurance contributions, doctors have warned the population not to give up on their regular medical check-ups. GPs may come across the signs of serious diseases such as cancer, and early detection means that patients may not have to go through surgery or lengthy periods of chemotherapy. A GP also reminds patients about healthy habits, such as cutting down on alcohol consumption and doing without red meat occasionally.	As more people are dismayed by increasing health insurance contributions, doctors have warned the population not to abandon their regular medical check-ups. GPs may discover the signs of serious diseases such as cancer, and early detection means that patients may not have to endure surgery or lengthy periods of chemotherapy. A GP also reminds patients about healthy habits, such as reducing alcohol consumption and forgoing red meat occasionally.

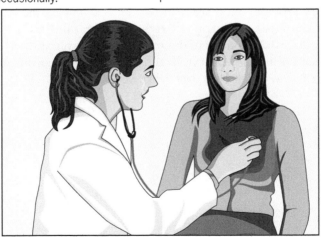

From *Communicative Activities for EAP*
© Cambridge University Press 2011   PHOTOCOPIABLE

Box 6.11b: Phrasal verbs and Latinate equivalents

Phrasal verbs	Latinate verbs
put off	*postpone*
come across	*encounter*
look at	*observe, examine, consider*
take up	*adopt, resume*
go through	*endure*
cut down on	*reduce*
do without	*forgo*
take care of	*tend, support*
look after	*protect*
ask for	*request*
take in	*absorb, grasp, understand*

Follow-up

Phrasal verbs are more common in oral academic English than in formal written texts. Provide a short academic written text and ask the students to use a thesaurus to replace Latinate verbs with phrasal verbs. They then briefly discuss the content of the article, using the phrasal verbs. A comprehensive list of phrasal verbs and their Latinate equivalents is available at http://www.btinternet.com/~ted.power/rp0780.html

6.12   Sorting nouns

Language Outline	Zero, definite and indefinite articles in descriptions Students discover rules for using articles.
Level	* * *
Time	30–40 minutes
Preparation	Photocopy a number of short texts from a class theme. The texts should come from the same genre: the example uses descriptions. The texts should contain a range of zero, definite and indefinite articles. See Box 6.12a. Provide a different text for each group. On the board, draw a table with three columns and write in the column headings: zero article, definite article and indefinite article. See Box 6.12b. *Note:* You may want to do Activity 6.2 on p. 252 in preparation for this activity.

Procedure

1   Divide the class into small groups and hand out the short texts. Allow students about five minutes to read and clarify the contents.

2   If necessary, explain the terms 'zero', 'definite' and 'indefinite' articles. Invite volunteers to provide examples to illustrate.

3   The groups copy the table on the board and create a list of the nouns in their text.

4   The students now discuss and decide why some nouns have a zero article, some have a definite article and some have an indefinite article. If necessary, you may want to use the prompts from Box 6.12c as you monitor their discussions.

5   When a number of rules have been 'discovered', create new groups consisting of one member of each of the original groups. This means that each group member has analysed a different text. The students compare their lists of nouns and share the outcomes of their discussions in Step 4.

6   Call the class together. On the board, create a list of 'discovered' rules and examples from the texts.

Box 6.12a: Describing ecosystems

Yellowstone National Park	Deserts
Greater Yellowstone is the last remaining large, nearly intact ecosystem in the northern temperate zone of the Earth and is partly located in Yellowstone National Park. Conflict over management has been controversial, and the area is a flagship site among conservation groups that promote ecosystem management.	Deserts take up about one-third of the Earth's land surface. Hot deserts usually have a large seasonal temperature range, with high daytime temperatures and low nighttime temperatures. In hot deserts the temperature in the daytime can reach 45°C/113°F or higher in the summer, and dip to 0°C/32°F or lower in the winter.

From *Communicative Activities for EAP*
© Cambridge University Press 2011   PHOTOCOPIABLE

Box 6.12b: Nouns analysed

Nouns from description of 'Yellowstone National Park'		
Zero article	**Definite article**	**Indefinite article**
Yellowstone Yellowstone National Park management conservation groups ecosystem management	the last ... intact ecosystem the northern temperate zone the Earth the area	a flagship site

Nouns from description of 'Deserts'		
Zero article	**Definite article**	**Indefinite article**
deserts hot deserts high daytime temperatures low nighttime temperatures	the Earth's land surface the temperature the daytime the summer the winter	a large ... temperature range

Box 6.12c: Prompts	
Prompts for using the zero article	• Is the noun countable or plural and does it have indefinite reference? (*deserts*) • Does the noun refer to a class of things? (*deserts*) • Does the noun refer to things in general? (*low nighttime temperatures*)
Prompts for using the definite article: *the*	• Does the noun refer back to something in the text? (*the area*) • Does the noun refer forward to something in the text? • Does the noun refer to some knowledge shared by the reader and the writer? (*the Earth*) • Does the noun represent a superlative? (*the last … ecosystem*)
Prompts for using the indefinite article: *a/an*	• Is it a singular countable noun and does it have indefinite reference? (*a flagship site*)

Follow-up

Other ecosystems which could be used in the activity include:

• aquatic
• coral reef
• prairie
• rainforest
• savannah
• tundra

Groups rewrite their text and remove all articles, thus creating a gap-fill exercise. At the bottom of the page they write the number of articles that have been removed. They swap texts and insert articles into the appropriate places. They then check each other's work.

6.13   Actors, actions and receivers

Language	Passive voice
Outline	Groups reflect on why passive and active voice are used in a text.
Level	*
Time	20–30 minutes
Preparation	Photocopy or project a paragraph which contains both active and passive voice. See Box 6.13a.

Procedure

1   On the board, write an active voice sentence. Underline sections of the text to demonstrate the word order in this sentence: the actor, then the action and then the receiver of the action. See Box 6.13a.

2   Explain to the class that to change this sentence into the passive voice, they should place the receiver first, then the verb *to be* + the past participle of the action + *by* and then the actor. See Box 6.13a. Raise the question: 'Why would a writer choose the passive voice over the active voice in a piece of text?' The students do not answer the question now, but they will be called upon to consider this question in more detail later in the activity.

3   Organize the class into groups of three or four and ask them to read the paragraph on the board and clarify any comprehension questions.

4   In their groups, the students now underline the passive verbs and then answer the question: 'Who is the actor in each passive construction?' See the words in bold in Box 6.13b. Warn the students that they will have to infer who the actor is in some instances. (Note that this investigation assists with reading comprehension.) Invite individuals to share their responses with the class.

5   The groups now discuss the following questions:
   • Why has the author chosen to use the passive voice and to omit the actor?
   • Why is the actor included in some passive constructions?
   • Why does the author use the active voice in some situations? See Box 6.13c. Invite volunteers to report back to the class.

6   Conclude the activity by reinforcing that writers use the passive voice as a tool for creating academic register.

Box 6.13a: Web accessibility

Active voice sentence:

Web accessibility (actor) **guarantees** (action) **universal inclusion of internet users** (receiver of the action), regardless of age or educational background.

Passive voice sentence:

Universal inclusion of internet users (receiver of the action), regardless of age or educational background, is **guaranteed by** (verb *to be* + past participle + *by*) **web accessibility.** (actor)

Accessibility is one of the key challenges that the internet must currently face to guarantee universal inclusion. Accessible Web design requires knowledge and experience from the designer, who can be assisted by the use of broadly accepted guidelines. ... Even if designers are convinced (or compelled) to create accessible products, they usually have to face a lack of knowledge and experience in accessible design. Therefore, methods, tools and criteria (usually provided as sets of guidelines) are needed to help designers with this difficulty. Guidelines have frequently been used to collect design knowledge and experience. Even if they may present problems, such as incoherence and unreliability, and may be difficult to handle (when the set of guidelines is too large), guidelines nevertheless prove to be the best method in order to transmit satisfactory design experiences either within large design groups or to the external world.

http://www.springerlink.com/content/r31k865algm7e38h/

From *Communicative Activities for EAP*

© Cambridge University Press 2011   PHOTOCOPIABLE

Box 6.13b: Web accessibility: analysed

Accessibility is one of the key challenges that the internet must currently face to guarantee universal inclusion. Accessible Web design requires knowledge and experience from the designer, who <u>can be assisted</u> **by the use of broadly accepted guidelines**. ... Even if designers <u>are convinced</u> **by experts in the field** (or [are] <u>compelled</u>) **by government regulators** to create accessible products, they usually have to face a lack of knowledge and experience in accessible design. Therefore, methods, tools and criteria ([which are] usually <u>provided</u> **by industry regulators** as sets of guidelines) <u>are needed</u> **by the games designers** to help designers with this difficulty. Guidelines <u>have frequently been used</u> **by games designers** to collect design knowledge and experience. Even if they may present problems, such as incoherence and unreliability, and may be difficult to handle (when the set of guidelines is too large), guidelines nevertheless prove to be the best method in order to transmit satisfactory design experiences either within large design groups or to the external world.

Box 6.13c: Reasons for using active and passive voice

Reasons for using the passive voice in actor-less sentences:

- The actor is not known.
- The actor can be inferred from the context.
- The writer wishes to avoid identifying the actor.
- The actor is not significant in the overall meaning of the text.
- The actor is repeated throughout the text.
- The writer wants to shift the focus from the human agent to an action, process or event.

Reasons for including the actor in active and passive sentences:

- The actor is essential in understanding the meaning of the text.
- The author wants to draw attention to the actor.
- In passive constructions, the author places the actor at the end of the sentence, where important information usually goes.

Follow-up
Students scan texts from their reading class and note passive constructions. They refer to the reasons in Box 6.13c and match one reason to each example they have highlighted.

6.14 Hunting for noun phrases

Language	Noun phrases: pre- plus post-modification
Outline	Groups locate a range of noun phrases.
Level	∗ ∗
Time	30–40 minutes
Preparation	On the board, write or project sentences which contain a variety of noun phrases. Use examples from a familiar context. See Box 6.14.
Background	Complex noun phrases are a feature of academic register. Students will be required to write such sentences in assignments. In addition, an understanding of the structure of these sentences will enhance their reading comprehension.

Procedure

1 Refer to the sentences on the board. See Box 6.14. Explain that writers use pre-modification and post-modification in academic writing. Ask the class to identify the nouns in the first sentence. Point out how the noun has been modified.

2 Divide the class into small groups and ask the students to decide how the nouns have been modified in each sentence on the board, i.e. pre-modification or post-modification.

3 Lead a class discussion in which you determine the grammar used in these constructions. Record this analysis following the sentences. See Box 6.14.

4 Set the groups the task of finding similar examples of pre- and post-modification using familiar academic texts. Go from group to group, offering incidental teaching when required.

5 Create pairs from different groups. The students share examples of pre-modification and post-modification from their texts.

6 Repeat Step 5 a number of times so that students have the chance to see most of the examples.

Box 6.14: Noun phrases

Sample sentences	Pre-modification	Post- modification
The **vitamins and minerals that our body needs, but which it cannot make itself**, include Vitamin C and the minerals iron and calcium.		Relative clause
Fibre is found in **foods derived from plants**, such as cereals, bread, fruits and vegetables.		Reduced relative clause / non-finite clause with -ed
Blood consists of a liquid part called plasma and **a cellular part consisting of red blood cells, white blood cells and platelets**.		Reduced relative clause / non- finite clause with -ing
The stomach is a **muscular bag** where both **mechanical and chemical digestion** take place.	Adjective phrase	
In most animals, blood is moved around the body through a network of tubes called **blood vessels**. (*Note*: while 'blood' acts as an adjective, you cannot say 'the vessels which are blood'. Therefore it creates a noun phrase. Compare this with 'muscular bag' in the previous example.)	Noun phrase	

Follow-up

- Students write a number of their sample sentences on the board. Call on volunteers to draw brackets around the noun phrases. They then underline the head noun and the verb which goes with this noun. Draw attention to the agreement between the subjects and their corresponding verbs.
- Students identify pre- and post-modification in their own writing. They suggest how they may further develop academic register through the use of noun phrases.

PHASE 3: PRODUCING

The focus in Phase 3 is access and output. Students incorporate knowledge of grammar to produce written and oral texts in a meaningful social context.

6.15 Noun conga

Language	Complex noun phrases
Outline	Groups take turns to add to a head noun.
Level	**
Time	20–30 minutes
Preparation	Choose a number of nouns from a class theme. Provide a piece of paper for each group. They will also need marker pens and scissors. If students are not familiar with pre-modification and post-modification of head nouns, then do Activity 6.14 on p. 281 as a lead-in to this activity.

Procedure

1   On the board, write a noun phrase from a class theme, e.g. Chief Executive Officers (CEOs).
2   Demonstrate how to modify this head noun. Add each modification one at a time, noting if it is pre- or post-modification. This demonstrates what the students will do in the activity. See Box 6.15. As you add a modification, draw attention to the grammar, e.g. adjective phrase, prepositional phrase. See Box 6.14.
3   Divide the class into small groups and distribute the marker pens, paper and scissors. On the board, write another noun taken from a current class theme. Each group will have a turn to modify this head noun. When it is their turn, they decide what they want to add and then write their text on

a strip of paper. The text should be large enough for the class to read it easily. One group member stands in front of the class holding their text.

4 The groups continue to add to the sentence. By this stage there should be a 'conga line' of students spread across the front of the classroom. Those in the line can signal that they have an idea, and a runner from their group could come to the front to retrieve their suggestion.

5 When all ideas have been exhausted, write the class's noun phrase on the board. Start again with a different head noun.

Box 6.15 Adding to the sentence conga

- CEOs
- These high-profile CEOs
- These high-profile, overpaid CEOs
- These high-profile, overpaid CEOs of companies
- These high-profile, overpaid CEOs of publicly listed companies
- These high-profile, overpaid CEOs of publicly listed companies identified in the report
- These high-profile, overpaid CEOs of publicly listed companies identified in the report, whose salaries are not determined by the shareholders

Follow-up

In their groups, the students jointly construct the remainder of the sentences on the board. Monitor their work and assist where needed. Display the students' writing and together decide which sentences provide good models for future writing.

6.16 Definition templates

Language	Language patterns in definitions
Outline	Groups create templates for defining terms
Level	**
Time	25–30 minutes
Preparation	Students will need access to the internet for this activity. Links to definitions can be found at http://www.definitions.net/# and http://dictionary.die.net/
Background	Students are regularly called upon to define terms. There are a number of grammatical structures which enable a writer to do this.

Procedure

1 Drawing on a class theme, write a definition on the board. The example in Box 6.16 uses medical terms.
2 Work with the students to identify the language pattern of the definition.
3 Divide the class into small groups and ask the students to decide on another term they would like to define. Each group should have a different term.
4 The students use an internet search engine to discover a definition for their term.
5 Next, the groups create a template based on their internet research. They write these definition templates on the board. See Box 6.16.
6 Lead a class discussion in which you reflect on the grammatical structures of the definitions. Ask the students to copy templates that they would like to use in their writing.

Box 6.16: Definition of terms

Definition 1:

Sleep apnoea is a sleep disorder characterized by pauses in breathing during sleep.

.... is .... characterized by
....

(http://en.wikipedia.org/wiki/Sleep_apnoea)

continued

Box 6.16: (*cont.*)

Definition 2:

A *cochlear implant* (CI) is a surgically implanted electronic device that provides a sense of sound to a person who is profoundly deaf or severely hard of hearing.

http://en.wikipedia.org/wiki/Cochlear_implant

.... is .... that
....

Definition 3:

Critical Care Units (or intensive care units [ICU]) can be defined as 'specialized sections of a hospital containing the equipment, medical and nursing staff and monitoring devices necessary to provide continuous and closely monitored health care to critically ill patients'.

© Cambridge University Press 2008

.... can be defined as ....
containing...
necessary to provide...
....

Follow-up

Using the templates from the activity, students generate definitions for other terms.

6.17 Softening a stance

Language	Modal expressions
Outline	Groups soften the stance of written statements.
Level	* * *
Time	20–30 minutes
Preparation	On the board, write a topic for discussion. A range of suitable topics can be found at http://www.globalissues.org/ The example looks at the causes of world poverty.

Procedure

1   Divide the class into groups and refer the students to the topic on the board.

2   Allow about 15 minutes for the students to decide on their stance and then write short statements in support of their point of view. Encourage a range of views.

3   Divide the board into columns: one for each group. Group members take turns to write one statement in their column. At any given time, there is one representative of each group at the board at the same time. Before writing, they should check whether their idea has already been recorded. If so, they will need an alternative idea. You would expect the tenor of these statements to be quite authoritative. See Box 6.17b.

4   When the columns each have four or five statements, stop the activity. On the board, write the language for expressing hedging. (Include the language from the left-hand column only.) Use the students' sentences to give a few examples of how to hedge ideas. See Box 6.17a.

5   The groups draw on the statements on the board to jointly construct a paragraph which encompasses a range of viewpoints. See Box 6.17b. They soften the stance of the statements by using modal expressions and hedging expressions from Box 6.17a.

6   Display the paragraphs and encourage the groups to read and comment on each other's work.

Box 6.17a: Modal expressions – hedging

Hedging + modality	Examples from Box 6.17b
Can to make fairly confident but not absolute assertions	*Some causes of poverty can be found within the poor country itself.*
Could, might to make more tentative assertions	*One external cause of poverty could be restrictive trade barriers.*
May to describe things which are likely to occur	*Government policies, for instance, may work against successful development.*
Would to make argumentative claims less direct: used in conjunction with speech act verbs, e.g. *advocate, argue, assert, seem*	*It would seem that policies such as providing a low-paid workforce and cheap resources are likely to attract investment.*
Hedging expressions: *apparently, evidently, usually, as a rule, broadly speaking, in some respects, in principle, generally speaking*	*Generally speaking, people remain poor for a range of reasons.*
Hedging expressions: impersonal 'it' construction with passive voice *... is believed to be* *... is claimed that* *... is assumed that* *... was considered to be* *... was decided to* *... has been suggested that*	*It has been suggested that external causes outweigh internal causes.*

Box 6.17b: Causes of world poverty

What are the causes of world poverty?	
List of statements	**Paragraph incorporating modal expressions**
1 The governments of poor countries pursue policies that work against successful development. 2 To attract investment, poor countries provide a low-paid workforce and cheap resources. 3 Workers in poor countries are exploited by powerful business interests. 4 Aid to poor countries does not go to the most needy but instead to corrupt government officials. 5 Wealthy nations provide aid as a way of promoting their own political power in a region. 6 Countries are poor because of ongoing regional conflicts. 7 Wealthy countries deny poorer countries access to their markets.	Generally speaking, people remain poor for a range of reasons. Some causes of poverty can be found within the poor country itself. Government policies, for instance, may work against successful development. It would seem that policies such as providing a low-paid workforce and cheap resources are likely to attract investment, but on the whole, the workers are usually trapped in the cycle of poverty. It has been suggested that external causes outweigh internal causes. One external cause of poverty could be restrictive trade barriers that tend to deny poorer nations access to the markets of wealthy countries.

Follow-up

From the students' work on the board, select sets of statements that could go together to form a number of paragraphs for the main body of an essay. Then allocate one set of statements to each group. Appoint one group to write an introduction to the essay and another group to write the conclusion. Each group then jointly constructs one paragraph. Collect all the paragraphs and publish the class essay.

6.18 Reporting findings

Language	Passive and active voice
Outline	Students use passive and active voice to report on research findings.
Level	* * *
Time	30–40 minutes
Preparation	This activity could follow a listening task. Photocopy an excerpt from a transcript, e.g. a discussion or interview about some form of research. See Box 6.18a. On the board, write or project examples of verbs which could be used when reporting findings or ideas. See Box 6.18b.
Background	This activity assumes that students are familiar with the passive voice. You could use Activity 6.13 on p. 278 as a preparation for this activity.

Procedure

1 Divide the class into two groups (A and B) and create pairs within each of the large groups.
2 Provide a copy of the transcript and allow a few minutes for the students to read it. This should not take long if you use material from a previous listening class.
3 The pairs use bullet points to summarize the main ideas in the text. See Box 6.18c.
4 Make sure the students are aware of the verb support on the board. See Box 6.18b.
5 Ask the pairs in Group A to write a brief report on the findings of the research, using mainly passive voice. Group B writes a similar report using mainly active voice. See Box 6.18c.
6 Create new pairs with one student from Group A and one from Group B. They swap reports and read each other's work.
7 Invite the pairs to write another report selecting sentences from their original work. As you monitor their writing, ask the students to provide reasons for choosing active or passive constructions. See Box 6.13c (on p. 280) and Box 6.18c.
8 Record the students' reasons on the board. If necessary, add to their list. See Box 6.13c for reasons for using active and passive voice.

Box 6.18a: Music therapy transcript

Interviewer: I suppose some of the scepticism about music therapy is engendered by … you hear these quick fixes, listen to Mozart for ten minutes a day and you'll get 20% smarter. What's your stance on these sorts of claims for music therapy?

Music therapist: Well, I think that there's been a real populist application and it's not really a scientific application at all and it's certainly no part of music therapy.

Interviewer: One of the criticisms about music therapy is that maybe it is that personal attention and relationship that's what the patients are responding to, rather than the music itself.

Music therapist: Sure, and that is one of the things that the research will explore further, but we can draw upon some of the music psychology literature that indicates very clearly the use of pre-recorded music and how it can promote change in people.

Interviewer: How do you assess the efficacy of the music therapy work that you do?

Music therapist: In my PhD research, I invited patients who experienced music therapy – staff, patients who overheard music therapy on the wards, visitors – to write anonymously: 'What did they think of the music therapy program?' And I collected over 250 response sheets and I analysed all of this data using qualitative research.

Interviewer: So when you evaluated these 200-odd surveys, what did you find?

Music therapist: What I found was that the patients were saying it helped take them to another space, another imagined space.

http://www.abc.net.au/rn/allinthemind/

From *Communicative Activities for EAP*

Box 6.18b: Verb support

Verbs for reporting		Passive constructions	Modal verbs
established reported examined produced alleged recorded analysed accepted	suggested claimed concluded debated justified interpreted argued assumed	Present Perfect: has/have/had suggested Simple tenses: was/were/is/are justified Impersonal 'it' with verbal verbs: It was concluded that …	can/could/may/ might/would

Box 6.18c: Summaries

Bullet points:

- Scepticism about music therapy
- Music therapy – 'quick fix'
- Patients respond to attention, not music
- Populist applications – not scientific application – no part of music therapy
- Music psychology literature – prerecorded music – promote change
- Patients, staff, visitors – write anonymously – qualitative research – 200 surveys
- MT takes patients to another imagined space

Summary in active voice
The interviewer suggested that music therapy is a 'quick fix' and that patients respond to the attention rather than the music itself. The music therapist asserted, however, that populist applications play no part in music therapy. The music psychology literature indicates that prerecorded music promotes change. In addition, patients, staff and visitors on music therapy wards report that the music took them to another imagined space.

continued

Box 6.18c: (*cont.*)

Summary in passive voice
It has been suggested that music therapy could be used as a 'quick fix' and that the attention rather than the music has been responsible for the patients' responses. It has also been asserted that populist applications play no part in music therapy. The music psychology literature indicated that change had been promoted by prerecorded music. It was also reported that patients, staff and visitors on music therapy wards were taken to another imagined space by music therapy.

Summary in active and passive voice
It has been suggested that music therapy could be used as a 'quick fix' and that patients respond to the attention rather than the music itself. Music therapists assert, however, that populist applications play no part in music therapy. The music psychology literature indicates that prerecorded music promotes change. In addition, patients, staff and visitors on music therapy wards reported that they were taken to another imagined space by music therapy.

Follow-up
Use academic texts from a reading class. Divide the text into small sections and allocate one section to each group. The students use passive and active voice constructions to write a brief report on the ideas represented in the written text and include appropriate referencing. Activity 4.1 on p. 153 explores how to incorporate a reference.

6.19   Students as teachers

Language	Academic register
Outline	Groups of students investigate grammar patterns and engage in a peer-tutoring activity.
Level	* * *
Time	30–40 minutes
Preparation	Students will need grammar books or online grammar explanations (see http://www.onestopenglish.com). Photocopy an authentic text which reflects academic register. See an example in Box 6.19a. Choose two grammar items from the text and create one activity for each grammar point. See Box 6.19b. Then design a 'culminating task' which will allow the students to use the grammar in a real context. See Box 6.19c.
Background	One of the ways writers achieve their purpose for writing is through their grammar choices. This activity explores how writers create academic register.

Procedure

1   Prepare the students for this activity by referring to the Background.

2   Divide the class into two large groups (A and B), and hand out the academic text. Then create small groups within the larger groups. Give one activity to Group A, the other activity to Group B. As each small group works on its activity, monitor their work and provide support where needed.

3   Now re-group the class into pairs drawing one person from Group A and the other from Group B. Based on their grammar activity, ask the students to 'teach' each other about the grammar they have learned through the exercise. They may use descriptions similar to those in 'Suggested responses' in Box 6.19b.

4   Write the 'culminating task' on the board. This task allows the pairs to use the grammar from Step 3. See Box 6.19c. Monitor the work of the pairs as they complete the task.

5   It may not be necessary to have open class feedback on the tasks if the pairs have performed it satisfactorily, but individuals could be invited to report on what they have learned from their colleagues.

Box 6.19a: Unit description – International Public Health

Unit of Study: MIPH5006 – Seminars in International Public Health

This unit aims to give students an insight into the realities of <u>prevention</u> and <u>control</u> of diseases and injury, and of health <u>promotion</u> in developing country populations **based on** real examples, and **presented by** a wide range of people with direct practical experience. The unit covers a variety of issues in health and development, disease <u>prevention</u> and <u>control</u> and health services in developing country settings.

Note: Nominalized words are underlined and relative participle clauses are in bold.

University of Sydney website (http://www.health.usyd.edu.au). Used with permission.

From *Communicative Activities for EAP*
© Cambridge University Press 2011   PHOTOCOPIABLE

Box 6.19b: Group activities

Group A	Group B
1 Use your dictionaries or online searches to explain the use of 'nominalization'.	1 Use your dictionaries or online searches to explain the use of 'relative participle clauses'.
2 Read the text and underline examples of nominalization. See Box 6.19a.	2 Read the text and highlight examples of past participles used in relative participle clauses. See Box 6.19a.
3 Rewrite the sentences, using the verb form rather than the nominalized form.	3 Rewrite the sentences and include the relative pronoun.
4 Write a similar sentence.	4 Write a similar sentence.
5 Rewrite the sentence in Step 4 and replace verb forms with nominalized forms.	5 Rewrite the sentence in Step 4 and replace the relative pronoun with a past participle.

continued

Box 6.19b: Group activities (*cont.*)

Suggested responses	Suggested responses
1 Nominalization: where the writer uses the noun form of the word instead of the verb form. 2 *prevention, promotion* 3 This unit aims to give students an insight into the realities of how to prevent and control diseases and injury and how to promote health in developing country populations.	1 Relative participle clause: where the relative pronoun has been omitted and the past participle is used like a defining relative clause. 2 *based on, presented by* 3 This unit aims to give students an insight into the realities of prevention and control of diseases and injury, and of health promotion in developing country populations, which is based on real examples and which is presented by a wide range of people with direct practical experience.
4 In this unit, students will study how to assess an injury and how to locate the cause of pain.	4 This unit of study aims to give students an insight into pain relief pharmaceuticals which is founded on extensive research and which is supported by practitioners in the field.
5 In this unit, students will study the assessment of an injury and the location of the cause of pain.	5 This unit of study aims to give students an insight into pain relief pharmaceuticals founded on extensive research and supported by practitioners in the field.

Box 6.19c: Culminating task

With your partner, use the grammar structures from the activities to write a unit descriptor for another health unit. Here are some examples:

Aged services
Disability services
Chronic disease control
Paramedic services
Pharmacology

Follow-up

From their reading of academic texts, ask the students to suggest other ways to achieve academic register. Language features could include: vocabulary choices, internal cohesion, sentence types and the generic structure of the text.

6.20 Notice the grammar: use the grammar

Language	Existential *there*; third person self-reference; rhetorical question; passive voice
Outline	Groups include particular grammar items as they compose a text from a list of main ideas.
Level	* * *
Time	30–40 minutes
Preparation	On the board, write or project a text taken from a class theme. (If necessary, adapt the text so that it includes the grammar items you want the students to use. See Box 6.20b.) From the text choose three or four grammar items for the focus of the activity. See Box 6.20a. Write the main ideas of the text in bullet points and photocopy these for the groups. See Box 6.20b.
Background	I have chosen an abstract for this activity because this text type contains the grammar items I want to explore. The activity could be adapted to accommodate any genre and its language features.

Procedure

1 Allow a few minutes for the students to read the text on the board and answer their comprehension questions.
2 Highlight and explore the language items you want to introduce. Record each grammar item on the board. See the left-hand column in Box 6.20a.

3 Remove the text from the board, and divide the class into small groups. Their task is to use the bullet points in the handout to re-create the text. They should include the grammar items from the board.

4 Go from group to group, monitoring their work and assisting as needed.

5 The groups display their writing. Allow time for the students to read each other's work.

Box 6.20a: Language features of academic register

Examples of language features which help to create academic register	
Existential *there*	There has been a longstanding and widely held expectation that tactile sensors would have a major impact on industrial robotics and automation.
	There is evidence that tactile sensing will soon play a major role in unstructured environments, particularly in areas such as medicine and surgery, health-care and service robotics, and automated natural product handling.
Third-person self-reference	This paper reports on the state of the art and shows that tactile sensing has undergone a major change of direction.
Rhetorical question	Has this technology failed to deliver its expected benefits to robotics applications, or have other factors influenced the development of the field?
Passive construction	However, this promise has not been realized, and few, if any, tactile sensors can be found in factory-based applications.

Box 6.20b: Abstract – robotics research

Over the past three decades, tactile sensing has developed into a sophisticated technology. There has been a longstanding and widely held expectation that tactile sensors would have a major impact on industrial robotics and automation. However, this promise has not been realized, and few, if any, tactile sensors can be found in factory-based applications. Has this technology failed to deliver its expected benefits to robotics applications, or have other factors influenced the development of the field? This paper reports on the state of the art and shows that tactile sensing has undergone a major change of direction. I revisit the original predictions and expectations, examine the implications of recent reviews, and show how the field has altered course. From current activities and recent trends, I determine the nature of new application areas and pressing developments that hold much promise for the future. There is evidence that tactile sensing will soon play a major role in unstructured environments, particularly in areas such as medicine and surgery, health-care and service robotics, and automated natural product handling.

✂---

Main ideas from the abstract

- Tactile sensing has developed into a sophisticated technology.
- Tactile sensors may have a major impact on industrial robotics and automation.
- Few if any tactile sensors can be found in factory-based applications.
- Tactile sensing has undergone a major change of direction.
- From recent reviews, it is clear that the field of industrial robotics has altered course.
- New applications areas and pressing developments hold much promise for the future.
- Tactile sensing will soon play a major role in unstructured environments such as medicine and surgery, health-care and service robotics, and automated natural product handling.

http://ijr.sagepub.com/cgi/content/abstract/19/7/636

From *Communicative Activities for EAP*

Follow-up

To make the activity more challenging, create bullet points from another article instead of using the main points from the model text. Groups use the bullet points to write a short text and include the nominated grammar items.

6.21   Soap box

Language	Conditional clauses
Outline	Students speak for one minute on a topic.
Level	* * *
Time	20–30 minutes
Preparation	Groups will need a pack of topic cards – one for each group member. Topics could be from a current class theme or could represent a range of topics from previous class themes. The topics should embody both real and unreal situations. See Box 6.21b. On the board, write or project the examples of conditional structures from Box 6.21a.
Background	This activity could be used to revise conditional constructions prior to a writing task or an oral exam.

Procedure

1   Refer to the conditional constructions on the board and briefly recap on how to express conditions in real and unreal situations.

2   Divide the class into small groups and distribute the cards, which are placed face down on the desk. Explain that each group member will have a turn to speak on a topic for one minute.

3   Give the signal for the first speaker to turn over the top card. Everyone in the group has a chance to read the topic and brainstorm ideas for about one minute. Encourage the students to use the conditional structures on the board.

4   The groups appoint a timekeeper. The first speaker then has one minute to address the topic in an uninterrupted speech.

5   Monitor the groups and offer feedback about content, accuracy and pronunciation, keeping in mind that communicating ideas is the focus of the activity.

6   When the time limit has expired, the next group member turns over a card. The procedure of brainstorming followed by a timed speech continues until each group member has had a chance to speak.

Box 6.21a: Conditional examples

Real situations: 'Things that are true, have happened, generally happen or are likely to happen.'	Unreal situations: 'Things that are untrue, or are imagined, have not happened, or are only remotely likely to happen.'
Present Simple *if* clause + Present Simple main clause Example: *If the value of the currency increases, then exports usually fall.*	**Simple Past *if* clause + modal verb (*would, could, might*)** Example: *If clean coal technology was commercially viable, then more countries would adopt this source of energy.*
Present Simple *if* clause + modal verb in main clause Example: *If the teeth are not cleaned regularly, then decay and gum disease may occur.*	**Past Perfect *if* clause + modal verb (*would have, could have, might have*)** Example: *If the United Nations had intervened earlier, then famine could have been avoided.*
Past Perfect *if* clause + modal verb in main clause Example: *If farmers had changed their practices earlier, then erosion would not have been so severe.*	**Future tense in main clause + *provided that / on the condition that, providing*** Example: *Banks will continue to lend money, provided that borrowers have secure employment.*
	***if* clause + modal verb + modal verb** Example: *If scientists could clone humans, then genetically identical cells could be used in organ transplants.*

Box 6.21b: Topic cards

Conditional questions	Business	World affairs	Economics	Environmental science	Health
Real situations	What are the benefits of online banking?	What are the implications for countries who accept refugees?	What usually happens if the value of the currency increases?	What are the consequences of deforestation?	What are the consequences if teeth are not cleaned regularly?
Unreal situations	If governments owned and controlled the banks, then how would consumers benefit?	Think of a country where the United Nations is involved. If the UN had intervened earlier, then what could have been avoided?	If every country in the world shared a common currency, what would be the implications?	If clean coal technology was commercially viable, then would this address climate change concerns?	If scientists could clone humans, then what could be the consequences?

From *Communicative Activities for EAP*

© Cambridge University Press 2011   PHOTOCOPIABLE

Follow-up

Hold a 'soap box' championship. Each team nominates a topic and a speaker. At the end of the speech, other teams have the opportunity to challenge the ideas put forward. Encourage the supporters of the speaker to participate with parliamentary-type interjections such as *Hear, hear! Bravo! Well said! Good point! Point taken!*

Appendix 1: Framework for speaking, listening, reading, writing

	Receptive skills			Productive skills	
	The reader	The listener	Code user	The speaker	The writer
Code breaker	The reader identifies: • patterns and conventions • phonological discriminations: words/sounds in sentences • sight vocabulary The reader uses: • context, grammar to confirm predictions	The listener identifies: • patterns and conventions • phonological discriminations: words/sounds in sentences • familiar vocabulary, e.g. numbers The listener uses: • context, grammar to confirm predictions • signals from the speaker, e.g. tone of voice, body language to comprehend		The speaker can create meaning through: • pronouncing words, phrases and sentences with appropriate stress, intonation, pausing, chunking in connected speech • using effective non-verbal communication The speaker can self-correct from a model	The writer can create meaning through: • writing words, phrases and simple sentences • using appropriate punctuation The writer can self-correct from a model

	Receptive skills			Productive skills	
	The reader	The listener	Text maker	The speaker	The writer
Text participant	To comprehend, the reader uses knowledge about: • texts/genres • intertextual relationships The reader can: • identify literal meanings • draw inferences • link to prior knowledge • interpret texts • evaluate texts	To comprehend, the listener uses knowledge about: • texts/genres • intertextual relationships The listener can: • identify literal meanings • draw inferences • link to prior knowledge • interpret texts • evaluate texts		The speaker can: • apply knowledge about genres to create texts • create intertextual links • express literal meanings • link texts to prior knowledge	The writer can: • apply knowledge about genres to create texts • create intertextual links • express literal meanings • link texts to prior knowledge

	Receptive skills			Productive skills	
	The reader	The listener		The speaker	The writer
Text user	To comprehend, the reader uses knowledge about: • different types of genres • social purposes of texts The reader can: • interact with others about texts • select texts to suit a purpose • adjust reading strategies to suit text type and reader purpose	To comprehend, the listener uses knowledge about: • different types of genres • social purposes of texts The listener can: • interact with others about texts • identify texts for a particular purpose • adjust listening strategies to suit text type and purpose for listening	Text user	The speaker can: • use genres and language features for a particular purpose, context and audience • interact with others about the text • adapt register according to audience, context and purpose	The writer can: • use genres and language features for a particular purpose, context and audience • interact with others about the text • adapt register according to audience, context and purpose

	Receptive skills			Productive skills	
	The reader	The listener	Text agent	The speaker	The writer
Text analyst	The reader can: • identify ideological meanings • detect beliefs, values, attitudes and judgements • recognize how an author uses vocabulary, grammar and text organization to achieve a purpose • accept, reject, challenge a text's position	The listener can: • identify ideological meanings • detect beliefs, values, attitudes and judgements • recognize how an author uses vocabulary, grammar and text organization to achieve a purpose • accept, reject, challenge a text's position		The speaker can: • use genres and language features to speak about values, attitudes and judgements within a social context • present alternative positions and points of view	The writer can: • use genres and language features to write about values, attitudes and judgements within a social context • present alternative positions and points of view

Source: Adapted from P. Freebody and A. Luke (1999) *Further Notes on the Four Resources Model*. Available at http://www.readingonline.org/research/lukefreebody.html

Appendix 2: Framework for vocabulary development and grammar

Vocabulary development		Grammar	
Phases of learning	**Knowledge and skills**	**Phases of learning**	**Knowledge and skills**
Noticing • input • intake • explicit instruction • implicit instruction • consciousness raising	• etymology • collocations • discover new words • record words	**Noticing** • input • intake • explicit instruction • implicit instruction • consciousness raising	• notice patterns • notice functions
Experimenting • acquisition • reasoning • hypothesizing • organizing	• syntactic structure • contextual clues • make associations • organize words into groups • lexical inferencing	**Experimenting** • acquisition • reasoning • hypothesizing • organizing	• discover rules • experiment with structures to achieve a purpose, in a context, for a particular audience
Producing • access • output • automatizing	• produce vocabulary in a meaningful social context for a particular audience	**Producing** • access • structuring and restructuring • output • automatizing	• produce grammar in a meaningful social context for a particular audience and purpose • move towards fluency and accuracy

Source: Adapted from T. Hedge (2000) *Teaching and Learning in the Language Classroom*. Oxford: Oxford University Press.

Further reading and resources

Alexander, O., Argent, S., and Spencer, J. (2008) *EAP Essentials: A Teacher's Guide to Principles and Practice*. Reading: Garner Publishing Ltd.

Brookfield, S. D., and Preskil, S. (1999) *Discussion as a Way of Teaching: Tools and Techniques for Democratic Classrooms*. San Francisco: Jossey-Bass Publishers.

Carter, R., and McCarthy, M. (2006) *Cambridge Grammar of English*. Cambridge: Cambridge University Press.

Dare, B., and Polias, J. (2001) 'Learning about language: scaffolding in ESL Classrooms', in J.Hammond (ed.), *Scaffolding: Teaching and Learning in Language and Literacy Education*. Sydney: PETA

De Silva Joyce, H., and Burns, A. (1999) 'Grammar teaching and written language', in *Focus on Grammar*. Sydney: National Centre for English Language Teaching and Research.

Ellis, R. (2000). 'Task-based research and language pedagogy', *Language Teaching Research*, 4(3), pp. 193–220.

Gerot, L. (1995) *Making Sense of Text*. Cammeray: Antipodean Educational Enterprises.

Freebody, P., and Luke, A. (1990) 'Literacies' programs: debates and demands in cultural context', *Prospect*, 5(3), pp. 7–16.

Freebody, P., and Luke, A. (1999) *Further Notes on the Four Resources Model*. Available at http://www.readingonline.org/research/lukefreebody.html

Halliday, M. A. K., and Matthiessen, C. M. I. M. (2004) *An Introduction to Functional Grammar*. London: Arnold.

Hedge, T. (2000) *Teaching and Learning in the Langugage Classroom*. Cambridge: Cambridge University Press.

Li, S., and Li, F. (2004) 'Intercultural communicative language teaching', *EA Journal*, 22(1), pp. 20–42.

Oxford Collocations Dictionary for Students of English (2002). Oxford: Oxford University Press.

Richards, J. (1999) 'Addressing the grammar gap in task-based learning', *TESOL in Context*, 9(1), pp. 3–10.

Richards, J., and Rodgers, T. (2001) 'Communicative language teaching', in J. Richards and T. Rodgers, *Approaches and Methods in Language Teaching*, 2nd edn. Cambridge: Cambridge University Press, pp. 153–77.

Riddell, C. (2000) 'They won't let me talk!' Exploring the rules of interaction in casual conversation with our ESL students', *TESOL in Context*, 10(1), pp. 13–14.

Scrivener, J. (1994) *Learning Teaching*. Oxford: Macmillan Heinemann English Language Teaching.

Swales, J. M. (2009) 'When there is no perfect text: approaches to the EAP practitioner's dilemma', *Journal of English for Academic Purposes*, 8, pp. 5–13.

Thompson, G. (1996) 'Some misconceptions about communicative language teaching', *ELT Journal*, 5(1), pp. 9–15.

Thornbury, S. (1997). *About Language*. Cambridge: Cambridge University Press.

Thornbury, S. (2005). *Beyond the Sentence*. Oxford: Macmillan.

Websites
Listening resources
(resources with audio)

    http://www.bbc.co.uk/keyskills/index.shtml
    http://www.themonthly.com.au/video
    http://fora.tv/
    http://www.thenakedscientists.com/
    http://www.bath.ac.uk/podcast/
    http://www.cam.ac.uk/video/itunesu.html
    http://www.aarp.org/
    http://www.howstuffworks.com/
    http://podcast.open.ac.uk/
    http://ethics.sandiego.edu/video/index.asp

http://audiovideo.economist.com/
http://www.ft.com/multimedia

(resources with audio and transcripts)
http://www.britishcouncil.org/learnenglish-podcasts
http://www.liverpoolmuseums.org.uk/
http://www.abc.net.au/rn/boyerlectures/index/
http://www.abc.net.au/rn/allinthemind/
http://www.videojug.com/
http://www.abc.net.au/health/minutes/
http://www.abc.net.au/rn/philosopherszone/default.htm
http://www.bbc.co.uk/radio4/reith2008/

Vocabulary resources

http://www.thefreedictionary.com/dictionary.htm (Medical, financial and legal dictionary. Terms are defined within a context. The dictionary also offers a guide to pronunciation and the etymology of the word.)

http://www.wordinfo.info/words/index/info/list (Words from Latin and Greek sources)

http://dictionary.reference.com/ (Dictionary and thesaurus plus word of the day, crosswords and word games)

http://www.merriam-webster.com/ (Dictionary and thesaurus plus medical dictionary)

http://english.glendale.cc.ca.us/roots.dict.html (Dictionary of Greek and Latin roots)

http://www.etymonline.com/ (Etymology dictionary)

http://dictionary.cambridge.org (Dictionary plus business, finance and education vocabulary)

http://encarta.msn.com/ (Dictionary, encyclopaedia plus pronunciation)

http://www.xiaolai.net/ocd/ (A collocations resource)

http://www.visualthesaurus.com/ (Visual thesaurus)

http://www.academicvocabularyexercises.com/ (Academic word list)

http://www.natcorp.ox.ac.uk/ (British National Corpus)

http://www.americancorpus.org/ (Corpus of Contemporary American English)

Index

Five-Minute Activities for Young Learners

Penny McKay and Jenni Guse

Five-Minute Activities for Young Learners is full of short, topical, low-resource ideas for teachers of English to children. Activities are organised around six themes:

- Animals
- Journeys
- Fantasy and adventure
- The world around us
- Healthy bodies
- About me.

These themes reflect the content covered in young learner English exams (for example the Cambridge Young Learner English Tests) and the curriculum in most primary classrooms.

Each theme contains activities at three levels of difficulty: one star (★) represents the lowest level of difficulty, while three stars (★★★) represent the most challenging tasks. Teachers can use the activities to meet a specific learning objective, to reinforce a teaching point or simply to fill a gap in the lesson.

All activities are hands-on and designed to appeal to children's sense of fun. They encourage meaningful language use and real communication appropriate to primary learners. Each activity also contains guidance and information on preparation, procedure, language focus, skills focus and thinking focus. Activities can be used flexibly in any order at any point in a teaching programme. In addition, the design of the activities allows teachers to adapt and apply the ideas to other themes.

This book will be of interest to both novice and experienced teachers who need a resource of enjoyable, achievable and motivating activities for the young learner classroom.

Paperback 978 0 521 69134 5

Advanced Skills

A resource book of advanced-level skills activities

Simon Haines

Advanced Skills is a lively collection of photocopiable activities for advanced-level students. The book is divided by skill into four sections. Each section has nine units on the same nine topic areas. While not specifically written as exam practice material, the book includes many tasks similar to those that students encounter in the main Cambridge exams (CAE, CPE, IELTS).

- *Advanced Skills* is organised around carefully selected topics so that the activities can be slotted into any lesson and used alongside any coursebook.

- All units integrate other skill areas while practising one key skill, preparing students for effective communication in everyday life.

- The book contains authentic material and realistic tasks that will engage and motivate students.

- Each unit lasts approximately 60 minutes and contains one to three photocopiable pages for students, together with a page of step-by-step teacher's notes to guide the busy teacher through the activity.

- The recordings offer a range of genres from radio and television broadcasts to political speeches and conversational dialogues. Students are exposed to a range of accents.

- The material offers teachers an original approach to nine familiar topics.

This resource book is accompanied by an audio CD to support the listening activities. There are recording scripts of the audio material at the back of the book.

Paperback 978 0 521 60848 0

Teaching Adult Second Language Learners

Heather McKay and Abigail Tom

Teaching Adult Second Language Learners addresses the special needs of adults studying English, particularly those who have immigrated to English-speaking countries. It provides a useful summary of the principles involved in teaching adults as well as a wealth of activities specially designed for adult learners.

The book is divided into three sections:

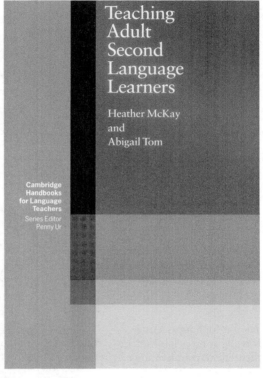

- Section I contains an introduction to the adult language learner. It also discusses assessment and placement of students, and the organization of courses and lesson organization.

- Section II gives teachers techniques for building community in the classroom.

- Section III provides activities designed for students at various levels that are organized thematically around topics such as self-identification, food, clothing, and work. Whenever possible, alternative activities are suggested to accommodate the needs of multilevel classes.

Paperback 978 0 521 64990 2

English for Academic Purposes

A guide and resource book for teachers

R. R. Jordan

This book provides a comprehensive overview of the field of English for Academic Purposes (EAP) for teachers. It looks not only at study skills, but also at other central concerns of EAP, such as needs analysis, syllabus and course design, methodology and materials, learning styles and cultural awareness, tests and exams, and academic style and genre analysis. Areas for potential research are also examined.

In addition to general EAP, the author also considers subject-specific language and the production of teaching materials.

The author adopts a user-friendly approach in which theoretical considerations are balanced with practical experience. Each chapter ends with questions and discussion activities which further explore the issues dealt with in the chapter. The book includes several appendices which are of practical use to teachers, as well as samples from published works and extensive bibliographies.

Paperback 978 0 521 55618 7

CAMBRIDGE LANGUAGE TEACHING LIBRARY

A series covering central issues in language teaching and learning,
by authors who have expert knowledge in their field.

For a complete list of titles please visit: http://www.cambridge.org/elt/cltl

A selection of recent titles in this series: